Adobe® Photoshop® 6.0

Classroom in a Book®

Adobe

www.adobe.com/adobepress

Contents

Getting Started

About Classroom in a Book 1

Prerequisites 2

Installing Adobe Photoshop and Adobe ImageReady 2

Starting Adobe Photoshop and Adobe ImageReady 2

Installing the Classroom in a Book fonts 3

Copying the Classroom in a Book files 3

Restoring default preferences 4

Additional resources 6

Adobe Certification 6

Getting to Know the Work Area

Lesson 1

Starting Adobe Photoshop and opening files 10

Using the tools 13

Entering values 16

Viewing images 17

Working with palettes 22

Using context menus 24

Using online Help 25

Using Adobe online services 28

Jumping to ImageReady 30

Review questions 32

Review answers 32

Working with Selections

Lesson 2

Selection tool overview 37

Getting started 38

Selecting with the rectangular marquee tool 38

Selecting with the elliptical marquee tool 39

Moving a selection 41

Selecting with the magic wand 44

Selecting with the lasso tool 45

Adding and subtracting selections 47

Selecting with the magnetic lasso 48

Transforming a selection 50

Combining selection tools 52

Cropping the completed image 53

For the Web: Creating evenly spaced buttons
for a Web page 55

Review questions 58

Review answers 58

Layer Basics

Lesson 3

Organizing artwork on layers 62

Getting started 63

Creating and viewing layers 63

Selecting and removing artwork on a layer 66

Rearranging layers 67

Changing the opacity and mode of a layer 68

Linking layers 70

Adding a gradient to a layer 71

Adding text 74

Applying a layer style 76

Flattening and saving files 79

Review questions 80

Review answers 80

Painting and Editing

Lesson 4

Getting started 84

Filling the background layer with color 85

Blending the lily image with the background 86

Painting the petals of the flowers 89

Correcting your work 91

Smoothing the edges of a paintbrush stroke 95

Creating a subtle overlay effect 96

Painting shadows in nontransparent areas 96

Adding a gradient to the background 98

Creating a glow effect with a custom airbrush 100

Creating a textured effect with a natural brush 101

Creating a patterned border 104

Review questions 107

Review answers 107

Masks and Channels   **Lesson 5**

Working with masks and channels 112

Getting started 113

Creating a quick mask 113

Editing a quick mask 115

Saving a selection as a mask 120

Editing a mask 122

Loading a mask as a selection and applying
an adjustment 124

Extracting an image 125

Applying a filter effect to a masked selection 132

Creating a gradient mask 134

Applying effects using a gradient mask 135

Review questions 137

Review answers 137

Photo Retouching   **Lesson 6**

Strategy for retouching 158

Resolution and image size 161

Getting started 163

Cropping an image 163

Adjusting the tonal range 166

Removing a color cast 168

Replacing colors in an image 169

Adjusting saturation with the sponge tool 171

Adjusting lightness with the dodge tool 172

Removing unwanted objects 173

Replacing part of an image 174

Applying the Unsharp Mask filter 176

Saving the image for four-color printing 177

On your own: Painting with the art history brush 178

Review questions 181

Review answers 181

Basic Pen Tool Techniques

Lesson 7

Getting started 186

Drawing paths with the pen tool 187

Drawing straight paths 188

Drawing curved paths 195

Combining straight and curved lines 200

Drawing a path around artwork 205

Review questions 213

Review answers 213

Vector Shapes and
Clipping Paths

Lesson 8

About bitmap images and vector graphics 218

Getting started 219

Creating the logo 220

Working with type 228

Re-creating the logo, using actions and styles 237

Review questions 241

Review answers 241

Advanced Layer
Techniques

Lesson 9

Getting started 246

Creating a layer clipping path 247

Creating layer sets 249

Creating an adjustment layer 251

Creating a knockout gradient layer 252

Importing a type layer 254

Applying layer styles 255

Duplicating and clipping a layer 255

Liquifying a layer 257

Creating a border layer 258

Flattening a layered image 259

Review questions 261

Review answers 261

Creating Special Effects

Lesson 10

Getting started 266

Saving and loading a selection 267

Hand-coloring selections on a layer 268

Combining and moving selections 273

Colorizing a selection 274

Using a grid 275

Changing the color balance 277

Applying filters 279

Improving performance with filters 282

For the Web: Animated rollover button 283

Review questions 286

Review answers 286

Setting Up Your Monitor for Color Management

Lesson 11

Getting started 290

Color management: An overview 291

Calibrating and characterizing your monitor
using Adobe Gamma 294

Saving the monitor profile 302

Review questions 303

Review answers 303

Producing and Printing Consistent Color

Lesson 12

Reproducing colors 309

Getting started 311

Specifying color management settings 311

Proofing an image 312

Identifying out-of-gamut colors 315

Adjusting an image and printing a proof 315

Saving the image as a separation 317

Selecting print options 318

Printing 320

Review questions 324

Review answers 324

Preparing Images for Two-Color Printing

Lesson 13

Printing in color 328

Using channels and the Channels palette 329

Getting started 329

Mixing color channels 330

Assigning values to the black and white points 334

Sharpening the image 335

Setting up for spot color 336

Adding spot color 338

For the Web: Creating two-color Web graphics 344

Review questions 347

Review answers 347

Optimizing Images for the Web

Lesson 14

Optimizing images using Photoshop or ImageReady ... 352

Getting started 354

Optimizing a JPEG image 354

Optimizing a GIF image 358

Controlling dither 365

Specifying background transparency 369

Creating an image map 373

Batch-processing file optimization 379

Review questions 381

Review answers 381

Creating Web Graphics
Using Slices and Rollovers

Lesson 15

Getting started 386

About slices 388

Slicing the image in Photoshop 388

Optimizing slices in Photoshop 392

Slicing the image in ImageReady 393

Optimizing slices in ImageReady 398

Creating rollovers 401

Previewing the completed banner in a browser 405

Saving the sliced images in ImageReady 406

Review questions 408

Review answers 408

Designing Web Pages
Using Multiple Adobe
Programs

Lesson 16

Getting started 414

Using Adobe Acrobat for design reviews 416

Creating the Web page in Adobe GoLive 422

Review questions 436

Review answers 436

Creating Animated Images
for the Web

Lesson 17

Creating animations in Adobe ImageReady 442

Getting started 443

Creating simple motion 444

Creating a transition between image states 455

Creating a two-step animation 457

Rotating and moving an object 458

Creating a montage sequence 463

Using advanced layer features to create animations ... 469

Review questions 474

Review answers 474

Index 477

Getting Started

Adobe® Photoshop® 6.0 delivers powerful, industry-standard image-editing tools for professional designers who want to produce sophisticated graphics for the Web and for print. Included with Photoshop 6.0 is ImageReady™ 3.0 and its powerful set of Web tools for optimizing and previewing images, batch-processing images with droplets in the Actions palette, and creating GIF animations. Photoshop and ImageReady combined offer a comprehensive environment for designing graphics for the Web.

About Classroom in a Book

Adobe Photoshop 6.0 Classroom in a Book® is part of the official training series for Adobe graphics and publishing software developed by experts at Adobe Systems. The lessons are designed to let you learn at your own pace. If you're new to Adobe Photoshop or ImageReady, you'll learn the fundamental concepts and features you'll need to master the programs. And if you've been using Adobe Photoshop or ImageReady for a while, you'll find that Classroom in a Book teaches many advanced features, including tips and techniques for using the latest version of these applications and for preparing images for the Web.

The lessons in this edition include new information on designing Web pages using multiple Adobe products, adding special effects, and creating slices and rollovers for Web graphics. In addition, existing lessons have been updated to incorporate new commands and tools.

Although each lesson provides step-by-step instructions for creating a specific project, there's room for exploration and experimentation. You can follow the book from start to finish or do only the lessons that correspond to your interests and needs. Each lesson concludes with a review section summarizing what you've covered.

Prerequisites

Before beginning to use *Adobe Photoshop 6.0 Classroom in a Book*, you should have a working knowledge of your computer and its operating system. Make sure you know how to use the mouse and standard menus and commands and also how to open, save, and close files. If you need to review these techniques, see the printed or online documentation included with your Windows® or Mac® OS documentation.

Installing Adobe Photoshop and Adobe ImageReady

Before you begin using *Adobe Photoshop 6.0 Classroom in a Book*, make sure that your system is set up correctly and that you've installed the required software and hardware. You must purchase the Adobe Photoshop 6.0 software separately. For system requirements and complete instructions on installing the software, see the *InstallReadMe* file on the application CD.

Photoshop and ImageReady use the same installer. You must install the applications from the Adobe Photoshop 6.0 Application CD onto your hard disk; you cannot run the program from the CD. Follow the on-screen instructions.

Make sure your serial number is accessible before installing the application; you can find the serial number on the registration card or CD sleeve.

Starting Adobe Photoshop and Adobe ImageReady

You start Photoshop and ImageReady just as you would any software application.

To start Adobe Photoshop or ImageReady in Windows:

1 Choose Start > Programs > Adobe > Photoshop 6.0 > Adobe Photoshop 6.0 or ImageReady 3.0.

In Photoshop, if you have deleted the preferences file, the Adobe Color Management Assistant appears.

2 Click Cancel to close the assistant without adjusting the monitor.

For instructions on how to calibrate a monitor, see Lesson 11, "Setting Up Your Monitor for Color Management," in this book.

To start Adobe Photoshop or Adobe ImageReady in Mac OS:

1 Open the Adobe Photoshop folder, and double-click the Adobe Photoshop or Adobe ImageReady program icon. (If you installed the program in a folder other than Adobe Photoshop, open that folder.)

In Photoshop, if you have deleted the preferences, the Adobe Color Management Assistant appears.

2 Click Cancel to close the assistant without adjusting the monitor. For instructions on how to calibrate a monitor, see Lesson 11, "Setting Up Your Monitor for Color Management," in this book.

The Adobe Photoshop or Adobe ImageReady application window appears. You can now open a document or create a new one and start working.

Installing the Classroom in a Book fonts

To ensure that the lesson files appear on your system with the correct fonts, you may need to install the Classroom in a Book font files. The fonts for the lessons are located in the Fonts folder on the *Adobe Photoshop Classroom in a Book* CD. If you already have these on your system, you do not need to install them. If you have ATM® (Adobe Type Manager®), see its documentation on how to install fonts. If you do not have ATM, installing it from the Classroom in a Book (CIB) CD will automatically install the necessary fonts.

You can also install the Classroom in a Book fonts by copying all of the files in the Fonts folder on the Adobe Photoshop Classroom in a Book *CD to the Program Files/Common Files/Adobe/Fonts (Windows) or System Folder/Application Support/Adobe/Fonts (Mac OS). If you install a Type 1, TrueType, OpenType, or CID font into these local Fonts folders, the font appears in Adobe applications only.*

Copying the Classroom in a Book files

The *Adobe Photoshop Classroom in a Book* CD includes folders containing all the electronic files for the lessons. Each lesson has its own folder, and you must copy the folders to your hard drive to do the lessons. To save room on your drive, you can install only the necessary folder for each lesson as you need it, and remove it when you're done.

To install the Classroom in a Book files:

1 Insert the *Adobe Photoshop Classroom in a Book* CD into your CD-ROM drive.

2 Create a folder named PS60_CIB on your hard drive.

3 Copy the lessons you want to the hard drive:

• To copy all of the lessons, drag the Lessons folder from the CD into the PS60_CIB folder.

• To copy a single lesson, drag the individual lesson folder from the CD into the PS60_CIB folder.

If you are installing the files in Windows, you need to unlock them before using them. You don't need to unlock the files if you are installing them in Mac OS.

4 In Windows, unlock the files you copied:

• If you copied all of the lessons, double-click the unlock.bat file in the PS60_CIB/Lessons folder.

• If you copied a single lesson, drag the unlock.bat file from the Lessons folder on the CD into the PS60_CIB folder. Then double-click the unlock.bat file in the PS60_CIB folder.

Note: As you work through each lesson, you will overwrite the Start files. To restore the original files, recopy the corresponding Lesson folder from the Classroom in a Book CD to the PS60_CIB folder on your hard drive.

Restoring default preferences

The preferences files store palette and command settings and color calibration information. Each time you quit Adobe Photoshop or Adobe ImageReady, the positions of the palettes and certain command settings are recorded in the respective preferences file. When you use the Photoshop color management assistant, monitor calibration and color space information is stored in the Photoshop preferences files as well.

Before beginning the Classroom in a Book, save your initial preferences file. This enables you to restore any custom settings you have when you are done with the book.

You must then restore the default preferences for Photoshop or ImageReady before you begin each lesson. This ensures that the tools and palettes function as described in this book. When you are finished with the book, you can restore your saved settings. Instructions for each of these processes are shown.

Important: *If you have adjusted your color display and color space settings, be sure to move the preferences file, rather than delete it, so that you can restore your settings when you are done with the lessons in this book.*

To save your current Photoshop preferences:

1 Exit Adobe Photoshop.

2 Locate and open the Adobe Photoshop 6 Settings folder.

Note: *The default location of the Adobe Photoshop 6 Settings folder varies by operating system; use your operating system's Find command to locate this folder.*

3 Drag the Adobe Photoshop 6 Prefs file from the Adobe Photoshop 6 Settings folder to your desktop.

To restore preferences to their default settings before each lesson:

1 Press and hold Shift+Alt+Control (Windows) or Shift+Option+Command (Mac OS) *immediately after* launching Photoshop or ImageReady.

2 Delete the preferences as the application starts up:

• For Photoshop, click Yes to delete the Adobe Photoshop preferences file.

• For ImageReady, click Erase to delete the ImageReady preferences file.

New Preferences files will be created the next time you start Photoshop or ImageReady.

3 If Photoshop asks whether you want to set custom color settings, click No.

To restore your saved settings after completing the lessons:

1 Exit Photoshop.

2 Drag the preferences file from the desktop back into the Adobe Photoshop 6 Settings folder.

3 In the warning dialog box that appears, confirm that you want to replace the existing version of the file.

Additional resources

Adobe Photoshop Classroom in a Book is not meant to replace documentation that comes with the program. Only the commands and options used in the lessons are explained in this book. For comprehensive information about program features, refer to these resources:

• The *Adobe Photoshop 6.0 User Guide*. Included with the Adobe Photoshop 6.0 software, this guide contains a complete description of all features.

• Online Help, an online version of the user guide, which you can view by choosing Help > Contents (Windows) or Help > Help Contents (Mac OS). (For more information, see Lesson 1, "Getting to Know the Work Area.")

• The Adobe Web site (www.adobe.com), which you can view by choosing Help > Adobe Online if you have a connection to the World Wide Web.

Adobe Certification

The Adobe Training and Certification Programs are designed to help Adobe customers improve and promote their product proficiency skills. The Adobe Certified Expert (ACE) program is designed to recognize the high-level skills of expert users. Adobe Certified Training Providers (ACTP) use only Adobe Certified Experts to teach Adobe software classes. Available in either ACTP classrooms or on-site, the ACE program is the best way to master Adobe products. For Adobe Certified Training Programs information, visit the Partnering with Adobe Web site at http://partners.adobe.com.

Lesson 1

1 Getting to Know the Work Area

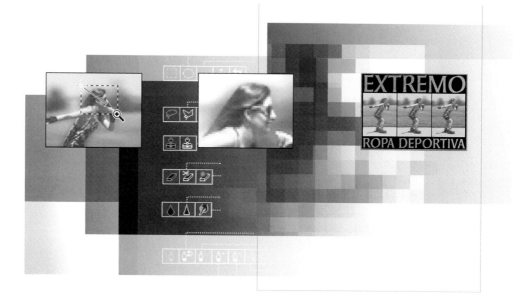

As you work with Adobe Photoshop and Adobe ImageReady, you'll discover that there is often more than one way to accomplish the same task. To make the best use of the extensive editing capabilities in these programs, you first must learn to navigate the work area.

In this lesson, you'll learn how to do the following:

• Open an Adobe Photoshop file.

• Select tools from the toolbox.

• Use viewing options to enlarge and reduce the display of an image.

• Work with palettes.

• Use online Help.

This lesson will take about 60 minutes to complete. The lesson is designed to be done in Adobe Photoshop, but information on using similar functionality in Adobe ImageReady is included where appropriate.

Before starting Adobe Photoshop, locate the Lesson01 folder on the *Adobe Photoshop 6.0 Classroom in a Book* CD, and copy the folder onto your hard drive. As you work on this lesson, you'll overwrite the start files. If you need to restore the start files, copy them from the *Adobe Photoshop Classroom in a Book* CD.

Before beginning this lesson, restore the default application settings for Adobe Photoshop. See "Restoring default preferences" on page 4.

Note: *Windows users need to unlock the lesson files before using them. For more information, see "Copying the Classroom in a Book files" on page 3.*

Starting Adobe Photoshop and opening files

The Adobe Photoshop and Adobe ImageReady work areas include the command menus at the top of your screen and a variety of tools and palettes for editing and adding elements to your image. You can also add commands and filters to the menus by installing third-party software known as *plug-in modules*.

In this part of the lesson, you'll familiarize yourself with the Adobe Photoshop work area and open a file in Adobe Photoshop.

1 Double-click the Adobe Photoshop icon to start Adobe Photoshop.

When you start Adobe Photoshop, the menu bar, the toolbox, the tool options bar, and four palette groups appear on the screen.

Both Photoshop and ImageReady work with bitmapped, digitized images (that is, continuous-tone images that have been converted into a series of small squares, or picture elements, called *pixels*). In Photoshop, you can also work with vector graphics, which are shapes made up of smooth lines that retain their crispness when scaled. You can create original artwork in both Photoshop and ImageReady, or you can bring images into the program by scanning a photograph, a transparency, a negative, or a graphic, by capturing a video image, or by importing artwork created in drawing programs. You can also import previously digitized images—such as those produced by a digital camera or by the Kodak° Photo CD process.

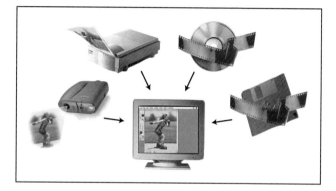

For information on the kinds of files you can use with Adobe Photoshop, see "About file formats" in Photoshop 6.0 online Help.

2 Choose File > Open, and open the file 01Start.psd from the Lessons/Lesson01 folder that you copied to your hard drive.

Using the tools

The toolbox contains selection tools, painting and editing tools, foreground and background color selection boxes, and viewing tools. This section introduces the toolbox and shows you how to select tools. As you work through the lessons, you'll learn more about each tool's specific function.

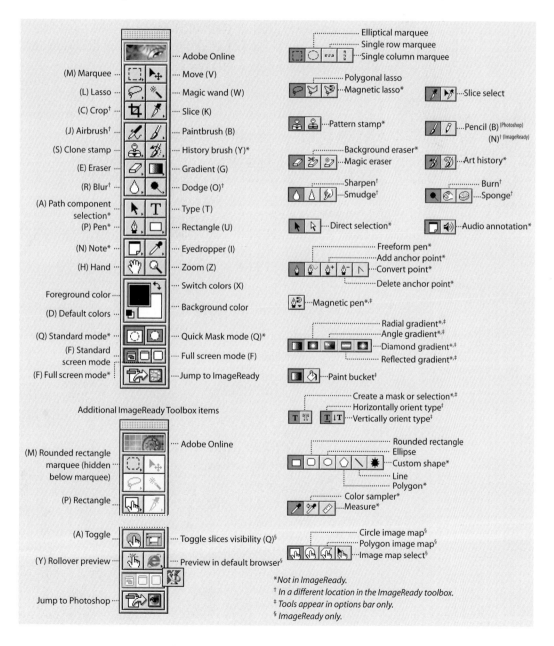

For an illustration of the tools, see figure 1-1 in the color section.

The work areas of Photoshop and ImageReady consist of a menu bar at the top of the work area, a floating toolbox on the left, a tool options bar below the menu bar, floating palettes on the right and bottom, and one or more document windows, which you open manually.

Together, Photoshop and ImageReady provide a consistent and integrated set of tools for producing sophisticated graphics for print and online viewing. ImageReady includes many tools that will already be familiar to users of Photoshop.

1 To select a tool, you can click the tool in the toolbox, or you can press the tool's keyboard shortcut. For example, you can press M to select a marquee tool from the keyboard. Selected tools remain active until you select a different tool.

2 If you don't know the keyboard shortcut for a tool, position the pointer over the tool until its name and shortcut are displayed.

Photoshop and ImageReady use the same keyboard shortcut keys for corresponding keys, with the exceptions of A, P, Q, and Y:

- *In Photoshop, press A for the selection tools; in ImageReady, press A to show or hide image maps.*

- *In Photoshop, press P for the pen tools; in ImageReady, press P for the image map tools.*

- *In Photoshop, press Q to switch between Quick Mask mode and Standard mode; in ImageReady, press Q to show or hide slices.*

- *In Photoshop, press Y for the history brush tools; in ImageReady, press Y for rollover preview.*

All keyboard shortcuts are also listed in the Quick Reference section of online Help. You'll learn how to use online Help later in this lesson.

Some of the tools in the toolbox display a small triangle at the bottom right corner, indicating the presence of additional hidden tools.

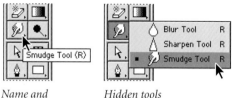

Name and   Hidden tools
shortcut displayed

3 Select hidden tools in any of the following ways:

• Click and hold down the mouse button on a tool that has additional hidden tools. Then drag to the desired tool, and release the mouse button.

• Hold down Alt (Windows) or Option (Mac OS), and click the tool in the toolbox. Each click selects the next hidden tool in the hidden tool sequence.

• Press Shift + the tool's keyboard shortcut repeatedly until the tool you want is selected.

Note: When you select a viewing tool to change the screen display of an image, you must return to the Standard screen mode to see the default work area displayed.

Standard
screen mode

Using the tool options bar

Most tools have options that are displayed in the tool options bar. The tool options bar is context sensitive and changes as different tools are selected. Some settings in the tool options bar are common to several tools (such as painting modes and opacity), and some are specific to one tool (such as the Auto Erase setting for the pencil tool).

You can move the tool options bar anywhere in the work area. In Photoshop, you can dock it at the top or bottom of the screen.

The Photoshop tool options bar includes a palette well for storing other palettes, providing quick access to palettes such as Swatches and Actions that you reference briefly while using the application. The palette well is available only when using a screen resolution greater than 800 pixels x 600 pixels (a setting of at least 1024 x 768 is recommended).

1 Select a tool in the toolbox or choose Window > Show Options to display the tool options bar.

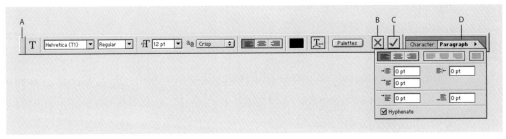

A. Title bar **B.** *Click the Cancel button to discard your changes.* **C.** *Click the OK button to commit your changes.* **D.** *Click the tab to display the palette stored in the palette well.*

Note: *In Photoshop (Windows) and ImageReady (Windows and Mac), you can double-click the title bar at the left edge to collapse the tool options bar, showing only the tool icon.*

2 Click the tool icon on the tool options bar, then choose Reset Tool or Reset All Tools from the context menu. This returns a tool or all tools to default settings.

3 Drag the title bar at the left edge of the options bar to move the tool options bar. In Photoshop, you can also grab the gripper bar at the left edge of the tool options bar. The gripper bar will appear only if the tool options bar is docked at the top or bottom of your screen.

Entering values

Some tool options bars and palettes contain options that let you enter values using any combination of sliders, angle controls, arrow buttons, and text boxes. As you do each lesson, whenever you're asked to enter a value, use one of the following methods.

To enter values, do one of the following:

• Type a value in the text box. To apply your entry, select a different option or text box in the palette, press Tab to go to a different text box in the palette, click the background in the composition, or press Enter or Return.

Note: *For certain options, you can use numeric shortcuts for entering percentages. For instance, typing 1 enters 10%, 2 enters 20%, 3 enters 30%, and so on.*

• Drag the slider to the desired value. Shift-drag to move the slider in increments of 10 units.

• Click the up arrow or down arrow button in the palette to increase or decrease the value.

• (Windows only) Click in the text field and then press the Up Arrow or Down Arrow key on the keyboard to increase or decrease the value.

• (Windows only) Use the mouse wheel to increase or decrease the value.

• Drag the angle control to the desired value. Shift-drag to change the angle in 15-degree increments.

To cancel values before you apply them, press the Escape key.

Viewing images

You can view your image at any magnification level from 0.25% (Photoshop) or 12.5% (ImageReady) to 1600%. Adobe Photoshop displays the percentage of an image's actual size in the title bar. When you use any of the viewing tools and commands, you affect the *display* of the image, not the image's dimensions or file size.

Using the View menu

To enlarge or reduce the view of an image using the View menu, do one of the following:

- Choose View > Zoom In to enlarge the display of the image.

- Choose View > Zoom Out to reduce the view of the image.

Each time you choose a Zoom command, the view of the image is resized. The percentage at which the image is viewed is displayed in the Title bar and in the lower left corner of the document window.

View percentage

You can also use the View menu or hand tool to fit an image to your screen.

1 Choose View > Fit on Screen. The size of the image and the size of your monitor determine how large the image appears on-screen.

2 Double-click the zoom tool (🔍) to return to a 100% view.

3 Double-click the hand tool (✋) to fit the image on your screen.

Using the zoom tool

In addition to the View commands, you can use the zoom tool to magnify and reduce the view of an image.

1 Select the zoom tool (🔍)and move the tool pointer onto the 01Start image. Notice that a plus sign appears at the center of the zoom tool.

2 Position the zoom tool over one of the skaters in the 01Start image, and click to magnify the image.

3 With the zoom tool selected and positioned in the image area, hold down Alt (Windows) or Option (Mac OS). A minus sign appears at the center of the zoom tool (🔍).

4 Click once; the magnification of the image is reduced by 100%.

You can also draw a marquee with the zoom tool to magnify a specific area of an image.

5 Draw a marquee around the head of one of the skaters using the zoom tool.

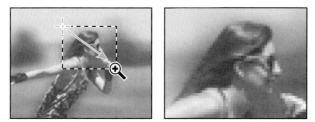

Area selected   *Resulting view*

The percentage at which the area is magnified is determined by the size of the marquee you draw with the zoom tool. (The smaller the marquee you draw, the larger the level of magnification.)

Note: You can draw a marquee with the zoom-in tool to enlarge the view of an image, but you cannot draw a marquee with the zoom-out tool to reduce the view of an image.

You can use the zoom tool to quickly return to a 100% view, regardless of the current magnification level.

6 Double-click the zoom tool to return the 01Start file to a 100% view.

Because the zoom tool is used frequently during the editing process to enlarge and reduce the view of an image, you can select it from the keyboard at any time without deselecting the active tool.

7 To select the zoom-in tool from the keyboard, hold down spacebar+Ctrl (Windows) or spacebar+Command (Mac OS). Zoom in on the desired area, and then release the keys.

8 To select the zoom-out tool from the keyboard, hold down spacebar+Alt (Windows) or spacebar+Option (Mac OS). Click the desired area to reduce the view of the image, and then release the keys.

Scrolling an image

You use the hand tool to scroll through an image that does not fit in the active window. If the image fits in the active window, the hand tool has no effect when you drag it in the image window.

1 Resize the image window to make it smaller than the image.

2 Select the hand tool. Then drag in the image window to bring another skater into view. As you drag, the image moves with the hand.

Like the zoom tool, you can select the hand tool from the keyboard without deselecting the active tool.

3 Select any tool but the hand tool.

4 Hold down the spacebar to select the hand tool from the keyboard. Drag to reposition the image. Then release the spacebar.

5 Double-click the zoom tool to return the image to 100% magnification.

Note: To return the window to its original size at 100% view, select Resize Windows to Fit in the zoom tool options bar, and then double-click the zoom tool.

Using the Navigator palette

The Photoshop Navigator palette lets you scroll an image at different magnification levels without scrolling or resizing an image in the image window. (ImageReady does not have a Navigator palette.)

1 If you don't see the Navigator palette, choose Window > Show Navigator to display it.

2 In the Navigator palette, drag the slider to the right to about 200% to magnify the view of the skater. As you drag the slider to increase the level of magnification, the red outline in the Navigator window decreases in size.

3 In the Navigator palette, position the pointer inside the red outline. The pointer becomes a hand.

Dragging slider to 200%   *200% view of image*   *View in Navigator palette*

4 Drag the hand to scroll to different parts of the image.

You can also draw a marquee in the Navigator palette to identify the area of the image you want to view.

5 With the pointer still positioned in the Navigator palette, hold down Ctrl (Windows) or Command (Mac OS), and draw a marquee over an area of the image. The smaller the marquee you draw, the greater the magnification level in the image window.

Using the Info bar

The Info bar is positioned at the lower left corner of the application window (Windows) or the document window (Mac OS). In Photoshop, you can choose from a pop-up menu to display information about a document's size, profile, scratch size, efficiency, timing, and current tool. In ImageReady, you can choose to display the original and optimized file size, optimized information, image dimensions, watermark strength, undo/redo status, original image in bytes, optimized image in bytes, the amount of optimized savings, and download times. You can also use the ImageReady Info bar to change the view of an image.

Photoshop Info bar   ImageReady Info bar

By default, the image's file size appears in the Info bar. The first value indicates the size if saved as a flattened file with no layer data; the second value indicates the size if saved with all layers and channels.

1 Position the pointer over the triangle in the Info bar and hold down the mouse button to display the pop-up menu.

In Photoshop, besides the file size, you can display the document profile, how efficiently Photoshop is operating and whether it's using the scratch disk (an Efficiency of less than 100%), the amount of time it took to complete the last operation, and the current tool.

💡 *In ImageReady, use the Info bar to change the view of an image by choosing a preset zoom percentage from the percentage pop-up menu in the Info bar. For complete information on the ImageReady Info bar options, see "Looking at the Work Area" in ImageReady 3.0 online Help.*

Working with palettes

Palettes help you monitor and modify images. By default, they appear in stacked groups. To show or hide a palette as you work, choose the appropriate Window > Show or Window > Hide command. Show displays the selected palette at the front of its group; Hide conceals the entire group.

Changing the palette display

You can reorganize your work space in various ways. Experiment with several techniques:

• To hide or display all open palettes and the toolbox, press Tab.

• To hide or display the palettes only, press Shift+Tab.

• To make a palette appear at the front of its group, click the palette's tab.

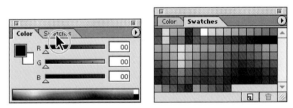

Click the Swatches tab to move it to the front.

• To move an entire palette group, drag its title bar.

• To rearrange or separate a palette group, drag a palette's tab. Dragging a palette outside of an existing group creates a new group.

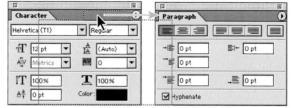

Palettes are grouped.   *Click the palette tab, and drag the palette to separate it
from the group.*

• To move a palette to another group, drag the palette's tab to that group.

• To dock a palette in the Photoshop tool options bar, drag the desired palette's tab into the palette well so that the palette well is highlighted.

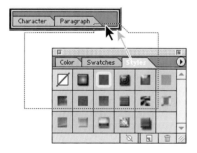

Note: *Palettes are considered hidden when stored in the tool options bar. Clicking on the title of a palette stored in the well shows the palette until you click outside the palette.*

• To display a palette menu, position the pointer on the triangle in the upper right corner of the palette, and hold down the mouse button.

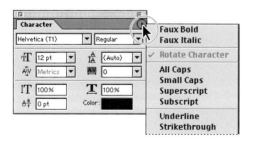

• To change the height of a palette, drag its lower right corner. To return the palette to default size, click the minimize/maximize box (Windows) or the resize box (Mac OS) in the right corner of the title bar. (A second click collapses the palette group.) You cannot resize the Info, Color, Character, and Paragraph palettes in Photoshop, or the Optimize, Info, Color, Layer Options, Character, Paragraph, Slice, and Image Map palettes in ImageReady.

Click to collapse or expand the palette.
A. Windows B. Mac OS

• To collapse a group to palette titles only, Alt-click the minimize/maximize box (Windows) or click the resize box (Mac OS). Or double-click a palette's tab. You can still access the menu of a collapsed palette.

Setting the positions of palettes and dialog boxes

The positions of all open palettes and movable dialog boxes are saved by default when you exit the program. Alternatively, you can always start with default palette positions or restore default positions at any time:

• To reset palettes to the default positions, choose Window > Reset Palette Locations (Photoshop), or choose Window > Arrange > Reset Palettes (ImageReady).

• To always start with the preset palette and dialog box positions, choose Edit > Preferences > General, and deselect Save Palette Locations. The change takes effect the next time you start Adobe Photoshop or Adobe ImageReady.

Using context menus

In addition to the menus at the top of your screen, context menus display commands relevant to the active tool, selection, or palette.

To display a context menu, position the pointer over the image or over an item in a palette and right-click (Windows) or Control-click (Mac OS).

Here we've used the blur tool (◊). The Sample Size options are displayed in the blur tool's context menu. You can also access these same options using the tool options bar.

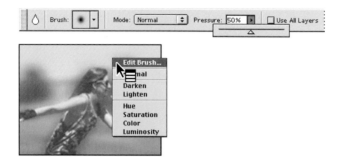

Using online Help

For complete information about using palettes, tools, and the application features, you can use online Help.

Adobe Photoshop and Adobe ImageReady each include complete documentation in online Help plus keyboard shortcuts, full-color galleries of examples, and more detailed information about some procedures.

Online Help is easy to use, because you can look for topics in several ways:

• Scanning a table of contents.

• Searching for keywords.

• Using an index.

• Jumping from topic to topic using related topic links.

First you'll try looking for a topic using the Contents screen.

1 Display online Help:

• In Windows, press F1, or choose Help > Contents to display the Help Contents menu.

• In Mac OS, choose Help > Help Contents (Photoshop) or Help > Help Topics (ImageReady).

Your browser will launch if it is not already running. The topics for the Photoshop 6.0 online Help system (all of the information in the Photoshop 6.0 User Guide) appears in the left frame of your browser window.

2 Drag the scroll bar or click the arrows for the left frame to navigate through the Help contents. The contents are organized in a hierarchy of topics, much like the chapters of a book.

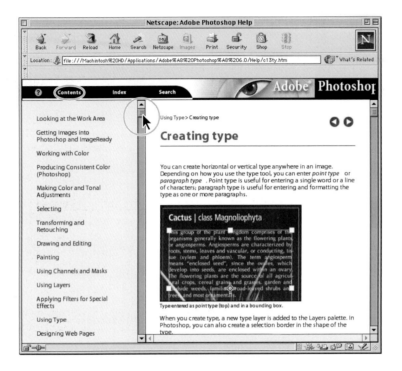

3 Position the pointer on Looking at the Work Area, and click to display its contents in the right window frame.

4 Locate the *Toolbox overview* topic, and click to display it. An illustration of the tools with brief descriptions appears.

The online Help system is interactive. You can click any text *link* to jump to another topic. Whenever you move the mouse pointer over a link or a hotspot, the mouse pointer changes to a pointing-finger icon.

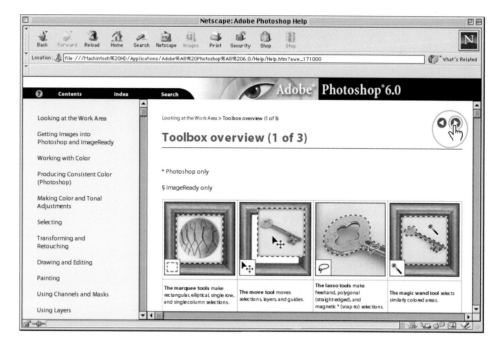

Using keywords, links, and the index

If you can't find the topic you are interested in by scanning the Contents page, then you can try searching using a keyword.

1 Click Search in the black tab area at the top of the Photoshop online Help window.

A search text box appears in the left frame.

2 Type a keyword in the text box and click the Search button. A list of topics based on your keyword search is displayed. If desired, click some of the links to go to the related topics.

You can also search for a topic using the index.

3 Click Index in the black tab area at the top of the Photoshop online Help window. A list of alphabetical letters displays in the left frame.

4 Click one of the letters to display index entries.

These entries appear alphabetically by topic and subtopic, like the index of a book.

5 Click the page number next to an entry to go to the corresponding topic page.

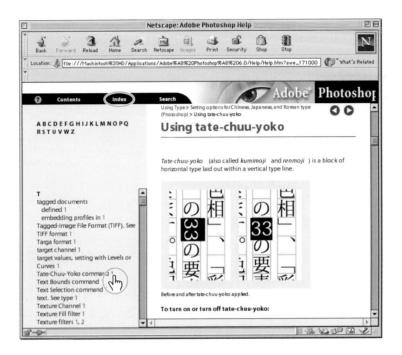

6 When you have finished browsing, click the Close box to close the Photoshop online Help window, or quit your browser application.

Using Adobe online services

Another way to get information on Adobe Photoshop or on related Adobe products is to use the Adobe online services. If you have an Internet connection and a Web browser installed on your system, you can access the U.S. Adobe Systems Web site (at www.adobe.com) for information on services, products, and tips pertaining to Photoshop.

Adobe Online provides access to up-to-the-minute information about services, products, and tips for using Adobe products.

1 In Photoshop or ImageReady, choose Help > Adobe Online, or click the icon () at the top of the toolbox.

2 Do any of the following:

• Select Refresh to make sure you have the latest version of the Adobe Online window and its buttons, as well as the latest bookmarks. It is important to refresh the screen so that the current options are available for you to choose from.

• Select Preferences to specify connection options. General preferences affect how Adobe Online interacts with all Adobe products installed on your system, and Application preferences affect how Adobe Online interacts with Photoshop and ImageReady. To see an explanation of each preference option, click Setup and follow the prompts. You also can set up an automatic refresh using the Update Options.

Note: *You can also set Adobe Online preferences by choosing Edit > Preferences > Adobe Online.*

3 If you selected Preferences in step 2, select configuration options in the Adobe Online Preferences dialog box and then click OK:

• Select Use System Default Internet Settings (Windows) or Use Internet Config settings (Mac OS) to use the Internet configuration currently used by your system, or enter new proxy and port settings for ImageReady to use.

• In the Update Options dialog box, select refresh and download options for updating Adobe Online.

When you set up Adobe Online to connect to your Web browser, Adobe can either notify you whenever new information is available or automatically download that information to your hard disk. If you choose not to use the Adobe automatic download feature, you can still view and download new files whenever they are available from within the Adobe Online window.

4 Click any button in the Adobe Online window to open the Web page to which the button is linked.

You can easily find information specifically on Photoshop and ImageReady—including tips and techniques, galleries of artwork by Adobe designers and artists around the world, the latest product information, and troubleshooting and technical information. Or you can learn about other Adobe products and news.

5 Click the bookmark button ( ) in the Adobe Online dialog box to view Web pages related to Photoshop and Adobe. These bookmarks are automatically updated as new Web sites become available.

6 Click Close to return to Photoshop or ImageReady.

Jumping to ImageReady

Now you'll switch to ImageReady. Jumping between the applications lets you use the full feature sets of both applications when preparing graphics for the Web or other purposes, yet still maintain a streamlined workflow. Jumping to another application also saves you from having to close the file in Photoshop and reopen it in the other application.

1 In Photoshop, click the Jump To ImageReady button ( ).

The 01Start.psd file opens in ImageReady.

You can jump between Photoshop and ImageReady to transfer an image between the two applications for editing, without closing or exiting the originating application. In addition, you can jump from ImageReady to other graphics-editing applications and HTML-editing applications installed on your system. For more information on jumping to other applications in ImageReady, see Photoshop 6.0 online Help.

2 Select Jump To, or choose File > Jump To > Adobe Photoshop to return to Photoshop.

Each time an image in Photoshop or ImageReady is updated with changes made in a jumped-to application, a single history state is added to the Photoshop or ImageReady History palette. You can undo the update in Photoshop or ImageReady as you would with other states in the History palette. For more information, see "Correcting your work" on page 91 in Lesson 4 of this book.

3 Close the file.

You're ready to begin learning how to create and edit images.

Making colors consistent between Photoshop and ImageReady

Although ImageReady 3.0 is capable of reading most profiles in Photoshop files, the RGB color display could vary between Photoshop and ImageReady. If a Photoshop file has a profile embedded, the Use Embedded Color Profile preview option communicates with Photoshop's color management system.

To adjust RGB color display in ImageReady to match color display in Photoshop:

Choose View > Preview > Use Embedded Color Profile.

ImageReady's Use Embedded Color Profile feature is available only if the Photoshop file has a profile embedded.

–From Adobe Photoshop 6.0 online Help

Review questions

1 Describe two ways to change your view of an image.

2 How do you select tools in Photoshop or ImageReady?

3 What are two ways to get more information about Photoshop and ImageReady?

4 Describe two ways to create images in Photoshop and ImageReady.

5 How do you switch between Photoshop and ImageReady?

Review answers

1 You can choose commands from the View menu to zoom in or out of an image, or to fit it to your screen; you can also use the zoom tools and click or drag over an image to enlarge or reduce the view. In addition, you can use keyboard shortcuts to magnify or reduce the display of an image. You can also use the Navigator palette to scroll an image or change its magnification without using the image window.

2 To select a tool, you can select the tool in the toolbox, or you can press the tool's keyboard shortcut. For example, you can press M to select a marquee tool. A selected tool remains active until you select a different tool.

3 Adobe Photoshop contains online Help, with all the information in the Photoshop 6.0 User Guide, plus keyboard shortcuts and some additional information and full-color illustrations. Photoshop also includes a link to the Adobe Systems home page for additional information on services, products, and tips pertaining to Photoshop. ImageReady 3.0 also contains online Help and a link to the Adobe home page.

4 You can create original artwork in Adobe Photoshop or ImageReady, or you can get images into the program by scanning a photograph, a transparency, a negative, or a graphic; by capturing a video image; or by importing artwork created in drawing programs. You can also import previously digitized images—such as those produced by a digital camera or by the Kodak Photo CD process.

5 You can click the Jump To button in the toolbox or choose File > Jump To to switch between Photoshop and ImageReady.

Lesson 2

2 | Working with Selections

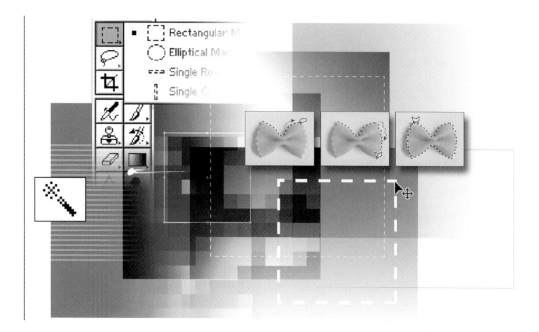

Learning how to select areas of an image is of primary importance—you must first select what you want to affect. Once you've made a selection, only the area within the selection can be edited. Areas outside the selection are protected from change.

In this lesson, you'll learn how to do the following:

- Select parts of an image using a variety of tools.
- Reposition a selection marquee.
- Deselect a selection.
- Move and duplicate a selection.
- Constrain the movement of a selection.
- Choose areas of an image based on proximity or color of pixels.
- Adjust a selection with the arrow keys.
- Add to and subtract from selections.
- Rotate, scale, and transform a selection.
- Combine selection tools.
- Crop an image.

This lesson will take about 40 minutes to complete. The lesson is designed to be done in Adobe Photoshop, but information on using similar functionality in Adobe ImageReady is included where appropriate.

If needed, remove the previous lesson folder from your hard drive, and copy the Lesson02 folder onto it. As you work on this lesson, you'll overwrite the start files. If you need to restore the start files, copy them from the *Adobe Photoshop Classroom in a Book* CD.

Note: *Windows users need to unlock the lesson files before using them. For information, see "Copying the Classroom in a Book files" on page 3.*

Selection tool overview

In Adobe Photoshop, you can make selections based on size, shape, and color using four basic sets of tools—the marquee, lasso, magic wand, and pen tools. You can reposition your selections using the move tool. You can also use the magic eraser tool to make selections in much the same way you use the magic wand tool.

Note: In this lesson, you will use the marquee, lasso, magic wand, and move tools; for information on the pen tools, see Lesson 7, "Basic Pen Tool Techniques."

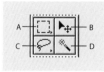

A. *Marquee tool*
B. *Move tool*
C. *Lasso tool*
D. *Magic wand tool*

The marquee and lasso tool icons contain hidden tools, which you can select by holding down the mouse button on the toolbox icon and dragging to the desired tool in the pop-up menu.

The *rectangular marquee tool* (⬚) lets you select a rectangular area in an image. The *elliptical marquee tool* (◯) lets you select elliptical areas. The *rounded rectangle marquee tool* (⬚) in ImageReady lets you select rectangular areas with rounded corners. The *single row marquee tool* (⋯) and *single column marquee tool* (⦙) let you select a 1-pixel-high row and 1-pixel-wide column. You can also use the *crop tool* (🔲) to crop an image.

The *lasso tool* (⌇) lets you make a freehand selection around an area. The *polygon lasso tool* (⋋) lets you make a straight-line selection around an area. The *magnetic lasso tool* (⋗) in Photoshop lets you draw a freehand border that snaps to the edges of an area.

The *magic wand tool* (⚲) lets you select parts of an image based on the similarity in color of adjacent pixels. This tool is useful for selecting odd-shaped areas without having to trace a complex outline using the lasso tool.

ImageReady includes the basic marquee selection tools, the lasso and polygon lasso tools, and the magic wand tool familiar to users of Photoshop. For more convenience in working with common shapes, ImageReady adds an extra marquee selection tool: the rounded rectangle marquee tool.

Getting started

Before beginning this lesson, restore the default application settings for Adobe Photoshop. See "Restoring default preferences" on page 4.

You'll start the lesson by viewing the finished lesson file to see the image that you'll create as you explore the selection tools in Photoshop.

1 Start Adobe Photoshop.

If a notice appears asking whether you want to customize your color settings, click No.

2 Choose File > Open, and open the 02End.psd file, located in the Lessons/Lesson02 folder on your hard drive.

An image of a face, constructed using various types of fruits and vegetables, is displayed.

3 When you have finished viewing the file, either leave the 02End.psd file open for reference, or close it without saving changes.

Selecting with the rectangular marquee tool

You'll start practicing selection techniques using the rectangular marquee tool.

1 Choose File > Open, and open the 02Start.psd file, located in the Lessons/Lesson02 folder on your hard drive.

2 Select the rectangular marquee tool (⬚).

3 Drag it diagonally from the upper left corner to the lower right corner of the melon to create a rectangular selection.

You can move a selection border after you've drawn it by positioning the pointer within the selection and dragging. Notice that this technique changes the location of the selection border; it does not affect the size or shape of the selection.

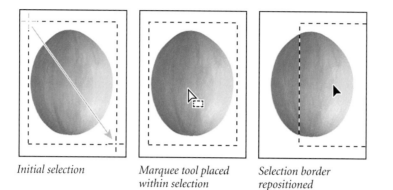

Initial selection   Marquee tool placed   Selection border
                     within selection   repositioned

4 Position the pointer anywhere inside the selection surrounding the melon. The pointer becomes an arrow with a small selection icon next to it.

5 Drag to reposition the border around the melon.

Note: Repositioning techniques for selection borders work with any of the marquee, lasso, and magic wand tools.

If you are still not happy with the selection after repositioning it, you can deselect it and redraw it.

6 Choose Select > Deselect, or click anywhere in the window outside the selection border to deselect the selection.

7 Reselect the melon using the rectangular marquee tool.

To back up one action at any point in the lesson, choose Edit > Undo. In ImageReady, you can set the number of undos in the ImageReady preferences. (The default is 32.)

Selecting with the elliptical marquee tool

Next you'll use the elliptical marquee tool to select eyes for the face. Note that in most cases, making a new selection replaces the existing selection.

1 Select the zoom tool (Q), and click twice on the blueberry to zoom in to a 300% view.

2 Select the elliptical marquee tool (○) hidden under the rectangular marquee tool.

3 Move the pointer over the blueberry, and drag it diagonally across the blueberry to create a selection. Do not release the mouse button.

Repositioning a selection border while creating it

If a selection border isn't placed exactly where you want it, you can adjust its position and size while creating it.

1 Still holding down the mouse button, hold down the spacebar, and drag the selection. The border moves as you drag.

2 Release the spacebar (but not the mouse button), and drag again. Notice that when you drag without the spacebar, the size and shape of the selection change, but its point of origin does not.

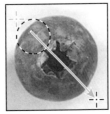  

Incorrect point of origin   *Corrected point of origin*   *Adjusted border*
(Click and drag)   *(Spacebar depressed)*   *(Spacebar released)*

3 When the selection border is positioned and sized correctly, release the mouse button.

Selecting from a center point

Sometimes it's easier to make elliptical or rectangular selections by drawing a selection from the center point of the object to the outside edge. Using this method, you'll reselect the blueberry.

1 Choose Select > Deselect.

2 Position the marquee tool at the approximate center of the blueberry.

3 Click and begin dragging. Then without releasing the mouse button, hold down Alt (Windows) or Option (Mac OS) and continue dragging the selection to the blueberry's outer edge.

Notice that the selection is centered over its starting point.

4 When you have the entire blueberry selected, release the mouse button first and then release Alt/Option.

If necessary, adjust the selection border using one of the methods you learned earlier.

Moving a selection

Now you'll use the move tool to move the blueberry onto the carrot slice to create an eye for the face. Then you'll duplicate and move the selection to make a second eye.

1 Make sure that the blueberry is selected. Then select the move tool (▸₊), and position the pointer within the blueberry's selection. The pointer becomes an arrow with a pair of scissors to indicate that dragging the selection will cut it from its present location and move it to the new location.

2 Drag the blueberry onto the carrot slice.

Move tool placed within blueberry selection   *Blueberry moved onto carrot slice*

3 Choose Select > Deselect.

4 Choose File > Save to save your work.

Moving and duplicating simultaneously

Next you'll move and duplicate a selection simultaneously.

1 Choose View > Fit on Screen to resize the document to fit on your screen.

2 Select the elliptical marquee tool (○).

3 Drag a selection around the carrot slice containing the blueberry. If necessary, adjust the selection border using one of the methods you learned earlier.

4 Select the move tool (⬈₊), hold down Alt (Windows) or Option (Mac OS), and position the pointer within the selection. The pointer becomes a double arrow, which indicates that a duplicate will be made when you move the selection.

5 Continue holding down Alt/Option, and drag a duplicate of the eye onto the left side of the melon face. Release the mouse button and Alt/Option, but do not deselect the eye.

Holding down Shift when you move a selection constrains the movement horizontally or vertically. Using this technique, you'll drag a copy of the left eye to the right side of the face so that the two eyes are level.

6 Hold down Shift+Alt (Windows) or Shift+Option (Mac OS), and drag a copy of the eye to the right side of the face.

7 Choose File > Save.

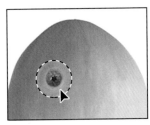

Eye moved onto left side of face   *Duplicate of eye moved with Shift+Alt/Option*

Moving with a keyboard shortcut

Next you'll select the kiwi fruit for the melon's mouth and then move it onto the melon using a keyboard shortcut. The shortcut allows you to temporarily access the move tool instead of selecting it from the toolbox.

1 Select the elliptical marquee tool (○).

2 Drag a selection around the kiwi fruit using one of the methods you learned earlier.

3 With the marquee tool still selected, hold down Ctrl (Windows) or Command (Mac OS), and position the pointer within the selection. A pair of scissors appears with the pointer to indicate that the selection will be cut from its current location.

4 Drag the kiwi mouth onto the face. Do not deselect.

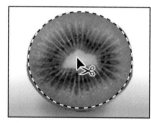
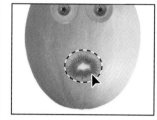

Selection to be cut   *Selection moved onto melon*

Moving with the arrow keys

You can make minor adjustments to the position of a selection using the arrow keys, which allow you to nudge the selection 1 pixel or 10 pixels at a time.

Note: The arrow keys adjust the position of a selection only if you've already moved the selection or if you have the move tool selected. If you try the arrow keys on a selection that has not yet been moved, they will adjust the selection border, not the part of the image that is selected.

1 Press the Up Arrow key (⬆) a few times to move the mouth upward.

Notice that each time you press the arrow key, the mouth moves in 1-pixel increments. Experiment with the other arrow keys to see how they affect the selection.

Sometimes the border around a selected area can distract you as you make adjustments. You can hide the edges of a selection temporarily without actually deselecting and then display the selection border once you've completed the adjustments.

2 Choose View > Show > Selection Edges or View > Show Extras.

The selection border around the mouth disappears.

3 Now hold down Shift, and press an arrow key.

Notice that the selection moves in 10-pixel increments.

4 Use the arrow keys to nudge the mouth until it is positioned where you want it. Then choose View > Show > Selection Edges or View > Show Extras.

5 Choose File > Save.

Copying selections or layers

You can use the move tool to copy selections as you drag them within or between images. Or you can copy and move selections using the Copy, Copy Merged, Cut, and Paste commands. Dragging with the move tool saves memory because the Clipboard is not used as it is with the Copy, Copy Merged, Cut, and Paste commands.

Keep in mind that when a selection or layer is pasted between images with different resolutions, the pasted data retains its pixel dimensions. This can make the pasted portion appear out of proportion to the new image. Use the Image Size command to make the source and destination images the same resolution before copying and pasting.

Photoshop and ImageReady contain several copy and paste commands:

• The Copy command copies the selected area on the active layer.

• The Copy Merged command makes a merged copy of all the visible layers in the selected area.

• The Paste command pastes a cut or copied selection into another part of the image or into another image as a new layer.

• (Photoshop) The Paste Into command pastes a cut or copied selection inside another selection in the same image or different image. The source selection is pasted onto a new layer, and the destination selection border is converted into a layer mask.

–From Adobe Photoshop 6.0 online Help

Selecting with the magic wand

The magic wand tool lets you select adjacent pixels in an image based on their similarity in color. You'll use the magic wand tool to select the pear tomato, which you'll use as a nose for the face.

1 Select the magic wand tool (✐).

The tool options bar allows you to change the way the tools work. In the tool options bar for the magic wand tool, the Tolerance setting controls how many similar tones of a color are selected when you click an area. The default value is 32, indicating that 32 similar lighter tones and 32 similar darker tones will be selected.

2 In the tool options bar, enter **50** in the Tolerance text box to increase the number of similar tones that will be selected.

Tolerance: 50   ☑ Anti-aliased ☑ Contiguous ☐ Use All Layers

3 Using the magic wand tool, click anywhere within the pear tomato. Most of it will be selected.

4 To select the remaining area of the pear tomato, hold down Shift, and click the unselected areas. Notice that a plus sign appears with the magic wand pointer, indicating that you're adding to the current selection.

Initial selection *Adding to selection* *Complete selection*
(Shift key depressed)

5 When the pear tomato is completely selected, hold down Ctrl (Windows) or Command (Mac OS), position the pointer within the selection, and drag the tomato nose onto the melon face.

6 Choose Select > Deselect.

7 Choose File > Save.

Selecting with the lasso tool

You can use the lasso tool to make selections that require both freehand and straight lines. You'll select a bow tie for the face using the lasso tool this way. It takes a bit of practice to use the lasso tool to alternate between straight-line and freehand selections—if you make a mistake while you're selecting the bow tie, simply deselect and start again.

1 Select the zoom tool, and click twice on the bow tie pasta to enlarge its view to 300%.

2 Select the lasso tool (🄿). Starting at the upper left corner of the bow tie pasta, drag to the right to create a freehand outline across the curves at the top of the bow tie. Continue holding down the mouse button.

3 To select the right edge of the bow tie, hold down Alt (Windows) or Option (Mac OS), release the mouse button, and then begin outlining with short, straight lines by clicking along the edge. (Notice that the pointer changes from the lasso icon to the polygon lasso icon.) When you reach the bottom right corner of the bow tie, do not release the mouse button.

Freehand outline with lasso tool   *Straight-line outline with polygon lasso tool*   *Completed selection (outline crosses starting point)*

4 Release Alt/Option, and drag to the left to create a freehand outline across the bottom of the bow tie. (The pointer returns to the lasso icon.)

5 Hold down Alt/Option again, and click the mouse button along the left edge of the bow tie to draw straight lines.

6 To complete the selection, make sure that the last straight line crosses the start of the selection, release Alt/Option, and then release the mouse button.

7 Choose View > Fit on Screen to resize the document to fit on your screen.

8 Hold down Ctrl (Windows) or Command (Mac OS), and drag the bow tie selection to the bottom of the melon face.

9 Choose File > Save.

Adding and subtracting selections

Holding down Shift while you are selecting an area adds to the current selection. Holding down Alt (Windows) or Option (Mac OS) subtracts from the selection. Now you'll use these techniques with the lasso tool to perfect a rough selection of the mushroom image. The mushroom will become a hat for the melon face.

1 Select the zoom tool (🔍), and click twice on the mushroom to enlarge its view to 300%.

2 Select the lasso tool (🏹), and drag a rough outline around the mushroom (include some of the area outside the mushroom and some of the stem).

3 Hold down Shift. A plus sign appears with the lasso tool pointer.

4 Drag the lasso tool around an area you want to add to the selection. Then release the mouse button. The area is added to the current selection.

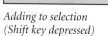

Initial selection   Adding to selection   Result
                         (Shift key depressed)

Note: *If you release the mouse button while drawing a selection with the lasso tool, the selection closes itself by drawing a straight line between the starting point and the point where you release the mouse. To create a more precise border, end the selection by crossing the starting point.*

Next you'll remove, or subtract, part of the selection.

5 Hold down Alt (Windows) or Option (Mac OS). A minus sign appears with the lasso tool pointer.

6 Drag the lasso tool completely around an area you want to remove from the selection. Then repeat the process until you've finished removing all the unwanted parts of the selection.

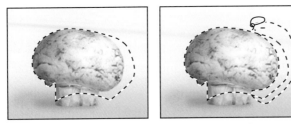 

Selection   *Subtracting from selection*   *Result*
              (Alt/Option depressed)

7 Choose View > Fit on Screen.

8 To move the mushroom hat onto the melon head, hold down Alt+Ctrl (Windows) or Option+Command (Mac OS), and drag a copy of the mushroom to the top of the melon.

9 Choose File > Save.

Selecting with the magnetic lasso

You can use the magnetic lasso tool in Photoshop to make freehand selections of areas with high-contrast edges. When you draw with the magnetic lasso, the border automatically snaps to the edge you are tracing. You can also control the direction of the tool's path by clicking the mouse to place occasional fastening points in the selection border. (There is no magnetic lasso tool in ImageReady.)

You'll now make an ear for the melon face by using the magnetic lasso to select the red part of the grapefruit slice.

1 Select the zoom tool (⚲), and click the grapefruit slice to zoom in to a 200% view.

2 Select the magnetic lasso tool (⌇) hidden under the lasso tool.

3 Now click once in the lower left corner of the red flesh of the grapefruit slice, release the mouse button, and begin tracing the outline of the flesh by dragging to the right over the curved upper edge.

Notice that the tool snaps to the edge and automatically puts in fastening points.

If you think the tool is not following the edge closely enough (in low-contrast areas), you can place your own fastening point in the border by clicking the mouse button. You can add as many fastening points as you feel are necessary. You can also remove fastening points and back up in the path by pressing Delete and moving the mouse back to the last remaining fastening point.

4 When you reach the lower right corner of the grapefruit flesh, double-click the mouse button, which signals the magnetic lasso tool to return to the starting point, and close the selection.

Notice that the tool automatically follows the remaining edge of the flesh as it completes the border.

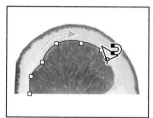
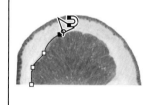
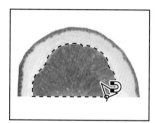

Laying down fastening points   *Removing fastening points*   *Double-clicking at corner to close path*

You can now move the selected part of the grapefruit next to the melon.

5 Double-click the hand tool (🖐) to fit the image on-screen.

6 Select the move tool, and drag the grapefruit ear to the middle of the left side of the melon face. Do not deselect.

7 Choose File > Save.

Softening the edges of a selection

You have two ways to smooth the hard edges of a selection.

Anti-aliasing smooths the jagged edges of a selection by softening the color transition between edge pixels and background pixels. Since only the edge pixels change, no detail is lost. Anti-aliasing is useful when cutting, copying, and pasting selections to create composite images. Anti-aliasing is available for the lasso, polygon lasso, magnetic lasso, elliptical marquee, and magic wand tools. (Select the tool to display its tool options bar.) You must specify the anti-aliasing option before using these tools. Once a selection is made, you cannot add anti-aliasing.

Feathering blurs edges by building a transition boundary between the selection and its surrounding pixels. This blurring can cause some loss of detail at the edge of the selection. You can define feathering for the marquee, lasso, polygon lasso, or magnetic lasso tool as you use the tool, or you can add feathering to an existing selection. Feathering effects become apparent when you move, cut, or copy the selection.

• To use anti-aliasing, select the marquee, lasso, polygon lasso, or magnetic lasso tool to display its tool options bar. Then select Anti-aliased in the tool options bar for the selected tool.

• To define a feathered edge for a selection tool, select the marquee, lasso, polygon lasso, or magnetic lasso tool to display its tool options bar. Then enter a Feather value in the tool options bar. This value defines the width of the feathered edge and can range from 1 to 250 pixels.

• To define a feathered edge for an existing selection, choose Select > Feather. Then enter a value for the Feather Radius, and click OK.

–From Adobe Photoshop 6.0 online Help

Transforming a selection

Next you'll use the Free Transform command to rotate and scale the melon's left ear, and then you'll duplicate and flip a copy to create a right ear.

1 Choose Edit > Free Transform.

A bounding box appears around the ear selection.

2 To rotate the ear, position the pointer outside a corner handle until you see a curved double-headed arrow (↳), and then drag in the direction you want the ear to rotate. Notice that the ear rotates around the selection's center point (✛).

3 To scale the ear, position the pointer directly on one of the corner handles, and drag to reduce the size of the ear. To scale the ear proportionately, hold down Shift as you drag.

4 To reposition the ear, place your pointer within the bounding box, but not on the center point, and drag. (If you place the pointer on the center point and drag, you will move the center point.)

[?] For information on working with the center point in a transformation, see "Transforming objects in two dimensions" in Adobe Photoshop 6.0 online Help.

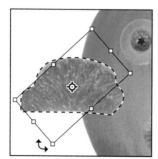 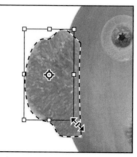 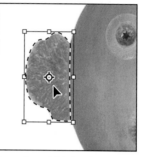

Dragging outside border to rotate ear   *Dragging on corner to scale ear*   *Dragging within border to reposition ear*

♀ *If you don't like the results of a Free Transform, press the Escape key and start over.*

5 When you have the ear positioned correctly, press Enter (Windows) or Return (Mac OS) to apply the transformation. The ear remains selected.

Now you'll move a copy of the ear to the right side of the face, flip the ear horizontally, and fine-tune its placement.

6 Position the pointer within the ear selection, hold down Shift+Alt (Windows) or Shift+Option (Mac OS), and drag a copy of the ear to the right side of the face.

7 With the duplicate ear still selected, choose Edit > Free Transform or Edit > Transform > Rotate.

A bounding box appears around the duplicate ear.

8 Choose Edit > Transform > Flip Horizontal.

9 If needed, place the pointer within the selection, and drag to reposition it next to the melon face.

10 If needed, choose Edit > Free Transform, rotate the ear to fit the right side of the face.

11 Press Enter (Windows) or Return (Mac OS) to complete the transformation.

12 Choose File > Save.

Combining selection tools

As you already know, the magic wand tool makes selections based on color. If an object you want to select is on a solid-colored background, it can be much easier to select the object and the background and then use the magic wand tool to subtract the background color, leaving the desired object selected.

You'll see how this works by using the rectangular marquee tool and the magic wand tool to select radish eyebrows for the face.

1 Select the rectangular marquee tool ([□]) hidden under the elliptical marquee tool (○).

2 Drag a selection around the radishes.

At this point, the radishes and the white background area are selected. You'll subtract the white area from the selection, resulting in only the radishes in the selection.

3 Select the magic wand tool; then hold down Alt (Windows) or Option (Mac OS). A minus sign appears with the magic wand pointer.

4 Click anywhere in the selected white area surrounding the radishes. Now only the radishes are selected.

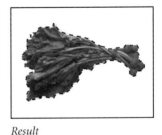

Initial selection   *Subtracting from selection with*   *Result*
                         Alt/Option magic wand

5 To duplicate and move the radish eyebrow to the melon face, hold down Alt+Ctrl (Windows) or Option+Command (Mac OS), and drag the radish above the left eye on the melon face. Do not deselect.

6 Hold down Shift+Alt+Ctrl (Windows) or Shift+Option+Command (Mac OS), position the pointer within the selection, and drag to duplicate and reposition another eyebrow above the right eye.

7 With the right eyebrow still selected, choose Edit > Free Transform or Edit > Transform > Rotate. A bounding box appears around the eyebrow.

8 Choose Edit > Transform > Flip Horizontal to adjust the right eyebrow. If you like, reposition the eyebrow using any of the methods you've learned. Then press Enter (Windows) or Return (Mac OS) to complete the transformation.

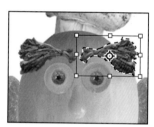

Left eyebrow placed with Alt+Ctrl/Option+Command

Right eyebrow placed with Shift+Alt+Ctrl/Shift+ Option+Command

Right eyebrow flipped horizontally

9 Choose File > Save.

Cropping the completed image

In both Photoshop and ImageReady, you can use either the crop tool or the Crop command to crop an image. You can also decide whether to delete the area outside of a rectangular selection, or whether to hide the area outside of the selection. You can use the Trim command to discard a border area around the edge of the image, based on transparency or edge color.

   In ImageReady, use the Crop command or the crop tool set to Hide when creating animated elements that move from off-screen into the live image area.

To complete the artwork, you'll crop the image to a final size.

1 Select the crop tool (⊨), or press C to switch from the current tool to the crop tool.

2 Move the pointer into the image window, and drag diagonally from the upper left corner to the lower right corner of the completed artwork to create a crop marquee.

After dragging in Photoshop, make sure that Perspective is not selected in the crop tool options bar.

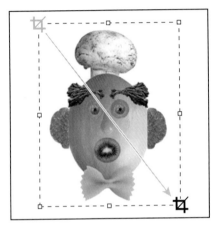

3 If you need to reposition the crop marquee, position the pointer anywhere inside the marquee and drag.

4 If you want to resize the marquee, drag a handle.

5 When the marquee is positioned where you want it, press Enter (Windows) or Return (Mac OS) to crop the image.

6 Choose File > Save.

The fruit-and-vegetable face is complete.

For the Web: Creating evenly spaced buttons for a Web page

One of the most common tasks when designing Web pages is to create a column of buttons that are used to link to other pages in the Web site. Using a background grid in Adobe Photoshop and the rectangular marquee tool, you can quickly create identical and evenly spaced buttons from selections. These buttons can then be stylized in ImageReady in preparation for the Web. Here's a way to create the column of buttons, and then to add a style to create the illusion of three-dimensional buttons.

1 In Adobe Photoshop, choose File > New. Name the new file, size it to fit the buttons you want to create (we chose 3 inches wide by 4.5 inches tall), select the Transparent option, and click OK.

2 Choose Edit > Preferences > Guides & Grid. Enter the height of your planned buttons in the Gridline Every text box (such as 0.5 inches), **1** in the Subdivisions text box, and click OK.

Note: *Grids are only available in Photoshop.*

3 Choose View > Show > Grid to make the grid visible.

4 Choose View > Snap To > Grid if the command is not already selected. (Snap to Grid is selected if there is a check mark next to the command.)

5 Select the rectangular marquee tool ( ), and draw a rectangular selection one grid line high by four grid lines wide (or as wide as you want your buttons to be). Notice that the marquee snaps to the nearest grid line.

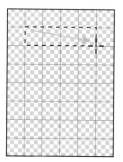

6 If you don't see the Color palette, choose Window > Show Color to display it.

7 Choose Web Color Sliders from the Color palette menu to ensure that you will choose a Web-safe color for your button.

8 Select a color in the Color palette (such as blue).

9 Select the paint bucket tool ( ) hidden under gradient tool ( ), and click in the selection to paint it.

10 To duplicate the rectangle, hold down the Shift+Ctrl+Alt keys (Windows) or the Shift+Command+Option keys (Mac OS), and drag two grid lines down from the original rectangle. (Holding Ctrl+Alt/Command+Option as you drag duplicates the selection. Holding down Shift constrains the newly created rectangle along the horizontal or— in this case—vertical axis). Repeat this process to add the third and fourth rectangles. You should now have four buttons spaced evenly by two grid lines each.

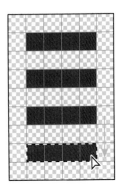

11 Choose File > Save to save your new buttons.

12 Click the Jump To ImageReady button in the toolbox to open the image in ImageReady.

13 Choose Window > Show Styles.

14 In the Styles palette, select a style (such as the Blue Glass button) to apply it to your rectangles.

You can also apply the style by dragging it from the Styles palette onto any of the buttons in the main window and releasing the mouse button. The button style is automatically applied to all of the buttons on the layer.

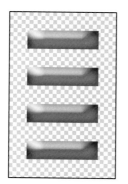

If you want, you can now add text to the buttons using the type tool (T). When you are finished, save your artwork. You can now use the buttons in your Web page design.

Review questions

1 Once you've made a selection, what area of the image can be edited?

2 How do you add to and subtract from a selection?

3 How can you move a selection while you're drawing it?

4 When drawing a selection with the lasso tool, how should you finish drawing the selection to ensure that the selection is the shape you want?

5 How does the magic wand tool determine which areas of an image to select? What is tolerance, and how does it affect a selection?

Review answers

1 Only the area within the selection can be edited.

2 To add to a selection, hold down Shift, and then drag or click the active selection tool on the area you want to add to the selection. To subtract from a selection, hold down Alt (Windows) or Option (Mac OS), and then drag or click the active selection tool on the area you want to remove from the selection.

3 Without releasing the mouse button, hold down the spacebar, and drag to reposition the selection.

4 To make sure that the selection is the shape you want, end the selection by dragging across the starting point of the selection. If you start and stop the selection at different points, Photoshop or ImageReady draws a straight line between the start point of the selection and the end point of the selection.

5 The magic wand selects adjacent pixels based on their similarity in color. The Tolerance setting determines how many color tones the magic wand will select. The higher the tolerance setting, the more tones the magic wand selects.

Lesson 3

3 | Layer Basics

Both Adobe Photoshop and Adobe ImageReady let you isolate different parts of an image on layers. Each layer can then be edited as discrete artwork, allowing unlimited flexibility in composing and revising an image.

In this lesson, you'll learn how to do the following:

- Organize your artwork on layers.

- Create a new layer.

- View and hide layers.

- Select layers.

- Remove artwork on layers.

- Reorder layers to change the placement of artwork in the image.

- Apply modes to layers to vary the effect of artwork on the layer.

- Link layers to affect them simultaneously.

- Apply a gradient to a layer.

- Add text and layer effects to a layer.

- Save a copy of the file with the layers flattened.

This lesson will take about 60 minutes to complete. The lesson is designed to be done in Adobe Photoshop, but information on using similar functionality in Adobe ImageReady is included where appropriate.

If needed, remove the previous lesson folder from your hard drive, and copy the Lesson03 folder onto it. As you work on this lesson, you'll overwrite the start files. If you need to restore the start files, copy them from the *Adobe Photoshop Classroom in a Book* CD.

Note: *Windows users need to unlock the lesson files before using them. For information, see "Copying the Classroom in a Book files" on page 3.*

Organizing artwork on layers

Every Photoshop file contains one or more *layers*. New files are generally created with a *background*, which contains a color or an image that shows through the transparent areas of subsequent layers. You can view and manipulate layers with the Layers palette.

All new layers in an image are transparent until you add artwork (pixel values). Working with layers is analogous to placing portions of a drawing on sheets of acetate: Individual sheets of acetate may be edited, repositioned, and deleted without affecting the other sheets, and when the sheets are stacked, the entire drawing is visible.

For complete information on backgrounds and converting backgrounds to layers, see Photoshop 6.0 online Help.

Getting started

Before beginning this lesson, restore the default application settings for Adobe Photoshop. See "Restoring default preferences" on page 4.

You'll start the lesson by viewing the final lesson file to see what you'll accomplish.

1 Start Adobe Photoshop.

If a notice appears asking whether you want to customize your color settings, click No.

2 Choose File > Open, and open the file 03End.psd file from the Lessons/Lesson03 folder.

3 When you have finished viewing the file, either leave it open for reference or close it without saving changes.

For an illustration of the finished artwork for this lesson, see the gallery at the beginning of the color section.

Creating and viewing layers

Now you'll open the start file and begin the lesson by working with the image as you learn about the Layers palette and layer options.

1 Choose File > Open, and open the file 03Start.psd from the Lessons/Lesson03 folder on your hard drive.

You'll add a new layer to the 03Start.psd file by bringing in an image from another file.

2 Choose File > Open, and open the Clock.psd file in the Lesson03 folder.

3 Select the move tool (⊹).

4 Hold down Shift and drag the image in Clock.psd into the 03Start.psd file. Place it on top of the image of the keyboard. (Holding down Shift when dragging artwork into a new file centers the art on the new file's image.)

The clock now appears on its own layer, Layer 1, in the 03Start.psd file's Layers palette.

Clock image in Clock.psd   *Clock image moved into 03Start.psd*

5 Close the Clock.psd file.

6 If the Layers palette is not showing, choose Window > Show Layers to display it. If you want to expand the Layers palette, click the minimize/maximize box (Windows) or the resize box (Mac OS) at the top of the palette.

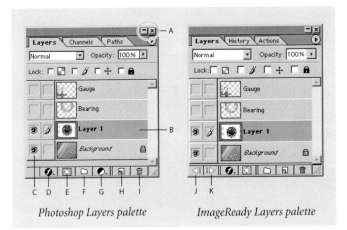

Photoshop Layers palette   *ImageReady Layers palette*

A. *Minimize/maximize or resize box* B. *New layer (clock image) added to palette*
C. *Show/hide column* D. *New layer styles* E. *New layer mask* F. *New layer set*
G. *New adjustment or fill layer* H. *New layer* I. *Trash* J. *Previous animation*
frame button K. *Next animation frame button*

You can use the Layers palette to hide, view, reposition, delete, rename, and merge layers. The Layers palette displays all layers with the layer name and a thumbnail of the layer's image. The thumbnail is automatically updated as you edit the layer.

You will now use the Layers Properties dialog box to rename Layer 1 with a more descriptive name.

7 With Layer 1 (the clock layer) currently selected in the Layers palette, choose Layer Properties from the palette menu.

8 In the Layer Properties dialog box, enter **Clock** in the Name text box and click OK.

Layer 1 is now named Clock in the Layers palette.

The Layers palette shows that the file contains three layers in addition to the Clock layer, some of which are visible and some of which are hidden. The eye icon (☻) to the far left of a layer name in the palette indicates that the layer is visible. You can hide or show a layer by clicking this icon.

9 Click the eye icon next to the Clock layer to hide the clock. Click again to redisplay it.

Creating a layered image

You can create a maximum of 8000 combined layers, layer sets, and layer effects per image, each with its own blending mode and opacity. However, the amount of memory in your system may limit the number of layers possible in a single image. Because each layer, layer set, and layer effect takes up part of that maximum value, a realistic maximum value would be closer to 1000 layers.

Newly added layers and layer sets appear above the selected layer in the Layers palette. You can add layers to an image in a variety of ways:

- *By creating new layers or converting selections into layers.*
- *By converting a background to a layer or adding a background to an image.*
- *By placing, dragging and dropping, or pasting selections or entire images into the image.*
- *By creating type using the type tool.*
- *By using the shape or pen tools to create a new layer that contains a layer clipping path.*

–From Adobe Photoshop 6.0 online Help

Selecting and removing artwork on a layer

Notice that when you moved the clock image onto the keyboard image in the start file, you also moved the white area surrounding the clock. This opaque area blocks out part of the keyboard image, since the clock layer sits on top of the keyboard, or background.

Now you'll remove the white area from around the clock image on the Clock layer by using the eraser tool.

1 Make sure that the Clock layer is selected. To select the layer, click the layer name in the Layers palette.

The layer is highlighted, and a paintbrush icon appears to the left of the layer name, indicating the layer is active.

2 To make the opaque areas on this layer more obvious, hide the keyboard by clicking the eye icon in the Layers palette to the left of the background name.

The keyboard image disappears, and the clock appears against a checkerboard background. The checkerboard indicates transparent areas on the active layer.

3 Select the magic eraser tool (✐), hidden under the eraser tool (⌀).

You can set how close the tolerance is for the magic eraser tool. Too low of a tolerance setting will leave white remaining around the clock. Too high of a tolerance setting will remove some of the clock image.

4 In the tool options bar, enter different values for Tolerance (we used 22), and then click the white area surrounding the clock.

Notice that the checkerboard fills in where the white area had been, indicating that this area is now transparent also.

5 Turn the background back on by clicking the eye icon column next to its name. The keyboard image now shows through where the white area on the Clock layer was removed.

Opaque white area   *Opaque area erased*   *Background turned on*

Rearranging layers

The order in which the layers of an image are organized is called the *stacking order*. The stacking order of layers determines how the image is viewed—you can change the order to make certain parts of the image appear in front of or behind other layers.

Now you'll rearrange layers so that the clock image moves in front of the other images in the file.

1 Make the Gauge and Bearing layers visible by clicking the eye icon column next to their layer names.

Notice that the clock image is partly covered up by the other images in the file.

Making all layers visible   *Result*

2 In the Layers palette, drag the Clock layer up to position it at the top of the palette. When you see a thick black line above the Gauge layer, release the mouse button.

The Clock layer moves to the top of the palette's stacking order, and the clock image appears in front of the other images.

Repositioning Clock layer   *Result*

Changing the opacity and mode of a layer

The clock image now blocks out any images that lie on layers below it. You can reduce the opacity of the clock layer, which allows other layers to show through it. You can also apply different blending modes to the layer, which affect how the clock image blends with the layers below it.

1 With the Clock layer selected, click the arrow next to the Opacity text box in the Layers palette, and drag the slider to 50%.

The clock becomes partially transparent, and you can see the layers underneath. Note that the change in opacity affects only the image areas on the Clock layer.

Changing opacity   *Result*

2 Next try applying some blending modes to the Clock layer to see their effects. Choose Difference and then Darken from the mode menu (to the left of the Opacity text box), and notice the effect on the clock image. Then select the Screen mode (the mode we used for our example) and change the opacity to 90%.

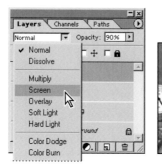 

Changing mode and opacity *Result*

3 Choose File > Save to save your work.

For complete information on blending modes, see Photoshop 6.0 online Help.

Setting layer blending options

The blending options in the Layer Style dialog box (Photoshop) and the Layer Options palette (ImageReady) let you change a layer's opacity and blending with the pixels underneath.

Keep in mind that a layer's opacity and blending mode interact with the opacity and mode of the tools you use to paint and edit the pixels on the layer. For example, suppose you are working on a layer that uses the Dissolve mode and an opacity of 50%. If you paint on this layer using the paintbrush tool set to Normal mode with an opacity of 100%, the paint will appear in Dissolve mode with a 50% opacity because this is the maximum the layer can display. On the other hand, suppose you are working on a layer created using Normal mode and 100% opacity. If you use the eraser tool with an opacity of 50%, only 50% of the paint will disappear as you erase.

–From Adobe Photoshop 6.0 online Help

For an illustration of some layer mode effects, see figure 3-1 in the color section.

Linking layers

An efficient way to work with layers is to link two or more of them together. By linking layers, you can move and transform them simultaneously, thereby maintaining their alignment with each other.

You'll now link the Clock and Bearing layers, and then reposition, scale, and rotate them together.

1 Select the move tool (⊹), and drag the clock to the lower-right corner of the collage so that just the top half of the clock face is visible.

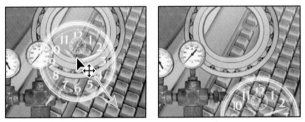

Dragging clock image   *Result*

2 With the Clock layer active in the Layers palette, click the small box to the right of the eye icon for the Bearing layer.

A link icon (⚟) appears in the box, indicating that the Bearing layer is linked to the Clock layer. (The active or selected layer does not display a link icon when you create linked layers.)

3 Position the move tool in the image window, and drag toward the top margin of the image. The clock and bearing images move simultaneously.

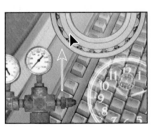

Linking Clock layer to   *Moving layers simultaneously*
Bearing layer

Now you'll try scaling and rotating the linked layers by using the Free Transform command.

4 Choose Edit > Free Transform. A transformation bounding box appears around the clock face.

5 To rotate the clock, position the pointer outside the transformation bounding box until you see a double-headed arrow. Then drag the face clockwise until the bottom left corner of the bounding box appears, and release the mouse button. The bearing rotates as well.

6 Hold down Shift, drag on the bottom corner handle of the bounding box, and scale the clock and bearing to a smaller size.

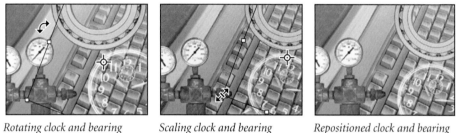

Rotating clock and bearing   *Scaling clock and bearing*   *Repositioned clock and bearing*

7 If necessary, position the pointer inside the bounding box, and drag to reposition the two images.

8 Press Enter (Windows) or Return (Mac OS) to apply the transformation changes.

9 Choose File > Save.

Adding a gradient to a layer

Next you'll create a new layer and add a gradient effect to it. You can add a layer to a file with the New Layer command, which creates a transparent layer with no artwork on it. If you then add a special effect to the layer, such as a gradient, the effect is applied to any layers stacked below the new layer.

In ImageReady, which does not have a gradient tool, you can apply a Gradient/Pattern layer effect from the Layers palette.

Note: *The Gradient/Pattern effects that you apply in ImageReady are not displayed when you view the file in Photoshop. However, the effects are preserved in the image. An alert icon in Photoshop indicates that the effects are present on the layer. The pattern and gradient effects are not altered in Photoshop unless you rasterize the layer on which the effects are applied.*

☒ For complete information on layers and layer effects, see Photoshop 6.0 online Help.

1 In the Layers palette, click the background to make it active.

2 Choose New Layer from the Layers palette menu.

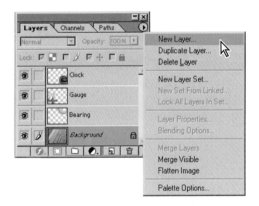

3 In the New Layer dialog box, enter **Gradient** in the Name text box and click OK.

The Gradient layer appears above the background in the Layers palette.

You can now apply a gradient to the new layer. A gradient is a gradual transition between two or more colors. You control the type of transition using the gradient tool.

4 Select the gradient tool (▨).

5 In the tool options bar, click the Linear Gradient button (▨). Then click the arrow (▾) next to the gradient color bar to display the gradient picker. Select Foreground to Transparent and then click on the document window to close the gradient picker.

6 Click the Swatches palette tab to bring it to the front of its palette group, and select a shade of purple that appeals to you.

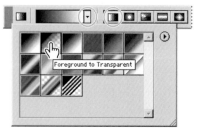 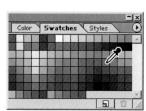

Tool options bar and gradient picker *Swatches palette*

7 With the Gradient layer active in the Layers palette, drag the gradient tool from the right to the left margin of the image.

The gradient extends over the width of the layer, starting with purple and gradually blending to transparent, and affects the look of the keyboard on the layer below it. Because the gradient partially obscures the keyboard, you'll now lighten the effect by changing the Gradient layer's opacity.

8 In the Layers palette, change the opacity for the Gradient layer to 60%. The full keyboard shows through the gradient.

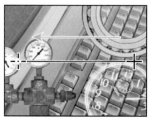  

Dragging the gradient tool *Gradient at 100% opacity* *Gradient at 60% opacity*
(right to left)

Adding text

Now you're ready to create and manipulate some type. You'll create text with the type tool, which places the text on its own type layer. You'll then edit the text and apply a special effect to that layer. ImageReady also has type creation and manipulation features, but it uses a palette to display type options, rather than a dialog box.

Now you'll add text to the image with the type tool.

1 In the Layers palette, click the Clock layer to make it active.

2 Select the type tool (T).

3 Click the image in the upper-left corner.

Notice that the Layers palette now includes a layer named Layer 1 with a "T" icon next to the name, indicating it is a type layer.

4 Click the small Default Foreground and Background Color box (▣) near the bottom of the toolbox to set the foreground color to black. This is the color you want for the text.

5 Choose a font from the Font menu in the tool options bar, and enter a point size in the Size text box (we used 60-point Arial® Regular). Choose Crisp from the Anti-Aliasing menu (ªa) in the options bar.

6 Type **Z2000**.

The text automatically appears on a new layer in the upper left corner of the image where you clicked.

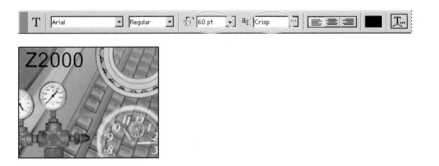

Now you'll reposition the text in the image.

7 Select the move tool (⊹), and drag the "Z2000" text until you can fully see it in the image.

Notice the layer's name changes to "Z2000" in the Layers palette.

For the Web: Ensuring Readability On-Screen

A monitor's resolution is much coarser than what even the least expensive inkjet or laser printer can produce, so a common publication-preparation problem to avoid is hard-to-read type. Text that looks fine on paper often does not look good on-screen. Fortunately, since you design electronic publications on-screen, you get a very good idea as you create your publications how readable their text is. Just be sure to check the on-screen text at actual size (if you have to zoom in, you know it's too hard for your readers to read). Be sure to proof the document in your browser so you will be able to view the same text quality that your readers will see.

Here are some basic guidelines for choosing readable typefaces for on-screen use:

Typeface selection Choose a simple font designed for on-screen use. Sans serif typefaces usually work better on-screen than serif faces, because a monitor cannot easily reproduce the serif font's details. Serif text is generally easier to read in printed documents because the serifs give more visual clues on what letters are being used. (Serifs are those little bars and curves that extend from the ends of letters; "sans" is French for "without," so sans serif means "without serifs.") Sans serif fonts with subtle changes in the characters' strokes (the lines and curves that comprise a character) are usually as hard to read on-screen as are serif fonts, so be cautious about using delicate sans serif fonts for on-screen publications. Instead, consider squared, simple serifs and even-stroke sans serifs in online publications, using fonts specifically designed for on-screen viewing whenever possible.

Text size Use larger sizes than what you would use in print. Typically, use 12-point type for body text in electronic publications. Remember that fine differences in point size are difficult to distinguish on-screen, so avoid sizes like 11.5 and 13 points—they are too close to 12-point type.

Text spacing Use more leading (line spacing) online than in print. Instead of the common 2 points of extra leading for print, use 4 or 6 extra points for on-screen publications. So, for 12-point text, you would ideally have 16- or 18-point leading on-screen.

–From Adobe Photoshop 6.0 online Help

Applying a layer style

You can enhance a layer by adding a shadow, glow, bevel, emboss, or other special effect from a collection of automated and editable layer styles. These styles are easy to apply and link directly to the layer you specify.

Applying layer styles

Layer styles are composed of one or more layer effects. You can apply layer styles to layers in any image. Once you apply a layer effect to a layer, you have created a custom layer style composed of that single effect. You can use a layer style either to replace all of the current layer effects applied to a layer, or to add layer effects while preserving the existing layer effects. After you have applied a layer effect, you can customize it. You can also save the resulting layer style for ease of reuse.

Layer styles are composed of a combination of one or more of the following effects:

• Drop Shadow to add a shadow that falls behind the contents on the layer.

• Inner Shadow to add a shadow that falls just inside the edges of the layer contents, giving the layer a recessed appearance.

• Outer Glow and Inner Glow to add glows that emanate from the outside or inside edges of the layer contents.

• Bevel and Emboss to add various combinations of highlights and shadows to a layer.

• Satin to apply shading to the interior of a layer that reacts to the shape of the layer, typically creating a satiny finish.

• Color, Gradient, and Pattern Overlay to overlay a color, gradient, or pattern on a layer.

• Stroke to outline the object on the current layer using color, a gradient, or a pattern. It is particularly useful on hard-edged shapes such as type.

The preset layer styles in the Styles palette, Styles pop-up palette (Photoshop), and the style libraries are composed of one or more of these layer effects and typically have been customized to create a specific result.

–From Adobe Photoshop 6.0 online Help

Layer styles are handled differently in Photoshop and ImageReady. In Photoshop, you use the Layer Styles dialog box to edit layer styles. In ImageReady, you use the Layer Options/Style palette along with the name of the effect you want to edit.

Modifying layer styles in Photoshop

Modifying layer styles in ImageReady

Individual effects can also be hidden temporarily by clicking the eye icon in the Layers palette or copied to other layers by dragging the effect onto the destination layer.

Now you'll apply a glowing yellow stroke around the type, and fill the type with a pattern. You'll begin by adding a glow.

1 With the Z2000 type layer still active, choose Layer > Layer Style > Outer Glow.

💡 *You can also call up the Layer Style dialog box by double-clicking the layer's name in the Layers palette or clicking the Add a Layer Style button (●) from the bottom of the Layers palette and choosing a command from the menu that appears.*

2 In the Layer Style dialog box, select Preview so that you can preview the effect.

3 In the Elements area, enter **10** for Spread. Then enter **10** for Size in pixels.

Next you'll add a yellow stroke to the text.

4 Select the Stroke check box in the left side of the Layer Style dialog box, and then click the name Stroke to display its individual options.

Selecting the Stroke check box applies default stroke settings but displays previous (Outer Glow) options.   *Clicking the Stroke name applies default stroke settings and displays stroke options for editing.*

5 In the Structure area, enter **1** for Size to create a 1-pixel-wide stroke. Click the Color box to display the color picker. Then choose a yellow color (we used R=255, G=255, and B=0) and click OK to apply and close the Color Picker dialog box.

6 Click the name Pattern Overlay in the left side of the Layer Style dialog box. This is the same as selecting Pattern Overlay and then clicking the name to display individual options. Enter **200** for Scale.

7 Click OK to apply the style to the type.

Layer effects are automatically applied to changes you make to a layer. You can edit the text and watch how the layer effect tracks the change.

8 Select the type tool (T) and select the text "Z2000." Change the text to **Z999**.

9 Drag or double-click the type tool in the text to select the "Z999" text. Enter a larger point size in the Font Size text box in the tool options bar (we used 72 points).

10 Notice that the layer style is applied to the text both as you type the new text and when you change to the larger font size.

11 Choose File > Save.

Flattening and saving files

When you have edited all the layers in your image, you can make a copy of the file with the layers flattened. Flattening a file's layers merges them into a single background, greatly reducing the file size. However, you shouldn't flatten an image until you are certain you're satisfied with all your design decisions. In most cases, you should retain a copy of the file with its layers intact, in case you later need to edit a layer.

To save a flattened version of the file, you will use the Flatten Image command.

1 Choose Flatten Image from the palette menu in the Layers palette. (You may need to select a different tool or layer to exit type-editing mode.)

2 Choose File > Save As.

3 In the dialog box, type the name **Flat03.psd** and click Save.

The Save As command saves a flattened version of the file while leaving the original file and all its layers intact. Your collage of business images is now complete.

Review questions

1 What is the advantage of using layers?

2 How do you hide or show individual layers?

3 How can you make artwork on one layer appear in front of artwork on another layer?

4 How can you manipulate multiple layers simultaneously?

5 When you've completed your artwork, what can you do to a file to minimize its size?

Review answers

1 Layers allow you to edit different parts of an image as discrete objects.

2 The eye icon to the far left of the layer name in the Layers palette indicates that a layer is visible. You can hide or show a layer by clicking this icon.

3 You can make artwork on one layer appear in front of artwork on another layer by dragging the layer name in the Layers palette or by using the Layer > Arrange > Bring to Front command.

4 You can link the layers you want to adjust by selecting one of the layers in the Layers palette, and then clicking the square box to the left of the Layer name of the layer to which you want to link it. Once linked, both layers can be moved, rotated, and resized together.

5 You can flatten the image, which merges all the layers onto a single background.

Lesson 4

4 Painting and Editing

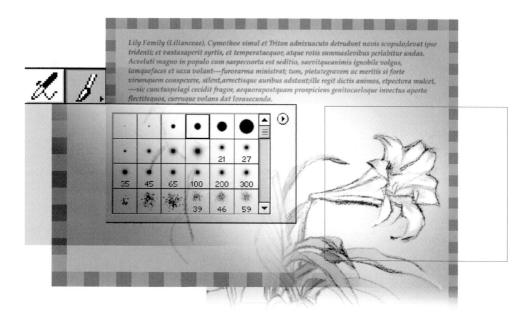

Adobe Photoshop allows you to do more than edit, enhance, or modify photographic images. You can also create graphics by painting and drawing. This lesson focusses on painting. You'll learn how to paint colors with soft edges and transitions, and then apply layer styles and filters to modify the layer's image data.

In this lesson, you'll learn how to do the following:

• Use the basic painting tools and experiment with different options for each tool.

• Work with colors, gradients, or patterns in a layer.

• Use layers to paint, adjust, add effects, and make color changes to specific portions of the image.

• Set the blending mode and opacity of a layer to adjust how colors and each element of the image combine with the others.

• Set the blending mode and opacity of a painting tool to adjust how a paint stroke combines with other pixels in the image.

• Use the eraser tool, history paint brush, and History palette to make corrections.

• Use a pattern from a different image to create a border.

• Create custom brushes and settings that appear in the tool options bar for any painting tool.

This lesson will take about 60 minutes to complete. The lesson is designed to be done in Adobe Photoshop.

If needed, remove the previous lesson folder from your hard drive, and copy the Lesson04 folder onto it. As you work on this lesson, you'll overwrite the start files. If you need to restore the start files, copy them from the *Adobe Photoshop Classroom in a Book* CD.

Note: Windows users need to unlock the lesson files before using them. For more information, see "Copying the Classroom in a Book files" on page 3.

Getting started

Before beginning this lesson, restore the default application settings for Adobe Photoshop. See "Restoring default preferences" on page 4.

You'll start the lesson by viewing the final Lesson file to see what you'll accomplish.

1 Start Adobe Photoshop.

If a notice appears asking whether you want to customize your color settings, click No.

2 Choose File > Open, and open the file 04End.psd from the Lessons/Lesson04 folder.

3 When you have finished viewing the file, either leave the 04End.psd file open for reference or close it without saving changes.

⚫ For an illustration of the finished artwork for this lesson, see the gallery at the beginning of the color section.

Filling the background layer with color

Throughout this lesson, you'll have the opportunity to use a variety of painting tools. First, you'll use the paint bucket tool to paint the background of the image with a light green color. The paint bucket tool fills a selection or a layer with the foreground color, the background color, or a pattern.

1 Choose File > Open, and open the file 04Start.psd from the Lessons/Lesson04 folder.

2 If the Layers palette is not showing, choose Window > Show Layers to display it.

There are nine layers in the Layers palette. Each layer allows you to paint, add an effect, or make color changes to specific portions of the entire image.

3 In the Layers palette, select the Background layer.

4 If guides are showing in the document window, choose View > Show Extras or View > Show > Guides to hide them for now. You'll be using these guides at the end of this lesson.

5 If the Color palette is not showing, choose Window > Show Color to display it.

6 Make sure that RGB Sliders is selected in the Color palette menu.

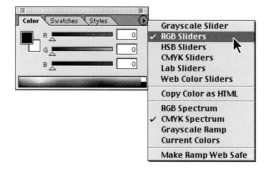

7 In the Color palette, enter **182** in the R text box, **201** in the G text box, and **139** in the B text box.

Notice that the light green color you specified in the Color palette is now the foreground color.

8 Select the paint bucket tool (🖌), hidden under the gradient tool (▦).

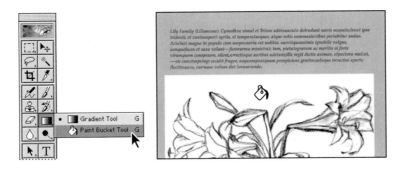

9 Click inside the image with the paint bucket tool to fill the Background layer with the current fill color.

10 Choose File > Save to save your work.

Blending the lily image with the background

The blending mode controls how pixels in an image are affected by painting and editing tools. It's helpful to think in terms of the following types of colors when visualizing a blending mode's effect:

• The *base color* is the original color in the image.

• The *blend color* is the color being applied with the painting or editing tool.

• The *result color* is the color resulting from the blend.

Throughout this lesson, you will learn how to specify a blending mode for a layer in the Layers palette and for a tool in the tool options bar.

▣ For complete information on the blending modes, see "Selecting a blending mode" in Photoshop 6.0 online Help.

Setting layer blending options

The blending options in the Layer Style dialog box (Photoshop) and the Layer Options palette (ImageReady) let you change a layer's opacity and blending with the pixels underneath.

Keep in mind that a layer's opacity and blending mode interact with the opacity and mode of the tools you use to paint and edit the pixels on the layer. For example, suppose you are working on a layer that uses the Dissolve mode and an opacity of 50%. If you paint on this layer using the paintbrush tool set to Normal mode with an opacity of 100%, the paint will appear in Dissolve mode with a 50% opacity because this is the maximum the layer can display. On the other hand, suppose you are working on a layer created using Normal mode and 100% opacity. If you use the eraser tool with an opacity of 50%, only 50% of the paint will disappear as you erase.

–From Adobe Photoshop 6.0 online Help

You'll use the Multiply blending mode to blend the white background of the Lily Image layer with the green background of the Background layer.

1 In the Layers palette, select the Lily Image layer.

2 Choose Blending Options from the Layers palette menu to open the Layer Style dialog box.

Choosing a blending mode option in the Layer Style dialog box

Choosing a blending mode option in the Layers palette

Double-clicking the layer in the Layers palette will also open the Layer Style dialog box.

3 In the Layer Style dialog box, select Preview, then choose different options from the Blend Mode menu and observe the effect that they have on the image. (You may need to move the dialog box to see the image better.)

Note: You can also choose a Blend Mode option and enter the Opacity at the top of the Layers palette.

4 Choose Multiply from the Blend Mode menu and click OK to close the Layer Style dialog box.

The Lily Image layer with the Normal blending mode

The Lily Image layer with the Multiply blending mode

The Multiply blending mode looks at the color information in each *channel* and multiplies the original color in the image by the color being applied. The resulting color is always darker. Multiplying any color with black produces black. Multiplying any color with white leaves the color unchanged. When you're painting with a color other than black or white, successive strokes with a layer set to the Multiply blending mode produce progressively darker colors.

Note: You'll learn about channels in the next lesson. For more information on channels, see Photoshop 6.0 online Help.

5 Choose File > Save.

Painting the petals of the flowers

Now that you've seen how the paint bucket tool can fill a layer with color, you'll use the paintbrush tool to apply color with brush strokes.

1 In the Layers palette, select the Flower layer.

2 Click the Switch Foreground and Background Colors icon (↰) so that the foreground fill color is white and the background fill color is green.

3 Select the paintbrush tool (✐).

When you select the paintbrush tool, the options change in the tool options bar to correspond with the paintbrush.

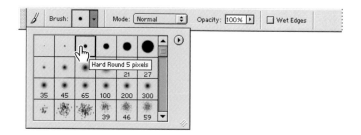

4 In the tool options bar, click the Brush arrow (▾) to display a palette of brush sizes, and select the Hard Round 5 Pixels brush size.

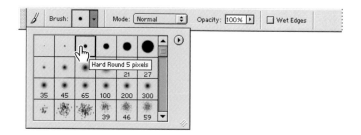

5 Enter **75%** in the Opacity text box for the brush strokes.

6 In the tool options bar, click the Brush Dynamics button (✐) to display the Brush Dynamics pop-up palette. Choose Fade from the Opacity menu, and enter **50** in the Steps text box.

The greater the number of steps you enter, the longer it takes for the brush stroke to fade away.

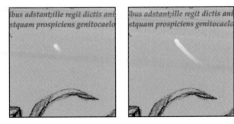

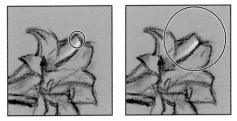

Brush stroke set to fade out to
0% opacity after a specified
number of steps

10 steps

50 steps

7 In the document window, use the paintbrush tool to apply a few strokes to a flower petal.

Notice that the white color of each stroke starts at 75% opacity and then fades out completely. An easy way to change the size of your strokes while you're painting is to press the [key to make the brush size smaller or the] key to make it larger.

8 Now paint all the flowers in the image white, changing the brush size and other paintbrush tool options as desired.

Note: *You can change the brush appearance on the screen by choosing Edit > Preferences > Display & Cursors. For Painting Cursors, select Standard ( ), Precise (-¦-), or Brush Size (○).*

The Brush Size pointer becomes larger when you
press the] key.

9 Choose File > Save.

Correcting your work

As you work on an image, you may want to undo an operation or correct a mistake. There are many ways to correct mistakes in Adobe Photoshop. In the following sections, you'll use the History palette, eraser tool, and history brush tools to revert your image to an earlier state.

Using the History palette

You can use the History palette to revert to a previous state of an image, to delete an image's states, and in Adobe Photoshop, to create a document from a state or snapshot.

1 Paint a few strokes with the paintbrush above the flowers in the image.

2 If the History palette is not showing, choose Window > History to display it.

Each stroke that you painted with the paintbrush is listed as a state in the History palette with the most recent state listed at the bottom.

3 In the History palette, select the Paintbrush state above the most recent state (at the bottom).

Notice that the last stroke you painted disappears in the image. You can select different Paintbrush states to step forward or backward in the history of the image.

For more information about the History palette, see Photoshop 6.0 online Help.

Using the eraser tool

The eraser tool changes pixels in the image as you drag through them. If you're working in the background or in a layer with transparency locked, the pixels change to the background color; otherwise, the pixels are erased to transparency. You can also use the eraser to return the affected area to a state selected in the History palette.

1 Select the eraser tool (⊘).

Options for the eraser tool appear in the tool options bar.

2 Drag the eraser tool over one of your paintbrush strokes.

Notice that an Eraser state is added to the History palette.

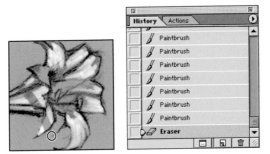

State of the eraser tool in Paintbrush mode added to the History palette.

3 In the tool options bar, choose a Brush size for the eraser, and enter a value of about **10%** to **20%** for the opacity.

The reduced opacity of the eraser tool produces a subtle effect when applying the tool.

You can also change the mode of the eraser from Paintbrush mode to Airbrush, Pencil, or Block mode. Changing to a different tool mode allows the eraser tool to erase using the attributes of the specified tool.

4 Drag the eraser tool over another paintbrush stroke.

Notice that the eraser tool softens the paintbrush stroke.

5 In the History palette, select the last state that you want to continue with.

6 Choose File > Save.

Using the history tools

The history tools paint strokes based on the selected state or snapshot in the History palette. In this section, you'll work with both history tools—the art history brush tool and the history brush tool.

The art history brush tool paints with a stylized stroke simulating the look of different paint styles.

1 In the History palette, click the Create New Snapshot button (▣).

A snapshot state appears at the top of the History palette.

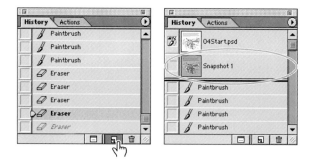

2 In the Layers palette, select the Lily Image layer.

3 Select the art history brush tool (✻) hidden under the history brush tool (✻).

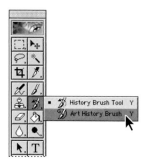

4 In the tool options bar, choose a small brush size (such as Hard Round 3 Pixels) and choose an option from the Style menu (such as Tight Long).

5 Using the art history brush tool, paint over the dark lines of the flowers and leaves. You can also experiment with just clicking on an area rather than dragging.

6 Choose a different style in the tool options bar and paint some more.

Before and after painting with the art history brush tool

The history brush tool paints a copy of the selected state or snapshot into the current image window. You'll use the history brush tool to remove the strokes you made with the art history brush tool—without affecting the original dark lines of the Lily Image layer. You'll also set the source for the history brush to be the snapshot you created at the beginning of this section.

7 Click in the empty box at the left of the Snapshot 1 thumbnail.

An icon (🖌) appears in the box, indicating that each stroke you make with the history brush tool will remove a state from the History palette that occurred after Snapshot 1 was created.

8 Select the history brush tool (🖌) and drag over the areas in the image that you painted with the art history brush tool.

Notice that the strokes you make with the history brush tool remove the strokes that you made with the art history brush tool and uncover the original dark lines of the image.

9 In the History palette, select the snapshot state that you created earlier.

10 Choose File > Save.

Smoothing the edges of a paintbrush stroke

Now you'll learn how to use the smudge tool to soften the edges of your paint strokes. The smudge tool simulates the actions of dragging a finger through wet paint. The tool picks up color where the stroke begins and pushes it in the direction you drag.

1 In the Layers palette, make sure the Flower layer is selected. (It was selected in the snapshot state you created.)

2 Select the paintbrush tool (✐).

3 In the tool options bar, click the Brush Dynamics button (✐) and choose Off from the Opacity menu.

4 Paint a few strokes on the flower petals.

5 Select the smudge tool (✐) hidden under the blur tool (◊).

6 Using the smudge tool, drag over your paintbrush strokes to smooth out their edges.

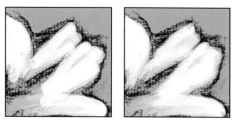

Before and after using the smudge tool

You can also use the smudge tool to create new strokes by selecting the Finger Painting option in the tool options bar.

7 In the History palette, select the Snapshot 1 state of the image.

8 Choose File > Save.

Creating a subtle overlay effect

Now you'll finish painting the flowers and apply the Overlay blending mode to the Flower layer that blends the color pixels of the flowers with the underlying pixels in the image to create a subtle overlay effect.

The Overlay blending mode multiplies or screens the colors, depending on the base color. Patterns or colors overlay the existing pixels while preserving the highlights and shadows of the base color. The base color is not replaced but is mixed with the blend color to reflect the lightness or darkness of the original color.

1 In the Color palette, select a yellow color for the foreground fill color.

2 Select the paintbrush tool (✒) and paint the flower pistils yellow.

3 In the Layers palette, double-click the Flower layer to display the Layer Style dialog box. Position the dialog box so you can see it and the image at the same time.

4 In the Layer Style dialog box, choose Overlay from the Blend Mode menu, and enter **70%** in the Opacity text box. Then click OK.

5 Choose File > Save.

Painting shadows in nontransparent areas

In this part of the lesson, you'll lock transparency on the Leaf layer to restrict your painting so you can only add shadows to colored pixels on the leaves and not to any transparent pixels between them.

1 In the Layers palette, select the Leaf layer.

2 In the Color palette, select a dark green color.

3 Use the paintbrush tool (✒) to paint a long stroke across several of the leaves.

Notice how your paintbrush stroke applies the dark green color everywhere it touches.

4 Choose Edit > Undo Paintbrush.

5 At the top of the Layers palette, click the Lock check box next to the Transparency icon (▧) to lock transparency for the selected Leaf layer.

6 Paint another long stroke across the leaves.

Notice how your paintbrush stroke does not apply the dark green color to transparent areas between the leaves.

Original image   *Paint stroke on unlocked layer*   *Paint stroke on locked transparency layer*

7 Choose Edit > Undo Paintbrush again.

8 Now, with the Leaf layer's transparency locked, paint dark green shadows behind the flowers and the leaves. (We used a Hard Round 5 Pixels brush. See the end file 04End.psd for comparison.)

9 In the Layers palette, enter **80%** in the Opacity text box to decrease the opacity of the selected Leaf layer.

10 Choose File > Save.

Adding a gradient to the background

The gradient tool options let you create straight-line, radial, angle, reflected, and diamond blends between colors. You can fill a background or a selection with a gradient.

1 In the Layers palette, select the Gradient layer.

2 Select the gradient tool (▨) hidden under the paint bucket tool (⬧).

You'll make a color gradient that starts with white on the left and gradually blends to brown on the right.

3 In the tool options bar, click the gradient sample box to display the Gradient Editor dialog box.

The Gradient Editor dialog box lets you define a new gradient by modifying a copy of an existing gradient. You can also add intermediate colors to a gradient, creating a blend between more than two colors.

4 In the Gradient Editor dialog box, double-click the color stop (⬧) located at the lower-left corner of the gradient bar, to select it and display the Color Picker dialog box.

*Double-clicking the color stops below the gradient bar
selects them and displays the Color Picker dialog box.*

5 In the Color Picker dialog box, select the white color in the upper-left corner, and click the cube icon (⬡) to adjust the color to a Web color.

💡 *Before selecting a color in the Color Picker, you can select Only Web Colors to limit your selection to Web-safe colors.*

6 Click OK.

7 In the Gradient Editor dialog box, double-click the color stop (🔒) located at the lower-right corner of the gradient bar, to display the Color Picker dialog box again.

8 In the Color Picker dialog box, select the check box for Only Web Colors, and then enter **147** in the R text box, **132** in the G text box, and **100** in the B text box.

After you enter each value, Photoshop immediately changes them to the closest Web value: 153 for R, 153 for G, and 102 for B.

9 Click OK to close the Color Picker, and then click OK to close the Gradient Editor dialog box.

Notice that the brown gradient you created appears in the tool options bar.

10 In the tool options bar, select the Radial Gradient icon (▨).

11 Using the gradient tool, drag from the center of the image to the edge of the document window and release the mouse.

Dragging the gradient tool from the center of the flowers

The white color of the gradient starts at the center and radiates out to brown on all the edges of the image. Now you'll blend the luminosity of the radial gradient with the green color of the Background layer.

12 In the Layers palette, choose Luminosity from the menu at the top of the palette to set the blending mode for the Gradient layer.

13 Choose File > Save.

Creating a glow effect with a custom airbrush

The airbrush tool paints soft-edged strokes. You can make adjustments in the airbrush tool options bar and save them as a custom airbrush for reuse.

1 In the Layers palette, select the Glow layer.

2 Select the airbrush tool ( ).

3 Hold down Alt (Windows) or Option (Mac OS) to change the pointer to an eyedropper ( ) and click on a flower petal to sample a light color from it.

The color you sampled appears in the foreground color fill box in the toolbox. Now you'll create a custom airbrush with a large diameter.

4 In the tool options bar, click the Brush Editor button ( ) to the left of the Brush arrow.

5 In the Brush Editor pop-up palette, enter **150** in the Diameter text box. Keep the Hardness at **0** and Spacing at **25**. Then enter **Glow Brush** in the Name text box.

6 Click the Create New Preset button ( ) in the upper-right corner of the Brush Editor.

Create New Preset button in the Brush Editor pop-up palette

Your new custom airbrush now appears in the list of brushes in the tool options bar.

If you have difficulty locating your new custom airbrush in the palette, click the triangle in the upper-right corner of the pop-up palette. Choose Small List from the palette menu. You can then scroll through a list of brushes and choose your new custom brush option. Use the palette menu to choose different configurations for viewing the brushes in the pop-up palette.

7 Click with your custom airbrush to paint a glow over the ends of the flowers.

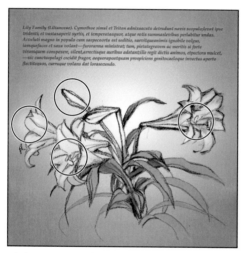

Click the ends of the flower with your custom airbrush tool.

8 At the top of the Layers palette, enter **80%** in the Opacity text box and choose Overlay from the menu to set the blending mode for the Glow layer.

9 Choose File > Save.

Creating a textured effect with a natural brush

Now you'll create a textured effect around the lilies, using a natural brush and applying different blending modes for the brush strokes.

Adobe Photoshop comes with bonus items, such as custom shapes and brushes, that you can add to your tool palettes. In this section of the lesson, you'll add natural brushes to the airbrush pop-up palette. Natural brushes simulate natural painting tools such as chalk, pencils, pens, and watercolors.

1 In the Layers palette, select the Natural Brush layer.

2 In the tool options bar for the airbrush tool, click the Brush arrow to display the Brush pop-up palette and then choose Natural Brushes 2.abr from the palette menu.

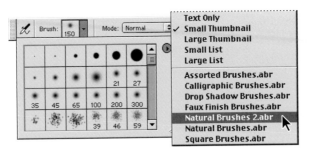

Palette menu in the Brush pop-up palette

3 In the dialog box, click Append to add the natural brushes to the Brush palette.

4 In the Brush palette, select the 118 Pastel Light 120 Pixels brush.

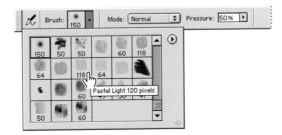

5 In the tool options bar, choose Screen from the Mode menu and enter **50%** in the Pressure text box.

6 In the toolbox, double-click the Set Foreground Color box (■) to display the Color Picker dialog box.

7 In the Color Picker dialog box, deselect Only Web Colors, and select a dark blue color or enter **65** in the R text box, **73** in the G text box, and **157** in the B text box.

8 Using the natural brush, click around the outer perimeter and in the center of the flowers to add blocks of color.

Don't worry about adding too much blue with the natural brush. You'll be applying a blending mode to the layer, which will cause most of the blue (the blend color) paint strokes to disappear and reveal the base color of the image.

Overlaid colors using the natural brush

9 In the tool options bar, choose Color Dodge from the Mode menu.

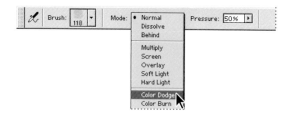

The Color Dodge blending mode looks at the color information in each channel and brightens the base color to reflect the blend color. Blending with black produces no change in the Color Dodge mode.

10 Click in the image to add more blocks of brighter color to the center of the flowers.

11 Choose Filter > Noise > Add Noise.

12 In the Add Noise dialog box, enter **10** in the Amount text box, select Gaussian for the Distribution, select Monochromatic, and click OK.

The Noise filters add or remove either pixels or *noise* (distortions, technically referred to as *stochastic variations*) with randomly distributed color levels. This helps to blend a selection into the surrounding pixels. Noise filters can create unusual textures or remove problem areas, such as dust and scratches from an image.

13 In the Layers palette, choose Difference from the Blend Mode menu, and enter **80%** in the Opacity text box for the Natural Brush layer.

The amount of blue (the blend color) remaining in the image depends on how much you applied with the natural brush in step 8.

The Difference blending mode looks at the color information in each channel and subtracts either the blend color from the base color or the base color from the blend color, depending on which has the greater brightness value. Blending with white inverts the base color values; blending with black produces no change.

14 Choose File > Save.

Creating a patterned border

As mentioned earlier in this lesson, you can fill a layer or selection with a color, texture, or pattern. You'll define a checkered pattern and use the paint bucket tool to paint the image border with it.

1 In the Layers palette, select the Pattern_Fill layer.

2 Choose File > Open and open the file Pattern_Check.psd from the Lessons/Lesson04 folder.

3 Choose Select > All.

4 Choose Edit > Define Pattern.

5 In the Pattern Name dialog box, enter **Checkered** for the Name and click OK.

6 Close the Pattern_check.psd file.

7 Select the paint bucket tool (⬦) hidden under the gradient tool (▨).

8 In the tool options bar, choose Pattern from the Fill menu. Then click the Pattern arrow (▾) to open the Pattern pop-up palette, and select the Checkered pattern you defined.

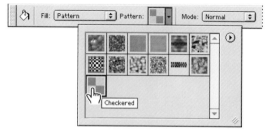

Selecting the Checkered pattern in the Pattern pop-up palette

9 Using the paint bucket tool, click in the 04Start.psd image.

The entire layer is filled with the checkered pattern. Now you'll use the guides included in the start file to help you cut out the central area of the pattern and create the border.

10 Choose View > Show Extras or View > Show > Guides.

11 Select the rectangular marquee tool (▢) and draw a rectangular marquee over the central area of the image that matches up with the guides.

To help you match your selection with the guides, make sure View > Snap To > Guides is active.

12 Choose Edit > Cut.

Selecting with the rectangular marquee tool

Selected area cut from the image

13 In the Layers palette, choose Multiply from the Blend Mode menu for the Pattern Fill layer.

The Multiply blending mode multiplies the original color of the image by the colors in the pattern to give a darker blend.

To view the image without guides showing, choose View > Show Extras or View > Show > Guides to hide the guides.

14 Choose File > Save.

Review questions

1 What is a blending mode, and what are the three types of color that are helpful for visualizing a blending mode's effect?

2 What do the History palette, eraser tool, and history brush tools have in common?

3 What is the difference between the art history brush tool and the history brush tool?

4 Why would you use the smudge tool?

5 How do you prevent layer properties from being changed?

6 Describe what the Gradient Editor dialog box is used for and how you display it.

7 What are noise filters used for?

Review answers

1 A blending mode controls how pixels in an image are affected by the tools or other layers. It's helpful to think in terms of the following colors when visualizing a blending mode's effect:

• The *base color* is the original color in the image.

• The *blend color* is the color being applied with the painting or editing tool.

• The *result color* is the color resulting from the blend.

2 The History palette, eraser tool, and history brush tools can all revert your image to an earlier state so you can undo an operation or correct a mistake.

3 The art history brush tool paints with a stylized stroke based on a selected state or snapshot. The stylized stroke of the art history brush tool simulates the look of different paint styles. The history brush tool paints a copy of the selected state or snapshot into the current image window. You can use the history brush tool to remove the strokes made with the art history brush tool.

4 You can use the smudge tool to soften the edges of your paint strokes. The smudge tool simulates the actions of dragging a finger through wet paint. The tool picks up color where the stroke begins and pushes it in the direction you drag.

5 Locking layers and layer sets makes certain properties of a layer unchangeable. You can lock transparent pixels to confine your painting and editing to those areas of a layer already containing pixels. You can also lock image pixels and the position of an image layer.

6 The Gradient Editor dialog box lets you define a new gradient by modifying a copy of an existing gradient. You can also add intermediate colors to a gradient, creating a blend between more than two colors. To display the Gradient Editor dialog box, select the gradient tool (⬛) and click the gradient sample box in the tool option bar.

7 Noise filters can create unusual textures or remove problem areas, such as dust and scratches from an image. The Noise filters add or remove either pixels or *noise* in an image with randomly distributed color levels.

Lesson 5

5 | Masks and Channels

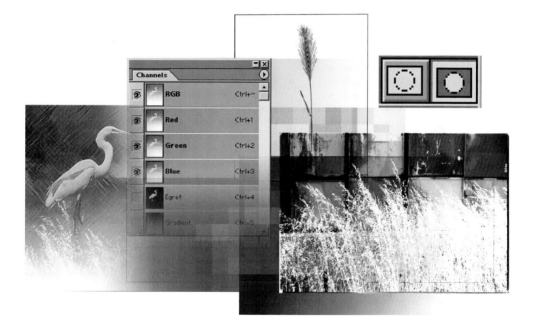

Adobe Photoshop uses masks to isolate
and manipulate specific parts of an
image. A mask is like a stencil. The cutout
portion of the mask can be altered,
but the area surrounding the cutout is
protected from change. You can create
a temporary mask for one-time use,
or you can save masks for repeated use.

In this lesson, you'll learn how to do the following:

• Refine a selection using a quick mask.

• Save a selection as a channel mask.

• View a mask using the Channels palette.

• Load a saved mask and apply effects.

• Paint in a mask to modify a selection.

• Make an intricate selection using the Extract command.

• Create and use a gradient mask.

This lesson will take about 70 minutes to complete. The lesson is designed to be done in Adobe Photoshop. ImageReady does not contain the advanced masking features available in Photoshop.

If needed, remove the previous lesson folder from your hard drive, and copy the Lesson05 folder onto it. As you work on this lesson, you'll overwrite the start files. If you need to restore the start files, copy them from the *Adobe Photoshop Classroom in a Book* CD.

Note: *Windows users need to unlock the lesson files before using them. For more information, see "Copying the Classroom in a Book files" on page 3.*

Working with masks and channels

Masks let you isolate and protect parts of an image. When you create a mask based on a selection, the area not selected is *masked* or protected from editing. With masks, you can create and save time-consuming selections and then use them again. In addition, you can use masks for other complex editing tasks—for example, to apply color changes or filter effects to an image.

In Adobe Photoshop, you can make temporary masks, called *quick masks*, or you can create permanent masks and store them as special grayscale channels, called *alpha channels*. Photoshop also uses channels to store an image's color information and information about spot color. Unlike layers, channels do not print. You use the Channels palette to view and work with alpha channels. ImageReady does not support channels, except for alpha channels used for PNG transparency and weighted optimization.

Getting started

Before beginning this lesson, restore the default application settings for Adobe Photoshop. See "Restoring default preferences" on page 4.

You'll start the lesson by viewing the finished image you'll create using masks and channels.

1 Start Adobe Photoshop.

If a notice appears asking whether you want to customize your color settings, click No.

2 Click Cancel to exit the color management dialog box if it appears.

3 Choose File > Open, and open the file 05End.psd from the Lessons/Lesson05 folder.

4 When you have finished viewing the file, either leave it open for reference or close it without saving changes.

For an illustration of the finished artwork for this lesson, see the gallery at the beginning of the color section.

Creating a quick mask

Now you'll open the start file and begin the lesson by using Quick Mask mode to convert a selection border into a temporary mask. Later you will convert this temporary quick mask back into a selection border. Unless you save a quick mask as a more permanent alpha channel mask, the temporary mask will be discarded once it is converted to a selection.

You'll begin by making a partial selection of the egret using the magic wand tool, and then you'll edit the selection using a quick mask.

1 Choose File > Open, and open the file 05Start.psd from the Lessons/Lesson05 folder.

2 Select the magic wand tool ( ).

3 In the tool options bar, enter **12** in the Tolerance text box.

4 Click anywhere in the white area of the egret to begin the selection process.

5 To extend the selection, hold down Shift and click the magic wand on another white portion of the egret. When you hold down Shift, a plus sign appears next to the magic wand tool. This indicates that the tool is adding to the selection.

Magic wand selection   *Selection extended*

The egret is still only partly selected. Now you'll add to this selection using a quick mask.

6 Select the Edit in Quick Mask mode button ( ) in the toolbox. By default, you have been working in Standard mode.

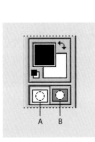 

A. *Standard mode*   *Quick mask selection*
B. *Quick Mask mode*   *showing red overlay*

In Quick Mask mode, a red overlay (similar to a piece of *rubylith*, or red acetate, that print shops used in the old days to mask an image) appears to mask and protect the area outside the selection. You can apply changes only to the unprotected area that is visible and selected. (It's possible to change the color of the red overlay; the color is only a matter of display.)

Note: *A partial selection must exist to see the overlay color in Quick Mask mode.*

Editing a quick mask

Next you will refine the selection of the egret by adding to or erasing parts of the masked area. You'll use the paintbrush tool to make changes to your quick mask. The advantage of editing your selection as a mask is that you can use almost any tool or filter to modify the mask. (You can even use selection tools.) In Quick Mask mode, you do all of your editing in the image window.

In Quick Mask mode, Photoshop automatically defaults to Grayscale mode. The foreground color defaults to black, and the background color defaults to white. When using a painting or editing tool in Quick Mask mode, keep these principles in mind:

• Painting with white erases the mask (the red overlay) and increases the selected area.

• Painting with black adds to the mask (the red overlay) and decreases the selected area.

Adding to a selection by erasing masked areas

You'll begin by painting with white to increase the selected area within the egret. This erases some of the mask.

1 To make the foreground color white, select the Switch Colors icon above the foreground and background color selection boxes.

Switch Colors icon

2 Select the paintbrush tool ( ).

3 In the tool options bar, make sure the mode is Normal, then click the arrow to display the Brushes pop-up palette, and select a medium brush from the first row of brushes.

Note: As you work, you may want to change the size of your brush. Simply click the Brushes pop-up palette again, and select a different-sized brush. You'll notice that the size of the tool brush pointer changes.

4 As you edit your quick mask, magnify or reduce your view of the image, as needed. When you zoom in, you can work on details of the image. When you zoom out, you can see an overview of your work.

You can zoom in or magnify your view in these ways:

• Select the zoom tool, and click the area you want to magnify. Each click magnifies the image some more. When the zoom tool is selected, you can also drag over the part of the image you want to magnify.

• Select the zoom tool from the keyboard by holding down Ctrl+spacebar (Windows) or Command+spacebar (Mac OS); then release the keys to go back to painting.

You can zoom back out in the following ways:

• Double-click the zoom tool to return the image to 100% view.

• Select the zoom tool. Hold down Alt (Windows) or Option (Mac OS) to activate the zoom-out tool, and click the area of the image you want to reduce.

• Select the zoom-out tool from the keyboard by holding down Alt+spacebar (Windows) or Option+spacebar (Mac OS) and click to reduce the view; then release the keys to go back to painting.

5 Using the paintbrush tool, begin painting over the red areas within the egret's body. As you paint with white, the red areas are erased.

Don't worry if you paint outside the outline of the egret's body. You'll have a chance to make adjustments later by masking areas of the image as needed.

Unedited mask   *Painting with white*   *Result*

6 Continue painting with white to erase all of the mask (red) in the egret, including its beak and legs. As you work, you can easily switch back and forth between Quick Mask mode and Standard mode to see how painting in the mask alters the selected area.

Standard mode

Notice that the selection border has increased, selecting more of the egret's body.

Edited mask in   *Quick mask selection*
Standard mode

For an illustration of the selection in Standard and Quick Mask modes, see figure 5-1 in the color section.

If any areas within the body of the egret still appear to be selected, it means that you haven't erased all of the mask.

Selection in Standard   *Erasing in Quick Mask*
mode   *mode*

7 Once you've erased all of the red areas within the egret, click the Standard mode icon again to view your quick mask as a selection. Don't worry if the selection extends a bit beyond the egret. You can fix that.

8 If you zoomed in on the image for editing, choose any of the techniques in step 4 to zoom out.

9 Choose File > Save to save your work.

Subtracting from a selection by adding masked areas

You may have erased the mask beyond the edges of the egret. This means that part of the background is included in the selection. Now you'll return to Quick Mask mode and restore the mask to those edge areas by painting with black.

1 Click the Edit in Quick Mask Mode button (▣) to return to Quick Mask mode.

2 To make the foreground color black, select the Switch Colors icon (↰) above the foreground and background color selection boxes. Make sure that the black color box now appears on top. Remember that in the image window, painting with black will add to the red overlay.

3 Choose a brush from the Brush pop-up palette. Select a small brush from the first row of brushes, because you'll be refining the edges of the selection.

4 Now paint with black to restore the mask (the red overlay) to any of the background area that is still unprotected. Only the area inside the egret should remain unmasked. Remember that you can zoom in and out as you work. You can also switch back and forth between Standard mode and Quick Mask mode.

Note: You can also use the eraser tool in Paintbrush mode to remove any excess selection and restore the mask.

Painting with black to restore mask

For an illustration of painting in Quick Mask mode, see figure 5-2 in the color section.

5 Once you're satisfied with your selection, switch to Standard mode to view your final egret selection. Double-click the hand tool (✋) to make the egret image fit in the window.

Using alpha channels

In addition to the temporary masks of Quick Mask mode, you can create more permanent masks by storing and editing selections in alpha channels. You create a new alpha channel as a mask. For example, you can create a gradient fill in a blank channel and then use it as a mask. Or you can save a selection to either a new or existing channel.

An alpha channel has these properties:

• *Each image can contain up to 24 channels, including all color and alpha channels.*

• *All channels are 8-bit grayscale images, capable of displaying 256 levels of gray.*

• *You can add and delete alpha channels.*

• *You can specify a name, color, mask option, and opacity for each channel. (The opacity affects the preview of the channel, not the image.)*

• *All new channels have the same dimensions and number of pixels as the original image.*

• *You can edit the mask in an alpha channel using the painting and editing tools.*

• *Storing selections in alpha channels makes the selections permanent, so that they can be used again in the same image or in a different image.*

–From Adobe Photoshop 6.0 online Help

Saving a selection as a mask

Now you'll save the egret selection as an alpha channel mask. Your time-consuming work won't be lost, and you can use the selection again later.

Quick masks are temporary. They disappear when you deselect. However, any selection can be saved as a mask in an alpha channel. Think of alpha channels as storage areas for information. When you save a selection as a mask, a new alpha channel is created in the Channels palette. (An image can contain up to 24 channels, including all color and alpha channels.) You can use these masks again in the same image or in a different image.

Note: *If you save and close your file while in Quick Mask mode, the quick mask will show in its own channel next time you open your file. However, if you save and close your file while in Standard mode, the quick mask will be gone the next time you open your file.*

1 To display the Channels palette, choose Window > Show Channels.

In the Channels palette, you'll see that your image by default already has color information channels—a full-color preview channel for the RGB image and a separate channel for the red, green, and blue channels.

2 With the egret selection still active, choose Select > Save Selection.

In the Save Selection dialog box, the name of your current document appears in the Destination pop-up menu, and New by default appears in the Channel pop-up menu.

3 Click OK to accept the default settings.

A new channel labeled Alpha 1 is added to the bottom of the Channels palette. All new channels have the same dimensions and number of pixels as the original image. You'll rename this new channel in a moment.

4 Experiment with looking at the various channels individually. Click in the eye icon column next to the channel to show or hide that channel. To show or hide multiple channels, drag through the eye icon column in the palette.

Alpha channel mask visible and selected; other channels hidden

Alpha channels can be added and deleted, and like quick masks, can be edited using the painting and editing tools. For each channel, you can also specify a name, color, mask option, and opacity (which affects just the preview of the channel, not the image).

To avoid confusing channels and layers, think of channels as containing an image's color and selection information; think of layers as containing painting and effects.

If you display all of the color channels plus the new alpha mask channel, the image window looks much as it did in Quick Mask mode (with the rubylith appearing where the selection is masked). It is possible to edit this overlay mask much as you did the quick mask. However, in a minute you will edit the mask channel in a different way.

5 When you have finished looking at the channels, click in the eye icon column next to the RGB channel in the Channels palette to redisplay the composite channel view.

6 Choose Select > Deselect to deselect everything.

7 To rename the channel, double-click the Alpha 1 channel in the Channels palette. Type the name **Egret** in the Channel Options dialog box, and click OK.

Editing a mask

Now you'll touch up your selection of the egret by editing the mask channel. It's easy to miss tiny areas when making a selection. You may not even see these imperfections until you view the saved selection as a channel mask.

You can use most painting and editing tools to edit a channel mask, just as you did when editing in Quick Mask mode. This time you'll display and edit the mask as a grayscale image.

1 With the Egret channel selected, click any eye icon appearing next to the other channels to hide all channels except the Egret channel. When only the Egret channel displays an eye icon, the image window displays a black-and-white mask of the egret selection. (If you left all of the channels selected, the colored egret image would appear with a red overlay.)

Look for any black or gray flecks within the body of the egret. You'll erase them by painting with white to increase the selected area. Remember these guidelines on editing a channel with a painting or editing tool:

• Painting with white erases the mask and increases the selected area.

• Painting with black adds to the mask and decreases the selected area.

• Painting with gray values adds to or subtracts from the mask in varying opacity, in proportion to the level of gray used to paint. For example, if you paint with a medium gray value, when you use the mask as a selection the pixels will be 50% selected. If you paint with a dark gray and then use the mask as a selection, the pixels will be less than 50% selected (depending on the gray value you choose). And if you paint with a light gray, when you use the mask as a selection, the pixels will be more than 50% selected.

2 Make sure that the Egret channel is the active channel by clicking on the channel in the Channels palette. A selected channel is highlighted in the Channels palette.

3 Now make sure that white is the foreground color. (If necessary, select the Switch Colors icon above the foreground and background color selection boxes.) Then select a small brush in the Brushes palette, and paint out any black or gray flecks.

Selection in channel   *Painting out black or gray*

4 If any white specks appear in the black area of the channel, make black the foreground color, and paint those out as well. Remember that when you paint with black, you increase the masked area and decrease the selection.

5 Choose File > Save.

Loading a selection using shortcuts

When you have finished modifying an alpha channel or simply want to use a previously saved selection, you can load the selection into the image. To load a saved selection using shortcuts, do one of the following in the Channels palette:

• Select the alpha channel, click the Load channel as selection button at the bottom of the palette, and then click the composite color channel near the top of the palette.

• Ctrl-click (Windows) or Command-click (Mac OS) the channel containing the selection you want to load.

• To add the mask to an existing selection, press Ctrl+Shift (Windows) or Command+Shift (Mac OS), and click the channel.

• To subtract the mask from an existing selection, press Ctrl+Alt (Windows) or Command+Option (Mac OS), and click the channel.

• To load the intersection of the saved selection and an existing selection, press Ctrl+Alt+Shift (Windows) or Command+Option+Shift (Mac OS), and select the channel.

–From Adobe Photoshop 6.0 online Help

Loading a mask as a selection and applying an adjustment

Now you'll load the Egret channel mask as a selection. The channel mask remains stored in the Channels palette even after you've loaded it as a selection. This means you can reuse the mask whenever you want.

1 In the Channels palette, click the RGB preview channel to display the entire image.

2 Choose Select > Load Selection. Click OK.

The egret selection appears in the image window.

Now that you've corrected any flaws in the selection by painting in the channel, you'll adjust the tonal balance of the egret.

3 Choose Image > Adjust > Auto Levels. This automatically adjusts the tonal balance of the colors in the selection.

Auto Levels defines the lightest and darkest pixels in each channel as white and black, and then redistributes the intermediate pixel values proportionately. Lesson 6, "Photo Retouching," takes you through basic image correction, including adjusting an image's tonal range.

4 Choose Edit > Undo to compare the adjustment you just made. Then choose Edit > Redo to reapply the adjustment.

5 Choose Select > Deselect.

6 Choose File > Save.

Extracting an image

Now you'll work with another masking and selection tool, the Extract command, to make some difficult selections—some marsh grasses and a foxtail.

The Extract command provides a sophisticated way to isolate a foreground object from its background. Even objects with wispy, intricate, or undefinable edges can be clipped from their backgrounds with a minimum of manual work.

You'll start with an image that consists of only one layer. You must be working in a layer to use the Extract command. If your original image has no layers, you can duplicate the image to a new layer.

Extracting an object from its background

You'll use the Extract command on a foxtail image set against a dark background.

1 Choose File > Open, and open the file Foxtail.psd from the Lessons/Lesson05 folder on your hard drive.

The Foxtail image has the same resolution as the Egret image, 72 pixels per inch (ppi). To avoid unexpected results when combining elements from other files, you must either use files with the same image resolution or compensate for differing resolutions.

For example, if your original image is 72 ppi and you add an element from a 144-ppi image, the additional element will appear twice as large because it contains twice the number of pixels.

For complete information on differing resolutions, see "About image size and resolution" in Adobe Photoshop 6.0 online Help.

2 Choose Image > Extract.

The Extract dialog box appears with the edge highlighter tool ( ) selected.

To extract an object, you use the Extract dialog box to highlight the edges of the object. Then you define the object's interior and preview the extraction. You can refine and preview the extraction as many times as you wish. Applying the extraction erases the background area to transparency, leaving just the extracted object.

If needed, you can resize the dialog box by dragging its bottom right corner. You specify which part of the image to extract by using the tools and previews in this dialog box.

Now you'll choose a brush size for the edge highlighter tool. You'll start with a fairly large brush.

3 Enter **20** in the Brush Size text box.

It's easiest to start with a large brush to highlight the general selection, and then switch to a finer brush to fine-tune the selection.

Edge highlighter tool selected; Brush Size set to 20

4 Using the edge highlighter tool, drag over the fuzzy ends and tip of the foxtail until you've completely outlined, but not filled, the foxtail. Draw the highlight so that it slightly overlaps both the foreground and background regions around the edge.

It's OK if the highlight overlaps the edge. The Extract command makes its selection by finding the difference in contrast between pixels. The foxtail has a well-defined interior, so make sure that the highlight forms a complete outline. You do not need to highlight areas where the object touches the image boundaries.

Now you'll highlight the fine stem.

5 Decrease the Brush Size to **5**.

6 If desired, select the zoom tool, or press spacebar+Ctrl (Windows) or spacebar+Command (Mac OS) and click to zoom in on the stem. You can also use the hand tool to reposition the image preview.

7 Using the edge highlighter tool, drag over the stem to select it.

If you make a mistake and highlight more than desired, select the eraser tool (⬦) in the dialog box and drag over the highlight in the preview.

8 Select the fill tool (⬦) in the Extract dialog box. Then click inside the object to fill its interior. You must define the object's interior before you can preview the extraction.

Highlighting edges of foxtail tip   *Highlighting stem and leaves; then filling*

The default Fill color (bright blue) contrasts well with the highlight color (green). You can change either color if you need more contrast with the image colors, using the Highlight and Fill menus in the Extract dialog box.

9 Click the Preview button to view the extraction.

You can control the preview using one of these techniques:

• To magnify the preview, select the zoom tool (⬦) in the Extract dialog box, and click in the preview. To zoom out, hold down Alt (Windows) or Option (Mac OS), and click with the zoom tool in the preview.

• To view a different part of the preview, select the hand tool in the Extract dialog box and drag the image in the preview.

💡 *To toggle quickly between the edge highlighter and eraser tools when one of the tools is selected, press **b** (edge highlighter) or **e** (eraser).*

10 To refine your selection, edit the extraction boundaries using these techniques:

• Switch between the Original and Extracted views using the Show menu in the Extract dialog box.

• Click a filled area with the fill tool to remove the fill.

• Select the eraser tool in the Extract dialog box, and drag to remove any undesired highlighting.

• Select the Show Highlight and Show Fill options in the Extract dialog box to view the highlight and fill colors; deselect the options to hide them.

• Zoom in on your selection using the zoom tool in the Extract dialog box. You can then use a smaller brush size as you edit, switching between the edge highlighter tool and the eraser tool as needed for more precise work.

• Switch to a smaller brush by entering a different size in the Brush Size text box and continue to refine the selection's border using the edge highlighter or to erase using the eraser tool.

11 When you are satisfied with your selection, click OK to apply the extraction.

Now you'll add the extracted image to the Egret image.

12 With the document window of the Foxtail image active, use the move tool (⊹) to drag the image to the right side of the Egret image. The foxtail is added as a new layer to the Egret image.

13 With the Egret image active, choose Edit > Transform > Scale to scale the foxtail. Drag the resize handles, holding down Shift to constrain the proportions, until the foxtail is about two-thirds the original image height. Press Enter (Windows) or Return (Mac OS) to apply the scaling.

Moving foxtail copy   *Scaling foxtail*   *Result*

14 In the Layers palette with the Foxtail layer (Layer 1) selected, decrease its opacity to **70%**.

15 Choose File > Save.

16 Save and close the Foxtail.psd image.

Extracting an intricate image

The Force Foreground option lets you make intricate selections when an object lacks a clear interior.

1 Choose File > Open, and open the file Weeds.psd image from the Lessons/Lesson05 folder on your hard drive.

2 Choose Image > Extract.

3 In the Extract dialog box, select the Force Foreground option.

You'll start by selecting the color on which to base your selection. The Force Foreground technique works best with objects that are monochromatic or fairly uniform in color.

4 Select the eyedropper tool (✐) in the Extract dialog box, and then click a light area of the weeds to sample the color to be treated as the foreground.

Force Foreground option   *Sampling foreground color*

5 Select the edge highlighter tool (✐) in the Extract dialog box.

6 For Brush Size, use the slider or enter a value to select a fairly large brush (about 20 or 30).

7 Drag to begin highlighting the wispy ends of the weeds where they overlap the dark background.

8 When you've enclosed the weed tips, drag to highlight the top third of the weeds fully. The highlight should be solid.

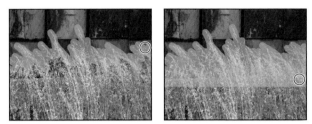

Highlighting weed edges   *Selecting top third of weeds*

9 Choose Black Matte from the Display menu in the Extract dialog box.

A black matte provides good contrast for a light-colored selection. For a dark selection, try the Gray or White Matte option. None previews a selection against a transparent background.

10 Click the Preview button to preview the extracted object.

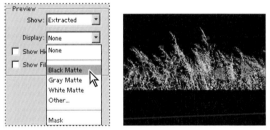

Black Matte option   *Preview*

11 To view and refine the extraction, use one of the following techniques:

• Use the Show menu to switch between previews of the original and extracted images.

• Select the Show Highlight or Show Fill option to display the object's extraction boundaries.

When you have finished editing, click Preview to view the edited extraction. You can edit and preview the extraction repeatedly until you achieve the desired result.

12 When you are satisfied with the selection, click OK to apply the final extraction. All pixels on the layer outside the extracted object are erased to transparency.

Once you've extracted an image, you can also use the background eraser and history brush tools to clean up any stray edges in the image.

Now you'll add the extracted weeds to the Egret image.

13 With the Weeds.psd file active, use the move tool (⤢) to drag the extracted selection to the Egret image. Position the weeds so that they fill the bottom third of the Egret image.

The selection is added to the Egret image as a new layer.

14 In the Layers palette, decrease the opacity of the new layer by entering a value of **70%**.

Weed image copy   New layer opacity set to 70%
added to egret image

15 Choose File > Save.

16 Save and close the Weeds.psd file.

Note: An alternate method for making intricate selections is to select areas by color. To do so, choose Select > Color Range. Then use the eye dropper tools from the Color Range dialog box to sample the colors for your selection. You can sample from your image window or the preview window.

Applying a filter effect to a masked selection

To complete the composite of the marsh grasses and Egret image, you'll isolate the egret as you apply a filter effect to the image background.

1 In the Channels palette, drag the Egret channel to the Load Channel as Selection button (▢) at the bottom of the palette. This loads the channel onto the image.

Next you'll invert the selection so that the egret is protected and you can work on the background.

2 Choose Select > Inverse.

The previous selection (the egret) is protected, and the background is selected. You can now apply changes to the background without worrying about the egret.

3 Click the Layers palette tab and make sure the background layer is selected. Then choose Filter > Artistic > Colored Pencil. Experiment with the sliders to evaluate the changes before you apply the filter.

Preview different areas of the background by dragging the image in the preview window of the Colored Pencil filter dialog box. This preview option is available with all filters.

Filter preview   *Filter applied*

4 Click OK when you're satisfied with the Colored Pencil settings. The filter is applied to the background selection.

You can experiment with other filter effects for the background. Choose Edit > Undo to undo your last performed operation.

5 Choose Select > Deselect to deselect everything.

6 Before you save your file, flatten your image to reduce the file size. Choose Layer > Flatten Image.

7 Choose File > Save.

Creating a gradient mask

In addition to using black to indicate what's hidden and white to indicate what's selected, you can paint with shades of gray to indicate partial transparency. For example, if you paint in a channel with a shade of gray that is at least halfway between white and black, the underlying image becomes partially (50% or more) visible.

You'll experiment by adding a gradient (which makes a transition from black to gray to white) to a channel and then filling the selection with a color to see how the transparency levels of the black, gray, and white in the gradient affect the image.

1 In the Channels palette, create a new channel by clicking the Create New Channel button ( ) at the bottom of the palette.

The new channel labeled Alpha 1 appears at the bottom of the Channels palette, and the other channels are hidden.

2 Double-click the new channel to open the Channel Options dialog box, and rename the channel **Gradient**. Click OK.

3 Select the gradient tool ( ).

4 In the tool options bar, click the arrow to display the Gradients pop-up palette and select the Black, White gradient.

5 Hold down Shift to keep the gradient vertical, and drag the gradient tool from the top of the document window to the bottom of the window.

The gradient is applied to the channel.

Applying effects using a gradient mask

Now you'll load the gradient as a selection and fill the selection with a color.

When you load a gradient as a selection and then fill the selection with a color, the opacity of the fill color varies over the length of the gradient. Where the gradient is black, no fill color is present; where the gradient is gray, the fill color is partially visible; and where the gradient is white, the fill color is completely visible.

1 In the Channels palette, click the RGB channel to display the full-color preview channel.

Next you'll load the Gradient channel as a selection.

2 Without deselecting the RGB channel, position the pointer over the Gradient channel. Drag from the channel to the Load Channel as Selection button (⬚) at the bottom of the palette to load the gradient as a selection.

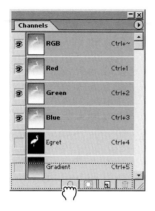

A selection border appears in the window. Although the selection border appears over only about half the image, it is correct.

3 Make sure that the foreground and background colors are set to their default (black and white). If necessary, click the Default Foreground and Background Colors icon (⬚) at the lower-left corner of the color selection boxes.

4 Press Delete to fill the gradient selection with the current background color, which is white.

5 Choose Select > Deselect to deselect everything.

6 Choose File > Save.

You have completed the Masks and Channels lesson. Although it takes some practice to become comfortable using channels, you've learned all the fundamental concepts and skills you need to get started using masks and channels.

Review questions

1 What is the benefit of using a quick mask?

2 What happens to a quick mask when you deselect?

3 When you save a selection as a mask, where is the mask stored?

4 How can you edit a mask in a channel once you've saved it?

5 How do channels differ from layers?

6 How do you use the Extract command to isolate an object with intricate borders from an image?

Review answers

1 Quick masks are helpful for creating quick, one-time selections. In addition, using a quick mask is an easy way to edit a selection using the painting tools.

2 The quick mask disappears when you deselect it.

3 Masks are saved in channels, which can be thought of as storage areas in an image.

4 You can paint directly on a mask in a channel using black, white, and shades of gray.

5 Channels are used as storage areas for saved selections. Unless you explicitly display a channel, it does not appear in the image or print. Layers can be used to isolate various parts of an image so that they can be edited as discrete objects with the painting or editing tools or other effects.

6 You use the Extract command to extract an object and the Extract dialog box to highlight the edges of the object. Then you define the object's interior and preview the extraction. Applying the extraction erases the background to transparency, leaving just the extracted object. You can also use the Force Foreground option to extract a monochromatic or uniform-colored object based on its predominant color.

Lesson 3

Lesson 4

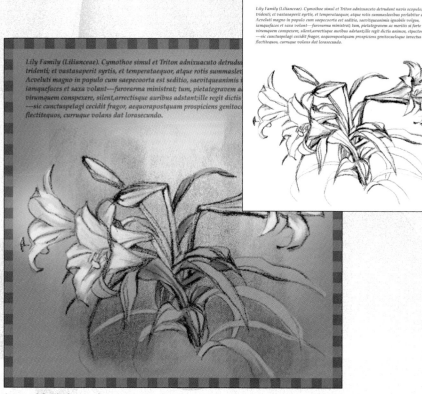

Start and finished artwork

Lesson 5

Lesson 6

Lesson 7

Lesson 8

Lesson 9

Lesson 10

Lesson 12

Start file

Corrected file

Lesson 14

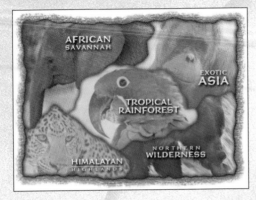 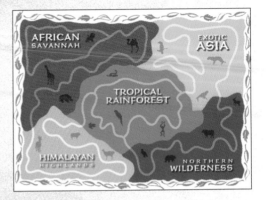

Lesson 15

Lesson 16

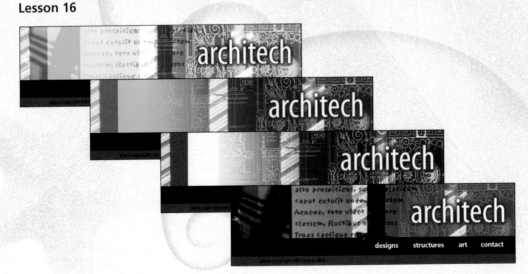

1-1: **Toolbox overview**

The marquee tools *make rectangular, elliptical, single row, and single column selections.*

The move tool *moves selections, layers, and guides.*

The lasso tools *make freehand, polygonal (straight-edged), and magnetic* (snap-to) selections.*

The magic wand tool *selects similarly colored areas.*

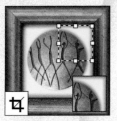

The crop tool *trims images.*

The slice tool *creates slices.*

The slice selection tool *selects slices.*

The airbrush tool *paints soft-edged strokes.*

The paintbrush tool *paints brush strokes.*

The pencil tool *paints hard-edged strokes.*

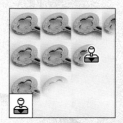

The clone stamp tool *paints with a sample of an image.*

The pattern stamp tool* *paints with part of an image as a pattern.*

The history brush tool* *paints a copy of the selected state or snapshot into the current image window.*

The art history brush tool* *paints with stylized strokes that simulate the look of different paint styles, using a selected state or snapshot.*

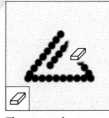

The eraser tool *erases pixels and restores parts of an image to a previously saved state.*

The background eraser tool* *erases areas to transparency by dragging.*

* Photoshop only
§ ImageReady only

1-1: **Toolbox overview (cont.)**

The magic eraser tool *erases solid-colored areas to transparency with a single click.*

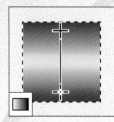

The gradient tools *create straight-line, radial*, angle*, reflected*, and diamond* blends between colors.*

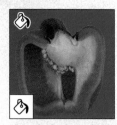

The paint bucket tool* *fills similarly colored areas with the foreground color.*

The blur tool *blurs hard edges in an image.*

The sharpen tool *sharpens soft edges in an image.*

The smudge tool *smudges data in an image.*

The dodge tool *lightens areas in an image.*

The burn tool *darkens areas in an image.*

The sponge tool *changes the color saturation of an area.*

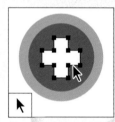

The path selection tools* *make shape or segment selections showing anchor points, direction lines, and direction points.*

The type tool *creates type on an image.*

The pen tools* *let you draw smooth-edged paths.*

The custom shape tool* *makes customized shapes selected from a custom shape list.*

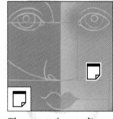

The annotations tool* *makes notes and voice annotations that can be attached to an image.*

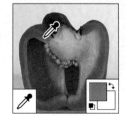

The eyedropper tool *samples colors in an image.*

The measure tool* *measures distances, locations, and angles.*

* *Photoshop only*
§ *ImageReady only*

1-1: Toolbox overview (cont.)

The hand tool *moves an image within its window.*

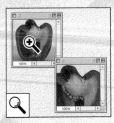

The zoom tool *magnifies and reduces the view of an image.*

The image map tools[§] *define image map areas in an image.*

The image map select tool[§] *selects image maps.*

The toggle image map visibility tool[§] *toggles between showing and hiding image maps.*

The toggle slices visibility tool[§] *toggles between showing and hiding slices in an image.*

The rollover preview tool[§] *previews rollover effects directly in ImageReady.*

The preview in default browser tool[§] *previews animations in a Web browser.*

* Photoshop only
§ ImageReady only

3-1: **Layer mode samples**

Layer 1

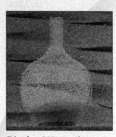

Background

Dissolve, 50% opacity

Multiply

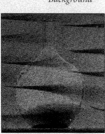

Screen

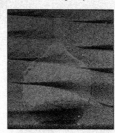

Overlay

Soft Light

Hard Light

Color Dodge

Color Burn

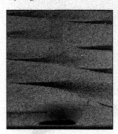

Darken

Lighten

Difference

Exclusion

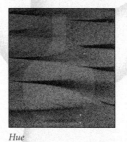

Hue

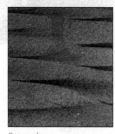

Saturation

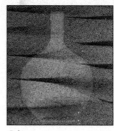

Color

Luminosity

4-1: **Application of brush stroke to background using blending modes**

Normal, 100% opacity

Normal, 50% opacity

Dissolve, 50% opacity

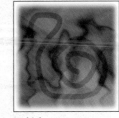

Multiply

Screen

Soft Light

Hard Light

Color Dodge

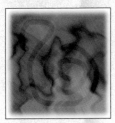

Color Burn

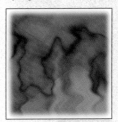

Darken

Lighten

Difference

Exclusion

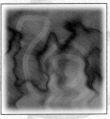

Hue

Luminosity

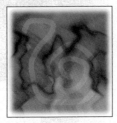

Saturation

Color

5-1: **Selecting in Standard mode and Quick Mask mode**

Lesson 5 start file

Standard mode

Quick Mask mode
A. Selected areas
B. Hidden areas

5-2: **Painting in Quick Mask mode**

Quick Mask mode

Painting with white

Resulting selection

Painting with black

Resulting selection

11-1: Setting the monitor's white point

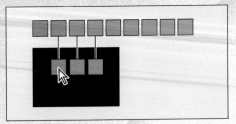

A shade cooler

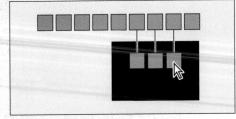

A shade warmer

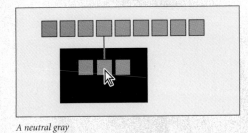

A neutral gray

12-1: RGB image with red, green, and blue channels

12-2: CMYK image with cyan, magenta, yellow, and black channels

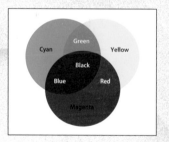

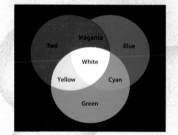

12-3: Color gamuts

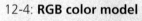

A. *Natural color gamut*
B. *RGB color gamut*
C. *CMYK color gamut*

12-4: RGB color model

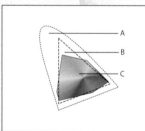

12-5: CMYK color model

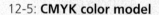

14-1: Optimized continuous-tone images

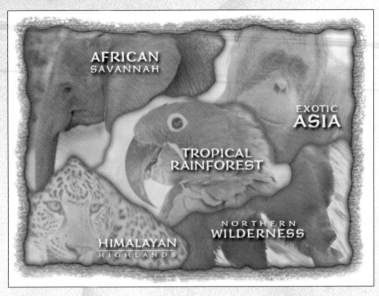

GIF, 128 colors,
88% dither

GIF, 128 colors,
No dither

GIF, 32 colors,
88% dither

GIF, 32 colors,
No dither

GIF, 64 colors,
88% dither

GIF, 64 colors,
No dither

GIF, Web palette,
auto colors

JPEG, Quality 60

JPEG, Quality 10

14-2: Optimized solid graphics

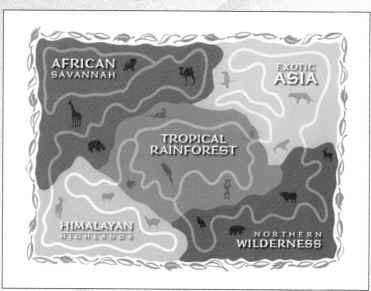

GIF, 128 colors,
88% dither

GIF, 128 colors,
No dither

GIF, 32 colors,
88% dither

GIF, 32 colors,
No dither

GIF, 64 colors,
88% dither

GIF, 64 colors,
No dither

GIF, Web palette,
auto colors

JPEG, Quality 60

JPEG, Quality 10

On your own: **Lesson 4—Painting with the history brush tools**

A. *Original charcoal drawing image*

B. *The art history brush tool paints stylized strokes based on a specific state or snapshot of the image. We softened the crisp lines delineating the petals and leaves using the art history brush tool.*

C. *The history brush tool paints with a specified copy of a previous state or snapshot, undoing changes made to an image. Once portions of the image are reverted as desired, you can apply other effects and painting tools. We added layers with a radial gradient, glow effects with the airbrush tool, and texture effects with the natural brush tool.*

Lesson 6

6 | Photo Retouching

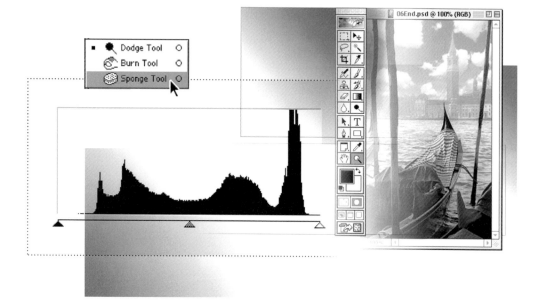

Adobe Photoshop and Adobe ImageReady include a variety of tools and commands for improving the quality of a photographic image. This lesson steps you through the process of acquiring, resizing, and retouching a photo intended for a print layout. The same workflow applies to Web images.

In this lesson, you'll learn how to do the following:

• Choose the correct resolution for a scanned photograph.

• Crop an image to final size.

• Adjust the tonal range of an image.

• Remove a color cast from an image using an adjustment layer.

• Use the Replace Color command to change the hue and saturation of a selected color in a photograph.

• Adjust the saturation and brightness of isolated areas of an image using the sponge and dodge tools.

• Use the clone stamp tool to eliminate an unwanted object from an image.

• Replace parts of an image with another image.

• Apply the Unsharp Mask filter to finish the photo-retouching process.

• Save an Adobe Photoshop file in a format that can be used by a page-layout program.

This lesson will take about 60 minutes to complete. The lesson is designed to be done in Adobe Photoshop, but information on using similar functionality in Adobe ImageReady is included where appropriate.

If needed, remove the previous lesson folder from your hard drive, and copy the Lesson06 folder onto it. As you work on this lesson, you'll overwrite the start files. If you need to restore the start files, copy them from the *Adobe Photoshop Classroom in a Book* CD.

Note: *Windows users need to unlock the lesson files before using them. For information, see "Copying the Classroom in a Book files" on page 3.*

Strategy for retouching

You can retouch photographic images in ways once available only to highly trained professionals. You can correct problems in color quality and tonal range created during the original photography or during the image's scan. You can also correct problems in composition and sharpen the overall focus of the image.

Photoshop provides a comprehensive set of color correction tools for adjusting the color and tone of individual images. ImageReady has a more basic set of color correction tools, including Levels, Auto Levels, Brightness/Contrast, Hue/Saturation, Desaturation, Invert, Variations, and the Unsharp Mask filter.

Basic steps

Most retouching follows these general steps:

• Check the scan quality and make sure that the resolution is appropriate for how the image will be used.

• Crop the image to final size.

• Adjust the overall contrast or tonal range of the image.

• Remove any color casts.

• Adjust the color and tone in specific parts of the image to bring out highlights, midtones, shadows, and desaturated colors.

• Sharpen the overall focus of the image.

Intended use

The retouching techniques you apply to an image depend in part on how the image will be used. Whether an image is intended for black-and-white publication on newsprint or for full-color Internet distribution will affect everything from the resolution of the initial scan to the type of tonal range and color correction that the image requires. Photoshop supports the CMYK color mode for preparing an image to be printed using process colors, as well as RGB and other color modes. ImageReady supports only RGB mode used for on-screen display.

To illustrate one application of retouching techniques, this lesson takes you through the steps of correcting a photograph intended for four-color print publication. The image is a scanned photograph of Venice that will be placed in an Adobe PageMaker® layout for an A4-size magazine. The original size of the photo is 5 inches by 7 inches, and its final size in the print layout will be 3.75 inches by 6 inches.

For more information about CMYK and RGB color modes, see Lesson 12, "Producing and Printing Consistent Color."

Original image

Image cropped and retouched

Image placed into page layout

For the Web: The printed page versus on-screen display

Although you can create publications for both paper and on-screen use, remember that a computer screen and a printed page are very different. Keep these differences in mind when you create publications for either medium—or for both media:

• Text can be small and still very legible on paper, because the dots of ink on paper are much finer than the dots of light used in a monitor. Therefore, avoid small text and finely detailed graphics on-screen. Note that this means it is more difficult to use formatting such as multiple columns effectively on-screen.

• Computer monitors come in all sizes, and you can rarely guarantee that your online readers all have the same monitor size. So design for the smallest monitor you expect people to have—typically a 15-inch monitor. By contrast, when you print to paper, you know what size the paper is and can design the publication accordingly. However, a page in an HTML or PDF publication can be any length.

• A computer screen is horizontal, while most printed pages are vertical. This fact fundamentally affects the format of your pages.

• A printed publication is usually read sequentially—even to flip through the publication the reader must turn from one page to the next. In an online publication, the reader can go anywhere any time, either by indicating what page to go to or by clicking on a link that goes to somewhere else, such as to another publication entirely.

–From the Official Adobe Electronic Publishing Guide, Chapter 1, "What Is Electronic Publishing?"

Resolution and image size

The first step in retouching a photograph in Photoshop is to make sure that the image is the correct resolution. The term *resolution* refers to the number of small squares known as *pixels* that describe an image and establish its detail. Resolution is determined by *pixel dimensions*, or the number of pixels along the width and height of an image.

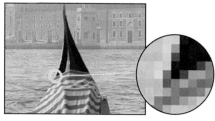

Pixels in a photographic image

Types of resolution

In computer graphics, there are different types of resolution:

The number of pixels per unit of length in an image is called the *image resolution*, usually measured in pixels per inch (ppi). An image with a high resolution has more pixels (and therefore a larger file size) than an image of the same dimensions with a low resolution. Images in Photoshop can vary from high resolution (300 ppi or higher) to low resolution (72 ppi or 96 ppi), whereas images in ImageReady are fixed at 72 ppi.

The number of pixels per unit of length on a monitor is the *monitor resolution*, usually measured in dots per inch (dpi). Image pixels are translated directly into monitor pixels. In Photoshop, if the image resolution is higher than the monitor resolution, the image appears larger on-screen than its specified print dimensions. For example, when you display a 1-inch-by-1-inch, 144-ppi image on a 72-dpi monitor, the image fills a 2-inch-by-2-inch area of the screen. ImageReady images have a consistent image resolution of 72 ppi and display at the monitor resolution.

3.75 in. x 6 in. @ 72 ppi;   *100% view on-screen*
file size 342K

3.75 in. x 6 in. @ 200 ppi;   *100% view on-screen*
file size 2.48 MB

The number of ink dots per inch produced by an imagesetter or laser printer is the *printer* or *output resolution*. Higher resolution printers combined with higher resolution images generally produce the best quality. The appropriate resolution for a printed image is determined both by the printer resolution and by the *screen frequency* or lines per inch (lpi) of the halftone screens used to reproduce images.

Keep in mind that the higher the image resolution, the larger the file size and the longer the file takes to download from the Web.

Resolution for this lesson

To determine the image resolution for the photograph in this lesson, we followed the computer graphics rule of thumb for color or grayscale images intended for print on large commercial printers: Scan at a resolution 1.5 to 2 times the screen frequency used by the printer. Because the magazine in which the image will be printed uses a screen frequency of 133 lpi, the image was scanned at 200 ppi (133 x 1.5).

[?] For complete information on resolution and image size, see Adobe Photoshop 6.0 online Help.

Getting started

Before beginning this lesson, restore the default application settings for Adobe Photoshop. See "Restoring default preferences" on page 4.

You'll start the lesson by viewing the finished Venice image that you'll retouch for the magazine layout.

1 Start Adobe Photoshop.

If a notice appears asking whether you want to customize your color settings, click No.

2 Choose File > Open, and open the file 06End.psd from the Lessons/Lesson06 folder.

3 When you have finished viewing the file, either leave the file open for reference or close it without saving changes.

For an illustration of the finished artwork for this lesson, see the gallery at the beginning of the color section.

Now you'll open the start file and begin the lesson by viewing the photograph you will be retouching. (Although the photograph for this lesson was originally scanned at 200 dpi, the file in which you will be working is actually a low-resolution file. The resolution was changed to limit the file size and to make work on the exercises more efficient.)

4 Choose File > Open, and open the file 06Start.psd from the Lessons/Lesson06 folder.

Cropping an image

Now you'll use the crop tool to trim and scale the photograph for this lesson so that it fits the space designed for it. You can use either the crop tool or the Crop command to crop an image.

You can decide whether to delete or discard the area outside of a rectangular selection, or whether to hide the area outside of the selection. In ImageReady, the Hide option is useful when creating animations with elements that move from off-screen into the live image area.

For more information on cropping, see "Cropping the completed image" on page 53.

1 Select the crop tool (⊟).

2 In the tool options bar, enter the dimensions of the finished image—**3.75** in the Width text box and **6** in the height text box.

Note: *In ImageReady, select the Fixed Size option in the tool options bar before entering the dimensions.*

3 Next draw a marquee around the image, making sure that you include the top of the tower and the orange tarp in the lower right gondola.

Notice that as you drag the marquee it retains the same proportion as the dimensions you specified for the target size. When you release the mouse button, the options change in the tool options bar, and a cropping shield will display outside the selected area. You can deselect this option in the tool options bar if you prefer not to see the shield.

After dragging the marquee in Photoshop, make sure that the Perspective option is not selected in the tool options bar.

Because the photograph was scanned in slightly crooked, you'll now use the crop tool to straighten the image before applying the new dimensions to it.

4 Move the pointer outside the crop marquee. The pointer turns into a curved double arrow (↱). Drag clockwise until the marquee is parallel with the image.

5 Place the pointer within the crop marquee, and drag until the right edge of the marquee lines up with the right edge of the image.

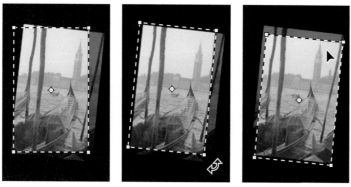

Initial crop marquee   *Marquee rotated*   *Marquee moved*

6 If necessary, fine-tune the size of the marquee by dragging a corner handle.

7 Press Enter (Windows) or Return (Mac OS). The image is now cropped.

Marquee resized   *Image cropped*

♀ *In Photoshop and ImageReady, you can use the Trim command to discard a border area around the edge of the image, based on transparency or edge color.*

8 Choose File > Save to save your work.

Adjusting the tonal range

The tonal range of an image represents the amount of *contrast*, or detail, in the image and is determined by the image's distribution of pixels, ranging from the darkest pixels (black) to the lightest pixels (white). You'll now correct the photograph's contrast using the Levels command.

1 Choose Image > Adjust > Levels, and make sure that the Preview option is checked in the Levels dialog box.

Notice the histogram in the Levels dialog box. The triangles at the bottom of the histogram represent the shadows (black triangle), highlights (white triangle), and midtones or gamma (gray triangle). If your image had colors across the entire brightness range, the graph would extend across the full width of the histogram, from black triangle to white triangle. Instead, the graph is clumped toward the center, indicating there are no very dark or light colors.

You can adjust the black and white points of the image to extend its tonal range.

2 Drag the left and right triangles inward to where the histogram indicates the darkest and lightest colors begin. Click OK to apply the changes.

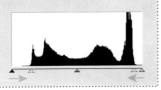

*Increasing shadows (black triangle)
and adding highlights (white triangle)*   *Result*

3 Choose Image > Histogram to view the new histogram. The tonal range now extends throughout the entire range of the histogram. Click OK.

Note: ImageReady does not have a Histogram command. To adjust and view a histogram, use the Levels command.

4 Choose File > Save.

Using the color adjustment tools

All Adobe Photoshop and ImageReady color adjustment tools work essentially the same way: by mapping existing ranges of pixel values to new ranges of values. The difference between the tools is the amount of control they provide.

You can use most color adjustment tools in three ways: applying them to one or more channels, to a regular layer, or to an adjustment layer. When you make color adjustments to a channel or a regular layer, you permanently alter the pixels on that layer.

If you make adjustments to an adjustment layer in Photoshop, your changes reside only in the adjustment layer and do not alter any pixels. At the same time, you can make adjustments to multiple layers at once. The effect is as if you are viewing the visible layers through the adjustment layer above them. This lets you experiment with color and tonal adjustments without permanently altering pixels in the image. You can even limit the adjustment to specific areas of the image by painting the layer mask of the adjustment layer. When you transfer an image with an adjustment layer to ImageReady, you can view the layers but not edit them.

–From Adobe Photoshop 6.0 online Help

You can also adjust the contrast (highlights and shadows) and the overall mix of colors in an image automatically using the Image > Adjust > Auto Contrast command. Adjusting the contrast maps the darkest and lightest pixels in the image to black and white.

This remapping causes the highlights to appear lighter and the shadows to appear darker and can improve the appearance of many photographic or continuous-tone images. (The Auto Contrast command does not improve flat-color images.)

The Auto Contrast command clips white and black pixels by 0.5%—that is, it ignores the first 0.5% of either extreme when identifying the lightest and darkest pixels in the image. This clipping of color values ensures that white and black values are representative areas of the image's content, rather than extreme pixel values.

Removing a color cast

Some images contain color casts (imbalances of color), which may occur during scanning or which may have existed in the original image. The photograph of the gondolas has a color cast—it's too red.

Note: To see a color cast in an image on your monitor, you need a 24-bit monitor (one that can display millions of colors). On monitors that can display only 256 colors (8 bits), a color cast is difficult, if not impossible, to detect.

Now you'll use a Color Balance adjustment layer to correct the photograph's color cast. An adjustment layer lets you edit an image as many times as you like without permanently changing the original pixel values. Using an adjustment layer to adjust color balance is a particular advantage for images you plan to print. After you see the color proof or printed copy, you can make additional changes to the image, if necessary.

Although ImageReady does not have adjustment layers, you can use the Auto Contrast or Variations command to perform a similar correction. However, the correction affects the entire image, not just a layer. For the greatest control, jump to Photoshop to use an adjustment layer, and then return to ImageReady.

1 Choose Layer > New Adjustment Layer > Color Balance.

2 In the New Layer dialog box, click OK to create the adjustment layer and to display the Color Balance dialog box.

3 To adjust the midtones so that they're less red, drag the top slider to the left (we used –15) and the middle slider to the right (we used +8).

4 Click OK to apply the changes to the Color Balance adjustment layer.

Notice that a Color Balance layer has appeared in the Layers palette.

5 In the Layers palette, click the eye icon next to the Color Balance layer to hide and show the layer. You'll see the difference between the adjusted colors and the original colors.

6 Choose File > Save.

Note: *When you double-click an adjustment layer in the Layers palette, the corresponding Layer Style dialog box appears, where you can edit the values of the adjustment layer.*

Adjusting color balance

Every color adjustment affects the overall color balance in your image. You have numerous ways to achieve similar effects, so determining which adjustment is appropriate depends on the image and on the desired effect.

It helps to keep a diagram of the color wheel on hand if you're new to adjusting color components. You can use the color wheel to predict how a change in one color component affects other colors and also how changes translate between RGB and CMYK color models. For example, you can decrease the amount of any color in an image by increasing the amount of its opposite on the color wheel—and vice versa. Similarly, you can increase and decrease a color by adjusting the two adjacent colors on the wheel, or even by adjusting the two colors adjacent to its opposite.

For example, in a CMYK image you can decrease magenta by decreasing either the amount of magenta or its proportion (by adding cyan and yellow). You can even combine these two corrections, minimizing their effect on overall lightness. In an RGB image, you can decrease magenta by removing red and blue or by adding green. All of these adjustments result in an overall color balance containing less magenta.

–From Adobe Photoshop 6.0 online Help

Replacing colors in an image

With the Replace Color command, you can create temporary masks based on specific colors and then replace these colors. *Masks* let you isolate an area of an image, so that changes affect just the selected area and not the rest of the image. Options in the Replace Color command's dialog box allow you to adjust the hue, saturation, and lightness components of the selection. *Hue* is color, *saturation* is the purity of the color, and *lightness* is how much white or black is in the image.

You'll use the Replace Color command to change the color of the orange tarp in the gondola at the lower right corner of the image. The Replace Color command is not available in ImageReady.

1 In the Layers palette, select the Background.

2 Select the zoom tool (🔍), and click once on the tarp to zoom in on it.

3 Select the rectangular marquee tool, and draw a selection around the tarp. Don't worry about making a perfect selection, but be sure to include all of the tarp.

4 Choose Image > Adjust > Replace Color to open the Replace Color dialog box.

By default, the Selection area of the Replace Color dialog box displays a black rectangle, representing the current selection.

You will now use the eyedropper tool to select the area of color that will be masked and replaced with a new color. Three eyedropper tools are displayed in the Replace Color dialog box.

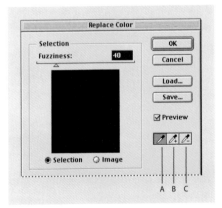

A. Select single color **B.** *Add to selection*
C. *Subtract from selection*

The first eyedropper tool (🖊) selects a single color, the eyedropper-plus tool (🖊) is used to add colors to a selection, and the eyedropper-minus tool (🖊) is used to subtract colors from a selection.

5 Select the eyedropper tool in the Replace Color dialog box, and click once on the orange tarp to select it.

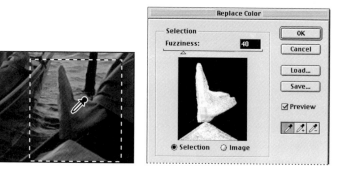

6 Then select the eyedropper-plus tool, and click and drag over the other areas of the tarp until the entire tarp is highlighted in white in the dialog box.

7 Adjust the tolerance level of the mask by moving the Fuzziness slider to **61**.

Fuzziness controls the degree to which related colors are included in the mask.

8 Select the eyedropper-minus tool ( ) and click in the black area around the selection in the Replace Color dialog box to remove any white.

9 In the Transform area of the Replace Color dialog box, drag the Hue slider to +**160**, the Saturation slider to –**20**, and the Lightness slider to –**40**.

The color of the tarp is replaced with the new hue, saturation, and lightness.

10 Click OK to apply the changes.

11 Double-click the hand tool ( ) to fit the image on-screen.

12 Choose Select > Deselect.

13 Choose File > Save.

Adjusting saturation with the sponge tool

Now you'll saturate the color of the gondolas in the foreground using the sponge tool. When you change the saturation of a color, you adjust its strength or purity. The sponge tool is useful in letting you make subtle saturation changes to specific areas of an image.

1 Select the sponge tool ( ), hidden under the dodge tool ( ).

ImageReady also has a sponge tool hidden under the clone stamp tool ( ).

2 In the tool options bar, choose Saturate from the Mode menu. To set the intensity of the saturation effect, enter **90** in the Pressure text box.

3 Click the arrow to display the Brush pop-up palette, and select a large, feathered brush from the second row of the Brushes palette.

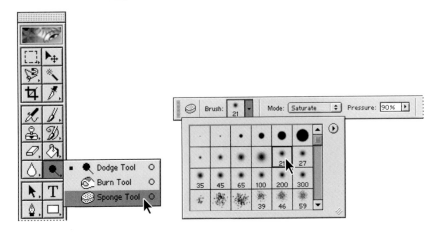

4 Drag the sponge back and forth over the gondolas to saturate their color. The more you drag over an area, the more saturated the color becomes.

Original   *Result*

Adjusting lightness with the dodge tool

Next you'll use the dodge tool to lighten the highlights along the gondola's hull and exaggerate the reflection of the water there. The dodge tool is based on the traditional photographer's method of holding back light during an exposure to lighten an area of the image.

1 Select the dodge tool (✹) hidden under the sponge tool (⬬).

ImageReady also has a dodge tool hidden under the clone stamp tool (♨).

2 In the tool options bar, choose Highlights from the Range menu, and enter **50** in the Exposure text box.

3 Select a medium, feathered brush from the second row of the Brush pop-up palette.

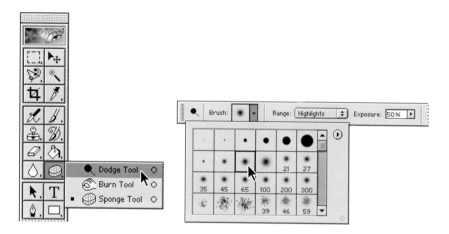

4 Drag the dodge tool back and forth over the gondola's hull to bring out its highlights.

Original   *Result*

Removing unwanted objects

You can remove unwanted objects from a photograph. Using the clone stamp tool, you can remove an object or area by "cloning" an area of the image over the area you want to eliminate.

You'll eliminate the small boat near the center of the image by painting over it with a copy of the water.

1 Select the zoom tool (🔍); then click the small boat to magnify that part of the image.

2 Select the clone stamp tool (📑).

3 In the tool options bar, make sure that the Aligned option is deselected. In the Brush pop-up palette, choose a medium-size brush from the second row.

Note: The Aligned option allows you to apply the entire sampled area, regardless of how many times you stop and resume painting. If Aligned is deselected, the sampled area is applied from the initial sampling point each time you stop and resume painting.

4 Center the clone stamp tool over the water between the large gondola and the post to its right. Then hold down Alt (Windows) or Option (Mac OS), and click to sample or copy that part of the image. Make sure that the area you sample will blend well with the area around the object you are removing.

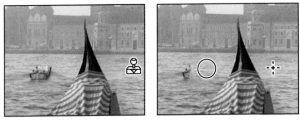

Clicking to sample image   *Dragging to paint over image*

5 Click or drag the clone stamp tool over the boat to paint over it with a copy of the water you just sampled. Notice the cross hair that follows your cursor as you paint; it represents the point from which the clone stamp tool is cloning.

6 Double-click the hand tool to fit the image on-screen.

7 Choose File > Save.

Replacing part of an image

Because the sky is fairly drab and overcast in this photograph, you'll replace it with a more interesting sky from another file. You'll begin by selecting the current sky.

1 Select the magic wand tool ( ).

2 In the tool options bar, enter **16** in the Tolerance text box.

3 Using the magic wand tool, click to select part of the sky. Then hold down Shift and click the rest of the sky to select it.

4 Choose File > Open and open the file Clouds.psd from the Lessons/Lesson06 folder.

5 Choose Select > All, and choose Edit > Copy to copy the selection to the Clipboard. Close the Clouds.psd file.

6 In the 06Start.psd file, choose Edit > Paste Into to paste the clouds into the current selection.

Notice that a new layer has been added to the Layers palette.

Note: ImageReady does not have a Paste Into command. To replicate the effect, select the sky as shown in step 3, and delete it. Open the Clouds.psd file, and copy it as in steps 4 and 5. Then choose Edit > Paste, and move the cloud layer beneath the boat layer.

7 Select the move tool ( ), and drag the clouds into the position you want.

Sky selected *Clouds pasted into sky* *Clouds moved into position*

Now you'll change the clouds' opacity to make them blend better with the rest of the image.

8 With the clouds layer still selected, adjust the Opacity in the Layers palette. Either use the slider bar or type any number from **01** (1%) to **100** (100%) in the Opacity text box (we used 55%).

9 Choose File > Save.

Opacity set to 55% *Result*

Now you'll flatten the image into a single layer so that you can apply the Unsharp Mask filter, the final step in retouching the photo. Because you may want to return to a version of the file with all its layers intact, you will use the Save As command to save the flattened file with a new name.

10 Choose Layer > Flatten Image.

11 Choose File > Save As. In the dialog box, type a new filename, and click Save.

Applying the Unsharp Mask filter

The last step you take when retouching a photo is to apply the Unsharp Mask filter, which adjusts the contrast of the edge detail and creates the illusion of a more focused image.

1 Choose Filter > Sharpen > Unsharp Mask.

2 In the Unsharp Mask dialog box, make sure that the Preview option is selected so that you can view the effect before you apply it. The preview will show in either the Unsharp Mask dialog box thumbnail or your document window. To get a better view, you can place the pointer within the preview window and drag to see different parts of the image. You can also change the magnification of the preview image with the plus and minus buttons located below the window.

3 Drag the Amount slider until the image is as sharp as you want (we used 60%).

4 Drag the Radius slider to determine the number of pixels surrounding the edge pixels that affects the sharpening. The higher the resolution, the higher the Radius setting should be. Since our image is only 72 dpi, we used a Radius of 0.5 pixel.

Note: *For high-resolution images, a Radius between 1 and 2 is recommended.*

5 If you desire, you can adjust the Threshold slider. This determines how different the sharpened pixels must be from the surrounding area before they are considered edge pixels and subsequently sharpened by the Unsharp Mask filter. The default Threshold value of 0 sharpens all pixels in the image.

6 Click OK to apply the Unsharp Mask filter.

[?] For complete information on the Unsharp Mask filter, see "Sharpening the image" in Adobe Photoshop 6.0 online Help.

Sharpening the image

Unsharp masking, or USM, is a traditional film compositing technique used to sharpen edges in an image. The Unsharp Mask filter corrects blurring introduced during photographing, scanning, resampling, or printing. It is useful for images intended for both print and online.

The Unsharp Mask filter locates pixels that differ from surrounding pixels by the threshold you specify and increases the pixels' contrast by the amount you specify. In addition, you specify the radius of the region to which each pixel is compared.

The effects of the Unsharp Mask filter are far more pronounced on-screen than in high-resolution output. If your final destination is print, experiment to determine what dialog box settings work best for your image.

–From Adobe Photoshop 6.0 online Help

Saving the image for four-color printing

Before you save a Photoshop file for use in a four-color publication, you must change the image to CMYK color mode so that it will be printed correctly in four-color process inks. You can use the Mode command to change the image's color mode.

[?] For complete information on color modes, see "Converting between color modes" in Adobe Photoshop 6.0 online Help.

You can perform these tasks in Photoshop only. ImageReady does not have printing capability. It uses only one color mode, RGB, for on-screen display.

1 Choose Image > Mode > CMYK Color.

You can now save the file in the correct format required for Adobe PageMaker and your publication. Because PageMaker uses the Tagged-Image File Format (TIFF) for images that will be printed in process or CMYK colors, you will save the photo as a TIFF file.

2 Choose File > Save As.

3 In the Save As dialog box, choose TIFF from the Format menu.

4 Click Save.

5 In the TIFF Options dialog box, select the correct Byte Order for your system and click OK.

The image is now fully retouched, saved, and ready for placement in the PageMaker layout.

On your own: Painting with the art history brush

In Photoshop, you can simulate the texture of painting with different colors and artistic styles using the art history brush tool. The art history brush paints with stylized strokes, using the source data from a specified history state or snapshot. The brush works well with realistic images to let you create painterly, impressionistic effects. Try out different settings to see the variety of effects you can create in the same image. (ImageReady does not have an art history brush.)

1 Choose File > Open, and open the image you want to paint.

2 Choose File > Save As, rename the file, and save it, to retain a copy of your original image for future use.

3 For a variety of visual effects, experiment with applying filters or filling the image with a solid color before painting with the art history brush tool. For example, add a layer to the image, fill it with white, and then use the art history brush tool to paint.

4 In the History palette, click the icon of the state or snapshot to use as the source for the art history brush tool. A brush icon appears next to the source history state.

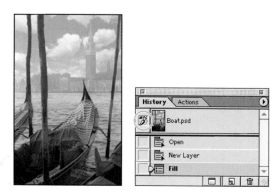

You can select any history state to be your source by clicking in the left column, and if you're not satisfied with an effect, you can return to a previous state or the snapshot by clicking the state thumbnail.

5 Select the art history brush tool (𝒷) hidden under the history brush tool (𝒷).

6 In the tool options bar, select a brush from the Brush pop-up palette. For interesting effects, try using a texture, noncircular, or custom brush. The brush corresponds to the size of individual paint strokes, not the total area covered by the paint.

7 Drag in the image to paint.

When you've practiced painting with the brush to see how it works, experiment with the settings to create various effects:

• Control the shape of the paint stroke by choosing an option from the Style pop-up menu in the tool options bar.

• Try out different blending modes using the Mode pop-up menu, and vary the opacity.

🔲 For information on setting tool options, see "Painting" in Adobe Photoshop 6.0 online Help.

• Vary how much the paint color changes from the color in the source state or snapshot by adjusting the Fidelity. The lower the fidelity, the more the color will vary from the source.

• Set the area covered by the paint strokes using the Area option. Try increasing the size to enlarge the covered area and increase the number of strokes.

• Control the distance between brush marks using the Spacing option. Type a number or use the slider to enter a value that is a percentage of the brush diameter.

• Select a small brush to maintain the image integrity and reveal the brush stroke. The larger the brush you use, the greater the distortion will be to the image.

If you are using a pressure-sensitive tablet, select either of the following Brush Dynamics options:

• Size to have increased pressure result in a larger area covered by the paint. Note that Size refers to the area of coverage, not the brush size.

• Opacity to have increased pressure result in more opaque paint.

Review questions

1 What does resolution mean?

2 How can you use the crop tool in photo retouching?

3 How can you adjust the tonal range of an image?

4 How can you correct a color cast in a photograph?

5 What is saturation, and how can you adjust it?

6 Why would you use the Unsharp Mask filter on a photo?

Review answers

1 The term *resolution* refers to the number of pixels that describe an image and establish its detail. The three different types of resolution include *image resolution*, measured in pixels per inch (ppi); *monitor resolution*, measured in dots per inch (dpi); and *printer or output resolution*, measured in ink dots per inch.

2 You can use the crop tool to trim, scale, and straighten an image.

3 You can use the black and white triangles below the Levels command histogram to control where the darkest and lightest points in the image begin and thus extend its tonal range.

4 In Photoshop, you can correct a color cast with a Color Balance adjustment layer. The adjustment layer lets you change the color of the image as many times as you like without permanently affecting the original pixel values.

5 Saturation is the strength or purity of color in an image. You can increase the saturation in a specific area of an image with the sponge tool.

6 The Unsharp Mask filter adjusts the contrast of the edge detail and creates the illusion of a more focused image.

Lesson 7

7 | Basic Pen Tool Techniques

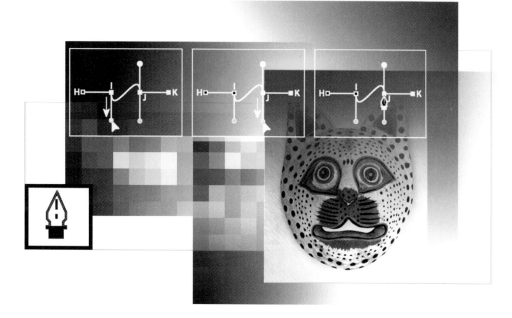

The pen tool draws precise straight or curved lines called paths. You can use the pen tool as a drawing tool or as a selection tool. When used as a selection tool, the pen tool always draws smooth, anti-aliased outlines. These paths are an excellent alternative to using the standard selection tools for creating intricate selections.

In this lesson, you'll learn how to do the following:

• Practice drawing straight and curved paths using the pen tool.

• Save paths.

• Fill and stroke paths.

• Edit paths using the path editing tools.

• Convert a path to a selection.

• Convert a selection to a path.

This lesson will take about 50 minutes to complete. The lesson is designed to be done in Adobe Photoshop. Adobe ImageReady does not have a pen tool and does not support paths.

If needed, remove the previous lesson folder from your hard drive, and copy the Lesson07 folder onto it. As you work on this lesson, you'll overwrite the start files. If you need to restore the start files, copy them from the *Adobe Photoshop Classroom in a Book* CD.

Note: *Windows users need to unlock the lesson files before using them. For information, see "Copying the Classroom in a Book files" on page 3.*

Getting started

You'll start the lesson by viewing a copy of the finished image that you'll create. Then you'll open a series of template files that guide you through the process of creating straight paths, curved paths, and paths that are a combination of both. In addition, you'll learn how to add points to a path, how to subtract points from a path, and how to convert a straight line to a curve and vice versa. After you've practiced drawing and editing paths using the templates, you'll open an image of the cat mask and practice making selections using the pen tool.

Before beginning this lesson, restore the default application settings for Adobe Photoshop. See "Restoring default preferences" on page 4.

1 Start Adobe Photoshop.

If a notice appears asking whether you want to customize your color settings, click No.

2 Choose File > Open, and open the file 07End.psd from the Lessons/Lesson07 folder on your hard drive.

3 When you have finished viewing the file, either leave it open for reference or close it without saving changes.

For an illustration of the finished artwork for this lesson, see the gallery at the beginning of the color section.

Now you'll open the first template for drawing straight paths.

4 Choose File > Open and open the file Straight.psd from the Lessons/Lesson07 folder.

5 If desired, select the zoom tool (Q), and drag over the image to magnify the view.

Drawing paths with the pen tool

The pen tool draws straight and curved lines called *paths*. A path is any line or shape you draw using the pen, magnetic pen, or freeform pen tool. Of these tools, the pen tool draws paths with the greatest precision; the magnetic pen and freeform pen tools let you draw paths as if you were drawing with a pencil on paper.

Paths can be open or closed. Open paths have two distinct endpoints. Closed paths are continuous; for example, a circle is a closed path. The type of path you draw affects how it can be selected and adjusted. Paths that have not been filled or stroked do not print when you print your artwork. (This is because paths are vector objects that contain no pixels, unlike the bitmap shapes drawn by the pencil and other painting tools.)

1 Select the pen tool (✎).

Press P on the keyboard to select the pen tool. Continue to press Shift+P to toggle between the pen and freeform pen tools.

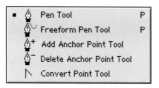

2 In the tool options bar, make sure the Create new work path (🗐) and the Auto Add/Delete options are selected. For this lesson, the Rubber Band option should not be selected.

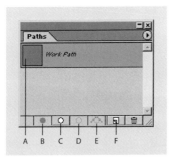

3 Click the Paths palette tab to bring the palette to the front of its group.

The Paths palette displays thumbnail previews of the paths you draw.

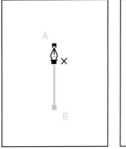

*A. Path thumbnail **B.** Fills path with foreground color **C.** Strokes path with foreground color **D.** Loads path as a selection **E.** Makes work path from selection **F.** Creates new path*

Drawing straight paths

Straight paths are created by clicking the mouse button. The first time you click, you set a starting point for a path. Each time thereafter that you click, a straight line is drawn between the previous point and the current point.

Click to set a starting point.

Click again to draw a straight line.

1 Using the pen tool, position the pointer on point A in the template and click the pen tool. Then click point B to create a straight-line path.

As you draw paths, a temporary storage area named Work Path appears in the Paths palette to keep track of the paths you draw.

You'll also notice that once you start using the pen tool, the tool options bar changes to a slightly different set of options. The Add to shape area option (▣) should be selected for this lesson.

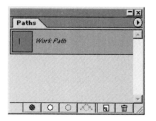

2 End the path in the image by clicking the pen tool (✒) in the toolbox.

The points that connect paths are called *anchor points*. You can drag individual anchor points to edit segments of a path, or you can select all the anchor points to select the entire path.

You'll learn more about anchor points later in this lesson.

3 In the Paths palette, double-click the Work Path to open the Save Path dialog box. Enter **Straight lines** in the Name text box, and click OK to rename the path.

The path is renamed, and remains selected in the Paths palette.

You must save a work path to avoid losing its contents. If you deselect the work path without saving and then start drawing again, a new work path will replace the first one.

About anchor points, direction lines, and direction points

A path consists of one or more straight or curved segments. Anchor points mark the endpoints of the path segments. On curved segments, each selected anchor point displays one or two direction lines, ending in direction points. The positions of direction lines and points determine the size and shape of a curved segment. Moving these elements reshapes the curves in a path.

A path can be closed, with no beginning or end (for example, a circle), or open, with distinct endpoints (for example, a wavy line).

Smooth curves are connected by anchor points called smooth points. Sharply curved paths are connected by corner points.

When you move a direction line on a smooth point, the curved segments on both sides of the point adjust simultaneously. In comparison, when you move a direction line on a corner point, only the curve on the same side of the point as the direction line is adjusted.

–From Adobe Photoshop 6.0 online Help

Moving and adjusting paths

You use the direct selection tool to select and adjust an anchor point, a path segment, or an entire path.

1 Select the direct selection tool (⬉) hidden under the path component selection tool (⬆).

💡 *To select the direct selection tool, press A. You can also select the direct selection tool when the pen tool is active by holding down Ctrl (Windows) or Command (Mac OS).*

2 Click the path in the window to select it, and then move the path by dragging anywhere on the path using the direct selection tool.

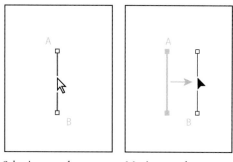

Selecting a path *Moving a path*

3 To adjust the angle or length of the path, drag one of the anchor points with the direct selection tool.

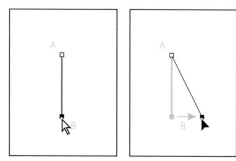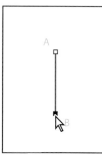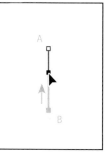

Adjusting the path angle *Adjusting the path length*

4 Select the pen tool.

5 To begin the next path, hold the pointer over point C. Click point C with the pen tool. Notice that an *x* appears in the pen tool pointer to indicate that you are starting a new path.

6 Click point D to draw a path between the two points.

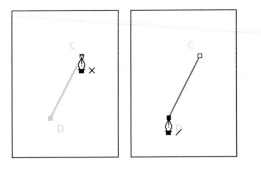

7 End the path using either of the following methods:

• Click the pen tool in the toolbox.

• Hold down Ctrl (Windows) or Command (Mac OS), and click away from the path. Holding down Ctrl/Command while the pen tool is active selects the direct selection tool.

8 Click point E to begin the next path. Then hold down Shift and click points F, G, H, and I. Holding down Shift as you click subsequent points constrains the path to a 45° angle.

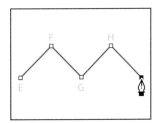

If you make a mistake while you're drawing, choose Edit > Undo to undo the last anchor point. Then click with the pen tool to continue.

9 End the path using one of the methods you've learned.

When a path contains more than one segment, you can drag individual anchor points to adjust individual segments of the path. You can also select all of the anchor points in a path to edit the entire path.

10 Select the direct selection tool (↖).

11 Try dragging individual anchor points to move segments of the zigzag path you just drew.

12 To select an entire path, Alt-click (Windows) or Option-click (Mac OS) with the direct selection tool. When an entire path is selected, all the anchor points are solid.

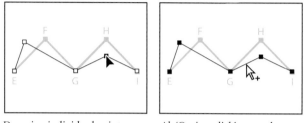

Dragging individual points   *Alt/Option-clicking to select entire path*

13 Drag the path to move the entire path; then choose Edit > Undo to undo the move.

Creating closed paths

Next you'll draw a closed path. Creating a closed path differs from creating an open path in the way that you end the path.

1 Select the pen tool (✒).

2 Click point J to begin the path; then click point K and point L.

When you position the pointer over the starting point to end the path, a small circle appears with the pen tool to indicate that the path will be closed when you click.

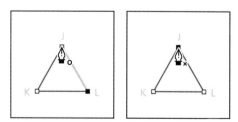

Circle indicating path will be closed, and result

3 To close the path, position the pointer over the starting point (point J), and click.

Closing the path ends the path. In contrast, to end an open path you must click the pen tool in the toolbox or Ctrl/Command-click away from the path.

If desired, practice drawing another closed path using the star shape on the template as a guide.

At this point, all of the paths you've drawn appear in the Straight Lines work path in the Paths palette. Each individual path on the Straight Lines path is called a *subpath*.

You can convert any path you have drawn into a selection and combine this selection with others. (You'll try this later.) You can also convert selection borders into paths and fine-tune them.

Painting paths

Painting paths adds pixels that appear when you print an image. Filling paints a closed path with color, an image, or a pattern. Stroking paints color along the path. To fill or stroke a path, you must first select it.

1 Click the Swatches palette tab to bring the palette forward. Click a swatch to select a foreground color to use to paint the path.

2 Select the direct selection tool (⬉).

3 In the image window, click the zigzag line with the direct selection tool to select it. Then choose Stroke Subpath from the Paths palette menu.

4 In the Stroke Subpath dialog box, choose Airbrush from the Tool menu, and click OK.

The path is stroked with the current airbrush settings.

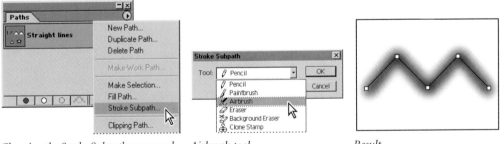

Choosing the Stroke Subpath command   Airbrush tool   Result

Note: You can select a painting tool and set attributes before you select the tool in the Stroke Subpath dialog box.

Now try filling one of the paths.

5 In the Swatches palette, click a swatch to select a different foreground color for the fill.

6 Click the triangular closed path with the direct selection tool. Then choose Fill Subpath from the Paths palette menu. The Fill Subpath dialog box appears.

7 In the Fill Subpath dialog box, click OK to accept the defaults.

The triangular path is filled with the foreground color.

Using the Fill Subpath command to fill a closed subpath   *Result*

8 To hide the paths, click below the pathnames in the blank area of the Paths palette.

9 Choose File > Close, and do not save changes.

Drawing curved paths

Curved paths are created by clicking and dragging. The first time you click and drag, you set a starting point for the curved path and also determine the direction of the curve. As you continue to drag, a curved path is drawn between the previous point and the current point.

As you drag the pen tool, Photoshop draws *direction lines* and *direction points* from the anchor point. Direction lines and points are used to edit the shape of curves and to change the direction of curves. You'll edit paths using the direction lines and direction points after you practice drawing curved paths.

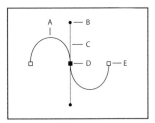

Direction lines and points setting
the curve direction
A. *Curved line segment* **B.** *Direction point*
C. *Direction line* **D.** *Selected anchor point*
E. *Unselected anchor point*

Like unpainted paths, direction lines and points do not print when you print your artwork because they are vector objects that contain no pixels.

1 Choose File > Open, and open the file Curves.psd from the Lessons/Lesson07 folder.

2 Select the pen tool (✎).

3 Click on point A of the first curve. Hold down the mouse button, and drag from point A toward the red dot. Then release the mouse button.

4 To complete the first curve of the path, drag from point B to the red dot. If you make a mistake while you're drawing, choose Edit > Undo New Anchor Point to undo the last point you drew. Then continue drawing the path.

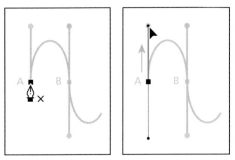
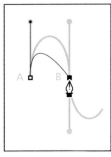
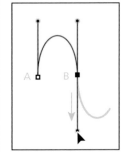

Position pointer on point A and drag to draw a curve.   *Drag again to complete the curve.*

5 Complete the curved path by dragging from point C to the red dot and from point D to the red dot. End the path using one of the methods you learned.

6 Now you'll save the temporary work path so that you don't lose its contents.

7 Double-click the Work Path in the Paths palette to open the Save Path dialog box. Enter **Curve1** in the Name text box, and click OK to rename the path.

The named path is selected in the Paths palette.

You must name the work path before you deselect it to prevent a new work path from replacing the first one as you start drawing again.

Creating separate paths

Now that you've created a new path in the Paths palette, as you continue to draw the path, you create a connected series of segments, or subpaths. Subpaths are saved automatically.

But sometimes you'll want to create separate named paths for each path you draw. To start a new Work Path, you click away from the current path in the Paths palette.

1 In the Paths palette, click in the blank area below the Curve1 path to deselect the path.

When you deselect a path in the Paths palette, any paths on the named path are deselected (hidden). To make them reappear, you click the desired path in the Paths palette (don't click the path now, because you're going to create a new one in a moment).

2 Drag up from point E to the red dot; then drag up from point F to the red dot. You'll notice that as soon as you begin drawing, a new Work Path appears in the Paths palette.

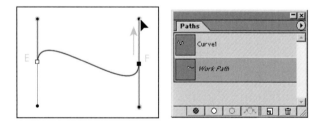

3 End the path using one of the methods you've learned.

4 Double-click the Work Path in the Paths palette, name the path **Curve2**, and then click OK.

5 Click away from the Curve2 path in the Paths palette to deselect it.

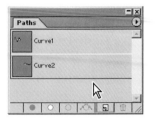

Now you'll create a closed curved path.

6 Drag up from point G to the red dot; then drag down from point H to the red dot. To close the path, position the pointer over point G, and click.

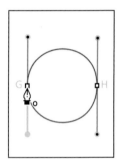

7 In the Paths palette, double-click the Work Path, save the path as **Closed Path**, and then click away from the path to deselect it.

Now you'll have a chance to edit the curved paths you've drawn.

8 Select the direct selection tool (⬉).

💡 *Press A, or hold down Ctrl (Windows) or Command (Mac OS) when the pen tool is active to select the direct selection tool from the keyboard.*

9 In the Paths palette, click the Curve2 path to select it; then click the path in the window to select it.

10 Click one of the anchor points in the curve; then drag a direction point at the end of the direction line emanating from the anchor point.

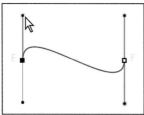
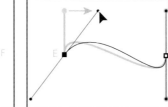

Dragging a direction point   *Direction of curve changes*

11 Now drag an anchor point to change the location of the curve.

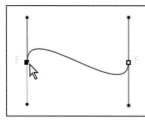
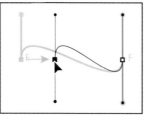

Dragging an anchor point   *Location of curve changes*

Stroking and filling paths

In addition to using the Stroke Path command, you can stroke or fill paths by dragging a named path onto a button at the bottom of the Paths palette. To determine which painting option you want to stroke a path with, you select the desired painting tool before you drag the path onto the Stroke Path with Foreground Color button.

1 Select the paintbrush tool ( ).

2 Drag the Curve1 path onto the Stroke Path with Foreground Color button ( ) at the bottom of the Paths palette to stroke the path with the current paintbrush settings.

Note: *You can also fill or stroke a path by clicking the Fill Path with Foreground Color button or the Stroke Path with Foreground Color button at the bottom of the Paths palette. Make sure that the path is selected in the palette before you click the button.*

3 Drag the Closed path onto the Fill Path with Foreground Color button ( ) at the bottom of the Paths palette to fill it with the current foreground color.

When you fill an open path, Photoshop automatically draws an invisible line between the starting point and the ending point, and fills the segments between them.

4 Choose File > Close, and do not save changes.

Combining straight and curved lines

Now that you've learned how to draw straight and curved paths individually, you'll put them together to create paths that combine straight and curved lines.

When you create a path that combines straight and curved lines, you create corner points to indicate the transition from a straight line to a curved line (or vice versa).

1 Choose File > Open, and open the file Combo.psd from the Lessons/Lesson07 folder.

2 Select the pen tool ( ).

3 Drag up from point A to the red dot; then drag from point B downward to the red dot.

At point B, you must create a corner point to change the direction of the next curve.

4 Alt-click (Windows) or Option-click (Mac OS) point B to set a corner point.

5 Now drag from the same point (point B) up to the red dot to change the direction of the next curve.

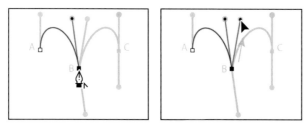

Alt-click (Windows) or Option-click (Mac OS) to set a corner point; then drag in the opposite direction.

6 Drag from point C to the red dot to complete the path. Then end the path using one of the methods you've learned.

7 To start the second path, which begins with a straight line, click point D with the pen tool; then hold down Shift, and click point E (don't drag).

8 Position the pointer on point E and drag to the red dot. Dragging from point E sets the direction of the next curve (which is an upward curve).

9 Drag from point F to the red dot; then Alt-click (Windows) or Option-click (Mac OS) point F to set a corner point.

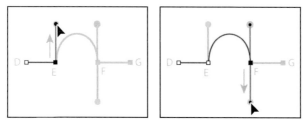

Drag in the direction of the curve from point E; then drag in the opposite direction to complete the curve before setting a corner point.

10 Hold down Shift, and click point G to create a straight line. Then end the path using one of the methods you learned.

11 To create the next path, click with the pen tool on point H, hold down Shift, and then click point I.

12 To set a curve at point I, Alt-drag (Windows) or Option-drag (Mac OS) to the red dot.

13 Drag from point J to the red dot.

14 Alt-click (Windows) or Option-click (Mac OS) point J to set a corner point.

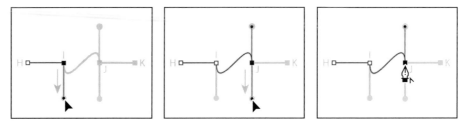

Creating an S-curve by dragging in the opposite direction of a curve; then setting a corner point

15 To complete the path, Shift-click point K. End the path using one of the methods you've learned.

16 Choose File > Close, and do not save changes.

Adding and subtracting anchor points

You can add points to a path to increase the number of segments in the path, and you can subtract unneeded or unwanted points from a path.

1 Choose File > Open, and open the file Edit.psd from the Lessons/Lesson07 folder.

Two paths have been named and saved in the Paths palette. You'll edit the paths using the pen tool and the convert-point tool.

2 In the Paths palette, click the Add and delete points path to make it the active path. Two subpaths appear in the document window.

3 Select the add-anchor-point tool (✎⁺) hidden under the pen tool (✎). Then position the pointer over the red dot at the center of the straight path, and click.

An anchor point with direction lines is added to the segment, and the pointer becomes a hollow arrow, which lets you select and manipulate the path.

4 Now select and drag the path upward.

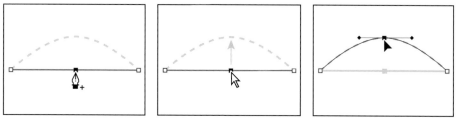

Clicking with the   *Dragging the anchor point*   *Result*
add-anchor-point tool

Next you'll subtract an anchor point from a path.

5 Select the direct selection tool (⬉) and select the second path.

You must select the path before you can delete points from the path. But you can select the path and the anchor points without first selecting a tool. If a path is selected, just move the pen tool over a segment to change it to the add-anchor-point tool. Move the pen tool over an end point to change the tool to the delete-anchor-point tool.

6 Select the delete-anchor-point tool (⬦⁻) hidden under the add-anchor-point tool (⬦⁺), position the pointer on the red dot over the center anchor point, and then click to remove the anchor point.

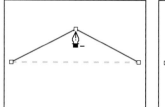

Clicking with the   *Result*
delete-anchor-point tool

Converting points

Sometimes, you may want to change a curve to a corner point or vice versa. Using the convert-point tool, you can easily make the adjustment.

Using the convert-point tool is very much like drawing with the pen tool. To convert a curve to a corner point, you click the anchor point, and to convert a corner to a curve, you drag on the anchor point.

1 In the Paths palette, select the Convert directions path.

The shaped path has both corner points and curves. You'll start by converting the corner points to curves, and then you'll convert the curves to corner points.

2 Select the convert-point tool (⌐) hidden under the delete-anchor-point tool (⌐).

3 Position the pointer on a point of the outer path; then click and drag to convert the point from a corner point to a curve.

4 Convert the rest of the corner points to smooth points to complete the outer path.

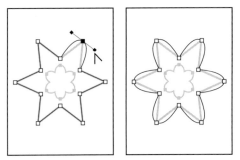

Changing corner points to curves with the convert-point tool

5 To convert the curves at the center of the shape to corner points, simply click the anchor point on each curve.

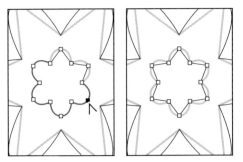

Converting curves to corner points with the convert-point tool

You can also use the convert-point tool to adjust only one side of a curved segment. You'll try this on the outer path.

6 Click the outer path with the direct selection tool; then click a curved segment so that direction lines and direction points emanate from one of the anchor points.

7 Select the convert-point tool again.

8 With the path still selected, position the convert-point tool directly on one of the direction points (at the end of a direction line), and drag. Only one side of the curve is adjusted.

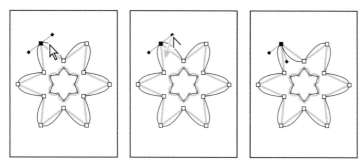

Select the path with the direct selection tool; then adjust part of a curved segment with the convert-point tool.

Remember that you can use the convert-point tool to convert a corner point to a curve, to convert a curve to a corner point, and to adjust one side of a curved segment.

9 Choose File > Close, and do not save changes.

Drawing a path around artwork

Now that you've had some practice using the templates, you'll use the pen tool to make selections in the image of the cat mask. You'll draw two paths around parts of the image. After you've drawn the paths, you'll convert them to selections. Then you'll subtract one selection from the other and apply a filter to the remaining selection. To complete the image, you'll apply another filter to everything.

When drawing a freehand path using the pen tool, use as few points as possible to create the shape you want. The fewer points you use, the smoother the curves.

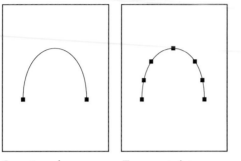

Correct number
of points

Too many points

1 Choose File > Open, and open the file Catmask.psd from the Lessons/Lesson07 folder.

First you'll use the pen tool to draw a path around the outside of the mask. Then you'll create a path selecting the area inside the mouth and converting the selection to a path.

2 Select the pen tool (✦), hidden under the convert-point tool (⊵).

💡 *Press P on the keyboard to select the pen tool. Pressing Shift+P repeatedly toggles between the pen and freeform pen tools.*

3 Position the pointer on point A, and drag to the red dot to set the first anchor point and the direction of the first curve.

4 Position the pointer on point B, and drag to the red dot.

5 At the tip of the ear, you'll need to set a corner point. Alt-click (Windows) or Option-click (Mac OS) point B to set a corner point. Remember, you set a corner point when the direction of the curve changes and no longer is smooth.

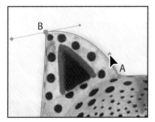

Setting an anchor point and
direction of curve at A

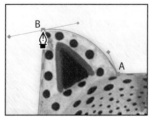

Setting a corner point at B

6 Now that you've set a corner point, position the pointer on point C, and drag to the red dot.

If you make a mistake while you're drawing, choose Edit > Undo to undo the step. Then resume drawing.

The next few points are simple curves.

7 Position the pointer on point D, and drag to the red dot; then do the same for points E and F.

At point G, you'll complete the curve from point F and then set another corner point at the tip of the ear.

8 Position the pointer on point G, and drag to the red dot. Then Alt-click (Windows) or Option-click (Mac OS) point G again to set a corner point.

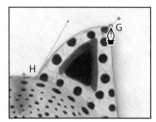

Dragging from point G;
then setting a corner point at G

9 Drag from point H to the red dot (below the anchor point) to complete the curve of the ear.

10 Still on point H, Alt-drag (Windows) or Option-drag (Mac OS) to the yellow dot on the left to set the direction of the final curve.

11 To complete the path, Alt-drag (Windows) or Option-drag (Mac OS) from point A to the yellow dot. (This adds a slight curve to the line between the ears.)

12 In the Paths palette, double-click the Work Path, enter **Face** in the Name text box, and click OK to save it.

13 Choose File > Save to save your work.

Converting selections to paths

Now you'll create a second path using a different method. First you'll use a selection tool to select a similarly colored area, and then you'll convert the selection to a path.

1 Click the Layers palette tab to display the palette, and then drag the Template layer to the Trash button at the bottom of the palette. You won't need this layer any longer.

2 Select the magic wand tool ( ).

3 In the Magic Wand tool options bar, enter **60** in the Tolerance text box.

4 Click the gray background where it shows through the cat's mouth.

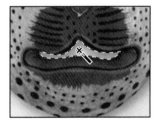

5 If you don't select the entire area the first time, Shift-click again on the mouth with the magic wand to add to the selection.

6 Click the Paths palette tab to bring the Paths palette to the front. Then click the Makes work path from selection button at the bottom of the palette.

The selection is converted to a path, and a new Work Path is created. You can convert any selection made with a selection tool into a path.

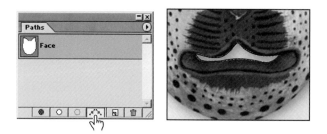

Note: If desired, use the tools you've learned to adjust the points on the path.

7 Double-click the Work Path, and name it **Mouth**; then click OK to save the path.

8 Choose File > Save to save your work.

Converting paths to selections

Just as you can convert selection borders to paths, you can convert paths to selections. With their smooth outlines, paths let you make precise selections. Now that you've drawn paths for the cat's face and mouth, you'll convert them to selections and apply a filter to the selection.

1 In the Paths palette, click the Face path to make it active.

2 Convert the Face path to a selection using either of the following methods:

• Choose Make Selection from the Paths palette menu, and click OK.

• Drag the Face path to the Load Path as Selection button (▢) at the bottom of the Paths palette.

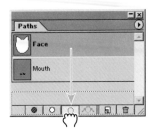

Next, you'll subtract the mouth selection from the face selection so that you can apply a filter without affecting the gray area of the background, which shows through the cat's mouth.

3 In the Paths palette, click the Mouth path; then choose Make Selection from the Paths palette menu.

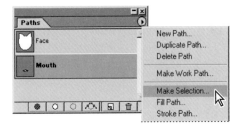

4 In the Make Selection dialog box, select Subtract from Selection in the Operation section, and click OK.

The Mouth path is simultaneously converted to a selection and subtracted from the Face selection.

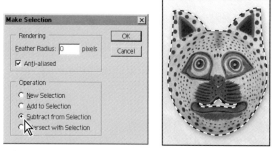

Subtracting the mouth selection   *Result*
from the face selection

5 Before adding a filter to the mask, make sure that the foreground is set to white and the background is set to black. If necessary, click the Default Foreground and Background Colors button (◼), and then click the Switch Foreground and Background Colors button (↰).

6 Choose Filter > Artistic > Neon Glow. Accept the defaults, and click OK to apply the filter.

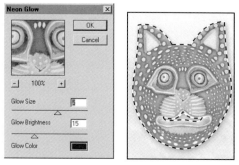

Neon Glow filter   *Result*

The filter has been applied to only the mask area. As a final step, you'll apply a textured filter to the entire image, including the background.

7 Choose Select > Deselect to deselect everything.

8 Choose Filter > Texture > Texturizer. Choose the Sandstone option from the Texture menu, and click OK to apply the settings.

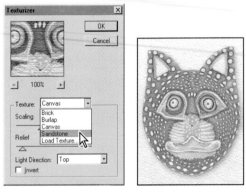

*Texturizer filter with   Result
Sandstone option*

9 Choose File > Save; then close the file.

You've completed the Basic Pen Tool lesson. Try drawing paths around different objects in your artwork to practice using the pen tool. With practice, you'll find that the pen tool can be invaluable for creating intricate outlines and selections.

Review questions

1 How do you modify individual segments of a path?

2 How do you select an entire path?

3 How do you add points to a path?

4 How do you delete points from a path?

5 When you drag with the pen tool to create a curved path, how does the direction in which you drag affect the curve?

6 How can the pen tool be useful as a selection tool?

Review answers

1 To modify individual segments of paths, you drag the anchor points on the path using the direct selection tool. You can also edit the shape of curved segments by dragging the direction points at the ends of the direction lines that extend from the anchor point of the curve.

2 To select an entire path, hold down Alt (Windows) or Option (Mac OS), and click the path using the direct selection tool. When an entire path is selected, all the anchor points are solid.

3 To add points to a path, you select the add-anchor-point tool hidden under the pen tool and then click the path where you want to add an anchor point.

4 To delete points from a path, you select the delete-anchor-point tool hidden under the pen tool and then click the anchor point you want to remove from the path.

5 The direction you drag with the pen tool defines the direction of the curve that follows.

6 If you need to create an intricate selection, it can be easier to draw the path with the pen tool and then convert the path to a selection.

Lesson 8

8 Vector Shapes and Clipping Paths

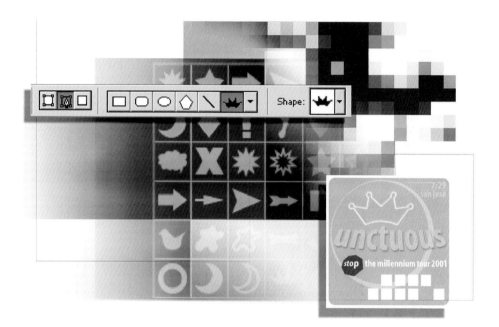

You can make simple illustrations using vector paths in Adobe Photoshop or Adobe ImageReady. Working with vectors allows you to create shapes, which can be filled or stroked, and use clipping paths to control what is shown in an image. This lesson will introduce you to advanced uses of vector shapes and clipping paths.

In this lesson, you'll learn how to do the following:

- Differentiate between bitmap and vector graphics.
- Use clipping paths to control what's shown in a layer.
- Create a logo using vector shapes and clipping paths.
- Work with text in Photoshop.
- Use actions and styles to re-create a vector graphic.

This lesson will take about 60 minutes to complete. The lesson is designed to be done in Adobe Photoshop, but information on using similar functionality in Adobe ImageReady is included where appropriate.

If needed, remove the previous lesson folder from your hard drive, and copy the Lesson08 folder onto it from the *Adobe Photoshop Classroom in a Book* CD.

Note: *Windows users need to unlock the lesson files before using them. For more information, see "Copying the Classroom in a Book files" on page 3.*

About bitmap images and vector graphics

Before working with vector shapes and clipping paths, you should understand the difference between *bitmap images* and *vector graphics*.

Computer graphics fall into two main categories—*bitmap* and *vector*. You can work with both types of graphics in Photoshop and ImageReady; moreover, a Photoshop file can contain both bitmap and vector data.

Bitmap images, technically called *raster images*, are based on a grid of colors known as pixels. Each pixel is assigned a specific location and color value. In working with bitmap images, you edit groups of pixels rather than objects or shapes. Because bitmap graphics can represent subtle gradations of shade and color, they are appropriate for continuous-tone images such as photographs or artwork created in painting programs. A disadvantage of bitmap graphics is that they contain a fixed number of pixels. As a result, they can lose detail and appear jagged when scaled up on-screen or if they are printed at a lower resolution than they were created for.

Vector graphics are made up of lines and curves defined by mathematical objects called *vectors*. These graphics retain their crispness whether they are moved, resized, or have their color changed. Vector graphics are appropriate for illustrations, type, and graphics such as logos that may be scaled to different sizes.

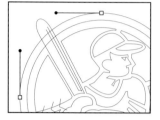

Logo drawn as vector art

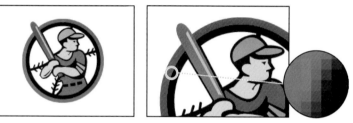

Logo rasterized as bitmap art

In the previous lesson, you learned how to use the pen tool to create simple shapes and paths. In this lesson, you'll learn advanced uses of paths and clipping paths to create a logo for a fictitious rock band named Unctuous. You'll learn how to add text to an image by incorporating the logo into a concert announcement.

Since logos and many other designs need to be reproducible and scaled, you'll also learn how to use actions to re-create the logo for use in a different image.

Getting started

Before beginning this lesson, restore the default application settings for Adobe Photoshop. See "Restoring default preferences" on page 4.

You'll start the lesson by viewing the final image, which is an example of a rock concert announcement incorporating the logo you'll create.

1 Start Adobe Photoshop.

If a notice appears asking whether you want to customize your color settings, click No.

2 Choose File > Open, and open the file 08End.psd from in the Lessons/Lesson08 folder.

If a notice appears asking whether you want to update the text layers for vector based output, click Update.

Note: *The update text layers notice might occur when transferring files between computers, especially between Windows and Mac OS.*

3 When you have finished viewing the 08End.psd file, leave it open for reference.

08End.psd

For a color illustration of the finished artwork for this lesson, see the gallery at the beginning of the color section.

Now you'll start the lesson by creating a new document for the logo.

Creating the logo

Logos need to be scalable yet retain a crispness to their appearance. You'll create shapes with paths, and use clipping paths to control what's being shown in your logo.

Using a shape for the logo's background

You can create a shape on a new layer. The shape is automatically filled with the current foreground color; however, you can easily change the fill to a different color, gradient, or pattern. The shape's outline is stored in a layer clipping path, which appears in the Paths palette. You can change the outline of a shape by editing its layer clipping path.

1 Choose File > New.

2 In the New dialog box, choose pixels for unit of measurement, and enter **400** in both the Width text box and the Height text box. Make sure the resolution is set for 72 pixels/inch and that White is selected for the background contents. Enter a name for this new document in the Name text box and click OK.

3 Drag the Paths palette from the Layers palette group. Since you'll be using both palettes frequently, it's easier to have them separate.

4 In the Color palette, set the foreground RGB color to an orange-yellow color by entering **228** in the R text box, **202** in the G text box, and **31** in the B text box.

5 Select the rounded rectangle tool (○) hidden under the rectangle tool (□).

6 In the tool options bar, enter **20px** in the Radius text box, and select the Create New Shape Layer option (▣).

7 Shift-drag to draw a shape that almost fills up the white area of the image, about 380 pixels square.

You've created a square shape with an orange-yellow fill. After drawing the shape, you'll see that there's a new layer named Shape 1 in the Layers palette. The left thumbnail in the palette shows that the entire layer is filled with the orange-yellow foreground color. The thumbnail on the right shows the layer clipping path. For clipping paths, like masks, white indicates the area where the image is exposed, and black indicates the areas where the image is blocked.

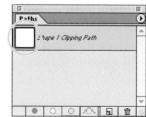

Clipping path in Layers palette   Clipping path in Paths palette

Subtracting shapes from the shape layer

After you create a shape layer (vector graphic), you can set options to subtract new shapes from the vector graphic. You can also use the path component selection tool and the direct-selection tool to move, resize, and edit shapes.

1 Select the rectangle tool (□) hidden under the rounded rectangle tool (○).

2 In the tool options bar, select the Subtract from Shape Area option (⬕).

3 Shift-drag to draw a small square.

You'll notice that the square is white because it is taking away a portion of the orange-yellow fill to show the white background.

4 Select the path component selection tool (▶) and move the pointer over the small square. Alt-drag (Windows) or Option-drag (Mac OS) to create a new square.

Note: Selecting a shape with the path component selection tool and selecting the Intersect Shape Areas option (⬕) in the tool options bar show the areas where two shapes overlap. Selecting the Exclude Overlapping Shape Areas option (⬕) excludes the area where two shapes or areas overlap.

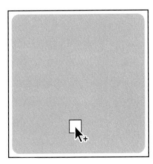

Moving the pointer over
the square using the path
component selection tool

Alt-dragging (Windows) or
Option-dragging (Mac OS)
to create a new square

Result

5 Shift-click to select both small squares with the path component selection tool. Then click the Align Top Edges button (▆) in the tool options bar.

6 Continue to Alt-drag (Windows) or Option-drag (Mac OS) to create new squares until you've created nine squares as shown in the 08End.psd image. Use the Align Top Edges button to align the squares, and the Distribute Horizontal Centers button (◆◆) to space the squares evenly apart.

7 Choose File > Save to save your work.

Next you'll add more elements to your logo, but you'll work with these elements on different layers. Throughout this lesson, you'll create new layers, so you can draw, edit, paste, and reposition elements on one layer without disturbing other layers.

Creating shapes from filled paths

So far, you've used the shape tools to create shape layers, which are fill layers with clipping paths. Now you'll learn to use a shape tool to create shapes as paths.

1 In the Layers palette, click the New Layer button ( ) to create a new layer.

2 Select the ellipse tool ( ).

3 In the tool options bar, select the Create New Work Path option ( ).

4 Shift-drag the ellipse tool to create a circle in the upper left portion of the document as in the 08End.psd image.

5 In the tool options bar, select the Exclude Overlapping Shape Areas option ( ) and then draw a second circle within the first.

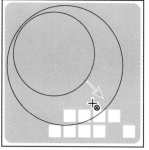
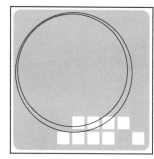

Drawing a second circle   *Result*

6 If needed, select the path component selection tool ( ) and move the circles as shown in the 08End.psd image.

Shift-click with the path component selection tool to select more than one circle.

💡 *To resize the circles (or any path), select the circles using the path component selection tool. Then choose Edit > Free Transform Path and use the handles to modify the size or outline shape.*

In the Paths palette, the thumbnail shows two clipping paths with a white area between them.

7 For a better view of the thumbnail, choose Palette Options from the Paths palette menu, and select the largest thumbnail option.

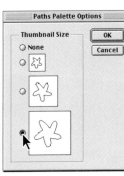

Default thumbnail   *Choosing largest thumbnail*   *Result*
                             option

8 Select the path component selection tool.

9 Shift-click to select both circles, and then click the Combine button in the tool options bar.

The two circle path components are now treated as one shape.

10 Click the Set Foreground Color box in the toolbox to open the Color Picker dialog box. Select white as the foreground color and click OK.

11 In the Paths palette, drag the work path to the Fill Path with Foreground Color button (⊡) at the bottom of the palette.

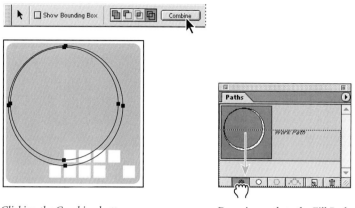

Clicking the Combine button, and result of the Combine option

Dragging path to the Fill Path with Foreground Color button

12 In the Layers palette with Layer 1 active, enter **40** in the Opacity text box.

Try different values for the Opacity to see the effects.

13 If needed, use the path component selection tool to move the circles as shown in the 08End.psd image.

14 If needed, use the move tool (⊹) to move the fill created by the two circles as shown in the 08End.psd image.

15 Choose File > Save.

Creating and working with custom shapes

Whenever you create a shape, you can save it as a custom shape for reuse. The saved shape appears in the Custom Shape pop-up palette.

1 Select the custom shape tool (✹) hidden under the ellipse tool (○).

2 In the tool options bar, click the arrow next to the Shape box to open the Custom Shape pop-up palette.

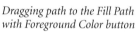

3 Click the triangle (⊙) in the upper-right corner of the pop-up palette and choose Custom Shapes.csh from the palette menu.

4 In the dialog box, click Append to add more shapes to the Custom Shape pop-up palette. If necessary, choose Small List from the palette menu for easier navigation through the palette.

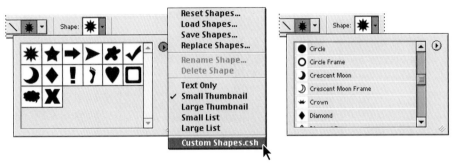

Selecting Custom Shapes.csh

New Custom Shapes list displayed in the Small List format

5 Select the crown shape in the Custom Shape pop-up palette. Then in the tool options bar, select the Add to Shape Area option (🖿).

6 Shift-drag to draw a crown shape within the work path. Use the path component selection tool (➤) to position the crown shape as shown in the 08End.psd image.

The crown is a component of the work path containing the two circles.

7 Click the Create a New Layer button (🖹) in the Layers palette to create another layer (Layer 2). This new layer will contain both the crown shape that you created in the work path, and the effect that you'll apply over the crown.

8 Select only the crown shape using the path component selection tool.

9 Select the paintbrush tool (✎) and choose a small brush size (such as Hard Round 3 Pixels) from the Brush pop-up palette in the tool options bar.

You'll apply this small paintbrush stroke when you choose Stroke Subpath in step 11.

10 If needed, use the Color Picker to make the foreground color white.

11 In the Paths palette, choose Stroke Subpath from the menu.

12 In the Stroke Subpath dialog box, choose the paintbrush from the tool menu and click OK.

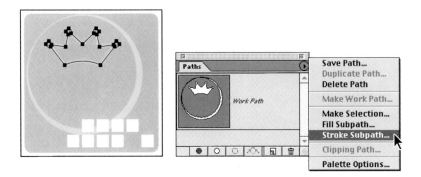

13 In the Layers palette, double-click Layer 2 to open the Layer Style dialog box.

14 In the Layer Style dialog box, select the Outer Glow and Bevel and Emboss options. Then select Bevel and Emboss to display options on the right side of the dialog box.

15 Choose Inner Bevel from the Style pop-up menu in the Structure section of the Layer Style dialog box. Then enter **71** in the Depth text box, and select Down for the Direction.

16 Leave the Outer Glow option at its default settings, and click OK.

17 In the Paths palette, double-click Work Path to open the Save Path dialog box. Enter **Band Logo** in the Name text box, and click OK.

18 Choose Edit > Define Custom Shape to add this logo to the Custom Shape pop-up palette in the tool options bar. Enter **Band Logo** for the name of the shape and click OK.

💡 *You can use the Preset Manager to save a library with your new custom shape. This ensures that your new custom shape will be available in Adobe Photoshop even if you restore the Adobe Photoshop preferences to their default settings. For information on using the Preset Manager, see Photoshop 6.0 online Help.*

19 Choose File > Save.

Working with type

Adobe Photoshop lets you create and edit type directly on-screen (instead of in a dialog box) and quickly change the font, style, size, and color of the type. You can apply changes to individual characters and set formatting options for entire paragraphs. In this part of the lesson, you'll learn to work with type by adding text to your logo.

Adding type to the image in edit mode

Clicking in an image with the type tool puts the type tool in edit mode. You can enter and edit characters when the type tool is in edit mode; however, you must commit changes to the type layer before you can perform other operations. Selecting another tool will automatically commit your text changes. If in the tool options bar you see the Commit Any Current Edits button (☑) and the Cancel Any Current Edits button (☒), the type tool is in edit mode.

1 Select the type tool (**T**).

2 In the tool options bar, choose a sans serif font, and then choose Bold and 100 pt for the type options. (We used Myriad Bold Condensed for the sans serif font.)

3 In the tool options bar, click the Set the Text Color box to open the Color Picker. Make sure Only Web Colors is deselected, and enter **249** in the R text box, **222** in the G text box, and **8** in the B text box. Click OK.

Your type will be a yellow color.

4 Type the word **unctuous**, the name of the fictitious rock band, on your logo.

Notice that typing creates a new layer, which is automatically named "unctuous" after you select another tool or click the Commit Any Current Edits button (✔).

5 In the tool options bar, click the Create Warped Text button (T̤) to open the Warp Text dialog box.

6 In the Warp Text dialog box, choose Shell Lower for Style. Enter **+20** in the Bend text box, and leave the other options at **0**.

You can experiment entering other values to see different effects.

Note: *Throughout this lesson, use the move tool (▸₊) to adjust the position of the text. You can also use the zoom tool (🔍) to enlarge areas for better viewing.*

7 Choose File > Save.

Applying a layer style to text

You can use the default layer styles, load libraries of layer styles, or create your own layer styles using the Styles palette. For more information about the Styles palette, see Photoshop 6.0 online Help.

1 In the Layers palette with the type layer selected, choose Overlay for the blending mode.

2 Click the Add a Layer Style button (●) at the bottom of the Layers palette, and choose Drop Shadow from the pop-up menu.

The Layer Style dialog box opens with the blending options for the drop shadow.

3 Enter **27** in the Opacity text box and click OK.

4 Select the Styles palette. Make sure the unctuous layer is selected, and click in an empty square in the Styles palette.

This opens the New Style dialog box.

5 Enter **Name Highlight** in the Name text box for the new style name and click OK.

This layer style is now saved. You'll use it later in this lesson.

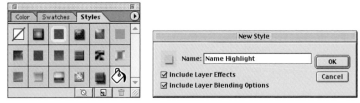

Clicking in an empty square in the Styles palette opens the New Style dialog box.

💡 *You can use the Preset Manager to save a library containing your new layer style. This ensures that your new layer style will be available in Adobe Photoshop even if you restore the Adobe Photoshop preferences to their default settings. For information on using the Preset Manager, see Photoshop 6.0 online Help.*

6 Choose File > Save.

Deselecting paths

Deselecting paths is sometimes necessary to see the appropriate tool options bar when you select a vector tool. Deselecting paths can also help you view certain effects that might be obscured if a path is highlighted.

Before proceeding to the next section of this lesson, make sure all paths are deselected.

1 Select the path component selection tool (▶).

2 In the tool options bar, click the Dismiss Target Path button (☑).

Your paths are now deselected.

Note: An alternate way to deselect paths is to click in the blank area below the paths in the Paths palette.

Blank area below the paths in the Paths palette

Dismiss Target Path button

Merging layers with text and a shape

By merging layers, layer clipping paths, clipping groups, linked layers, or adjustment layers, you can combine several layers into one and keep your file size manageable. When you've finalized the characteristics and positioning of a layer's contents, you can then merge the layer with one or more other layers to create partial versions of your composite image.

In this section, you'll create a shape and text in separate layers, and then merge the two layers together.

1 In the Layers palette, click the New Layer button (⬜) to create another layer.

2 Select the polygon tool (◇) hidden under the custom shape tool (♛).

3 In the tool options bar, select the Create Filled Region button (□), and enter **8** in the Sides text box.

4 Click the Set Foreground Color box in the toolbox to open the Color Picker dialog box. Enter **228** in the R text box, **45** in the G text box, and **31** in the B text box. Click OK.

Now you'll draw an eight-sided polygon shape with a red fill to create a stop sign.

5 Drag the polygon tool to draw a stop sign.

While drawing the stop sign, you can drag the polygon tool in a circular motion to rotate the stop sign to the desired position. You can also use the path component selection tool to move the stop sign to the position shown in the 08End.psd image.

6 Select the type tool (**T**).

7 In the tool options bar, choose the same sans serif font you used for the unctuous text, and choose 30 pt for the font size.

8 In the tool options bar, click the Set the Text Color box to open the Color Picker dialog box, and select white as the text color. Click OK.

9 Type **stop** anywhere in the image.

This automatically creates a new layer above the polygon shape layer.

10 Select the move tool (▶✛).

11 Move the "stop" text over the stop sign shape as shown in the 08End.psd image.

Make sure that the "stop" layer is still selected before proceeding to the next step.

12 In the Layers palette, choose Merge Down from the options menu.

The "stop" layer and polygon shape layer are now merged into a single layer, Layer 3.

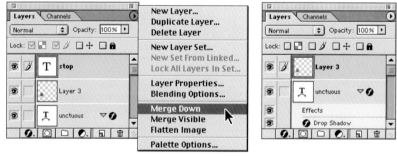

Choose Merge Down from the Layers palette options menu.   *Merged layers*

13 With Layer 3 selected, choose Edit > Transform > Distort. Drag the handles to skew the stop sign until it appears as shown in the 08End.psd image.

14 Press Enter (Windows) or Return (Mac OS) to apply the transformation.

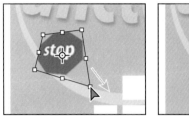 

Dragging distort handles   *Result*

15 Choose File > Save.

Creating work paths from type

Creating a work path from type lets you work with characters as vector shapes. A work path is a temporary path that appears in the Paths palette. Once you create a work path from a type layer, you can save and manipulate it like any other path. The original type layer remains intact and editable as text.

1 Select the type tool (T).

Keep the font, size, and color the same as the "stop" text.

2 Type **the millennium tour 2001** anywhere in the image.

A type layer is automatically created.

3 Select the move tool (⊹) and move the "the millennium tour 2001" type next to the stop sign shape as shown in the 08End.psd image.

4 Select the type tool.

5 In the tool options bar, click the Right Align Text button (≡).

6 Type **7/29** in the upper-right corner of the image as shown in the 08End.psd image.

7 Press Enter (Windows) or Return (Mac OS), and then type **san josé**.

This is the text you'll use to generate your paths.

💡 *To type an e with an acute accent, type **Alt 0233** (Windows) using the numeric keypad, or **Option-e** + **e** (Mac OS).*

8 In the tool options bar, click the Commit Any Current Edits button (☑) to commit the type change.

9 If needed, select the move tool and move the "7/29 san josé" type as shown in the 08End.psd image.

10 With the "7/29 san josé" layer selected, choose Layer > Type > Create Work Path.

A new work path (named Work Path) appears in the Paths palette.

11 In the Layers palette, select the "7/29 san josé" layer and drag it to the Trash button (🗑) at the bottom of the palette.

Creating work paths from type leaves the original type layer intact. If you don't drag the "7/29 san josé" type layer to the trash, it shows up and visually competes with the vector clipped layer you'll create from the work path.

New 7/29 Work Path   Dragging 7/29 layer to the trash

12 Select the path component selection tool (▶).

13 Adjust the position of the work path outlines as shown in the 08End.psd image.

14 Select the direct-selection tool (▷) hidden under the path component selection tool (▶).

15 Shift-click to select the two top left points of the **7**, then Shift-drag to the left.

16 Click outside the work path to deselect.

Note: *The direct-selection tool can be used to edit any path.*

Using the direct-selection tool   *Shift-dragging the points left*
to choose points

17 Choose File > Save.

Creating a clipping path from a work path

Now you'll create a layer that has a clipping path made from the previous work path.
A layer clipping path creates a sharp-edged shape on a layer and is useful anytime you
want to add a design element with clean, defined edges. Once you create a layer with a
layer clipping path, you can apply one or more layer styles to it or edit it if needed.

1 In the Layers palette, click the New Layer button (⊡) to create another layer (Layer 4).

2 Select the gradient tool (▣).

3 If needed, click the Set Foreground Color box in the toolbox to open the Color Picker
dialog box. Select white as the foreground color and click OK.

4 In the tool options bar, click the gradient picker to open the Gradient Editor
dialog box.

5 Choose the Foreground to Transparent fill in the Gradient Editor dialog box and
click OK.

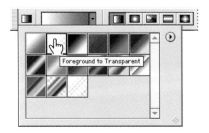

6 Shift-drag the gradient tool from right to left in the image.

The gradient covers the entire image, with the lower layers showing through the transparent areas.

Make sure Work Path is selected in the Paths palette before proceeding to the next step.

7 Choose Layer > Add Layer Clipping Path > Current Path.

This creates a new path named Layer 4 Clipping Path. The thumbnail for this clipping path appears both in the Paths palette and in Layer 4 of the Layers palette.

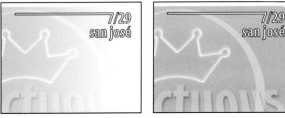

Gradient over the image   Clipped gradient

8 Click the link icon (⌗) in Layer 4 to unlink the path from the gradient layer.

Make sure the gradient layer is selected and not the clipping path.

9 If needed, select the path component selection tool and click the Dismiss Target Path button (☑) in the tool options bar.

This deselects all paths.

Note: You can also click in the blank area below the paths in the Paths palette to deselect all paths.

10 Select the move tool (▸₊).

11 Adjust where the gradient falls as it shows through the clipping path.

Refer to the 08End.psd image if necessary.

12 Choose File > Save.

Re-creating the logo, using actions and styles

Logos need to be scalable so they can be used in a variety of settings. Now that you've created a logo using vector shapes and paths, you'll re-create the logo in a different image using actions.

Automating tasks can save you time and ensure consistent results for many types of operations. Using *actions* is one of several ways in Adobe Photoshop and Adobe ImageReady to automate tasks. An action is a series of commands that you play back on a single file or a batch of files. To learn more about recording actions, see Photoshop 6.0 online Help.

Preparing to record a new action

You use the Actions palette to record, play, edit, and delete individual actions. The Actions palette also lets you save and load action files.

You'll start by opening a new document and preparing to record a new action in the Actions palette.

1 Choose File > New.

2 In the New dialog box, choose pixels for the unit of measurement, and enter **300** in the Width text box and **100** in the Height text box. Make sure the resolution is set for 72 pixels/inch and that White is selected for the background contents. Enter a name for this new document in the Name text box, and click OK.

This new document provides the background for the logo you'll create.

3 If needed, choose Window > Show Actions to open the Actions palette.

4 In the Actions palette, click the Create New Set button (□).

Clicking the Create New Set button

5 In the New Set dialog box, enter **My Actions** in the Name text box and Click OK.

A new set named My Actions appears in the Actions palette. In Photoshop, actions are grouped into sets for better organization.

Recording a new action

When you create a new action, the commands and tools you use are added to the action until you stop recording.

Your new action will be added to the My Actions set in the Actions palette.

1 In the Actions palette, click the Create New Action button (▣).

Clicking the Create New Action button

2 In the New Action dialog box, enter **Create Logo** in the Name text box and click the Record button (●).

The recording process starts automatically.

3 In the Layers palette, click the New Layer button (▣) to create another layer.

4 Select the custom shape tool (✳).

5 In the tool options bar, choose Band Logo from the Custom Shape picker.

6 If needed, click the Set Foreground Color box in the toolbox to open the Color Picker dialog box. Select any color but white as the foreground color and click OK. (We selected black.)

7 Shift-drag the custom shape tool within the image area to create the band logo.

8 In the Layers palette, with Layer 1 selected, click the Add a Layer Style button (⦿), and choose Bevel and Emboss from the pop-up menu.

The Layer Style dialog box opens.

9 In the Layer Style dialog box, click OK to accept the default values.

10 Select the type tool (**T**).

11 In the tool options bar, choose the same sans serif font you used for "unctuous" in "Adding type to the image in edit mode" on page 228 of this lesson, and enter **20 pt** for the font size.

12 Click the Set the Text Color box to open the Color Picker dialog box. Enter **249** in the R text box, **222** in the G text box, and **8** in the B text box to select yellow for the text color.

13 Type the word **unctuous**.

14 In the tool options bar, click the Create Warped Text button (𝒯) to open the Warp Text dialog box. Apply the same warp text you used in steps 5 and 6 in "Adding type to the image in edit mode" on page 228 of this lesson.

15 In the Styles palette, click the Name Highlight style.

The text seems to partially vanish, but an overlay is added to the white background.

16 In the Actions palette, click the Stop button (■) to end the recording.

Clicking the Stop button

To see the overlay effect, try adding different colors to the background layer using the paint bucket tool.

17 Choose File > Save, and close the document window.

Playing an action

Once you've recorded an action, you can select it in the Actions palette and use it as an automated task.

Now you'll re-create the logo by selecting and playing your newly recorded action. You'll start by viewing the Road_final.psd image, which shows your newly recorded logo re-created in a photographic image.

1 Choose File > Open, and open the file Road_final.psd from the Lessons/Lesson08 folder.

2 When you have finished viewing the Road_final.psd image, leave it open for reference.

3 Choose File > Open and open the Road.psd file from the Lessons/Lesson08 folder.

4 In the Actions palette, select the Create Logo action and click the Play button (▷).

The logo you recorded is re-created in the Road.psd image.

Road_final.psd

5 Choose File > Save.

Review questions

1 What is the difference between a bitmap image and a vector graphic?

2 What does a clipping path do?

3 What tools are used to move and resize paths and shapes?

4 Does the type tool create vector shapes?

5 What is the purpose of merging layers?

6 How do you automate tasks?

Review answers

1 Bitmap or raster images are based on a grid of pixels and are appropriate for continuous-tone images such as photographs or artwork created in painting programs. Vector graphics are made up of shapes based on mathematical expressions and are appropriate for illustrations, type, and drawings that require clear, smooth lines.

2 A clipping path stores the outline of a shape in the Paths palette. You can change the outline of a shape by editing its layer clipping path.

3 You use the path component selection tool (▶) and the direct-selection tool (▷) to move, resize, and edit shapes. You can also modify and scale a shape or path by choosing Edit > Free Transform Path.

4 No, the type tool adds text, not vector shapes, to an image. If you want to work with the characters as vector shapes, you must create a work path from the type. A work path is a temporary path that appears in the Paths palette. Once you create a work path from a type layer, you can save and manipulate it like any other path. You cannot edit characters in the path as text. However, the original type layer remains intact and editable.

5 Merging combines several layers into one to keep your file size manageable. When you've finalized the characteristics and positioning of a layer's contents, you can merge the layer with one or more other layers to create partial versions of your composite image.

6 Using actions is one of several ways that Adobe Photoshop and Adobe ImageReady provide to automate tasks. An action is a series of commands that you play back on a single file or batch of files.

Lesson 9

9 | Advanced Layer Techniques

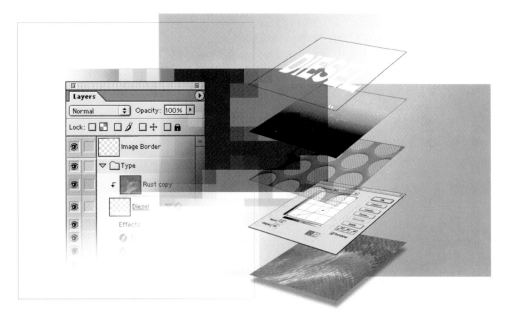

*Once you've learned basic layer
techniques, you can begin to create
more complex effects in your artwork
using layer masks, clipping groups,
and style layers.*

In this lesson, you'll learn how to do the following:

• Create clipping groups, which let you use an image on one layer as a mask for artwork on other layers.

• Create layer sets to organize and manage layers.

• Add adjustment layers to an image, and use them to apply color and tonal adjustments without permanently changing pixel data.

• Create knockout layers to use one layer selectively to reveal others.

• Import layers from other Photoshop files.

• Work with type layers.

• Duplicate and clip layers.

• Add layer styles to a layer, and apply the effects to multiple layers.

• Rasterize layers.

• Convert clipping paths to masks.

• Liquify a layer, giving it a melted appearance.

• Flatten and save layered files, greatly reducing their file size.

This lesson will take about 60 minutes to complete. The lesson is designed to be done in Adobe Photoshop, but information on using similar functionality in Adobe ImageReady is included where appropriate.

If needed, remove the previous lesson folder from your hard drive, and copy the Lesson09 folder onto it. As you work on this lesson, you'll overwrite the start files. If you need to restore the start files, copy them from the *Adobe Photoshop Classroom in a Book* CD.

Note: Windows users need to unlock the lesson files before using them. For information, see "Copying the Classroom in a Book files" on page 3.

Getting started

Before beginning this lesson, restore the default application settings for Adobe Photoshop. See "Restoring default preferences" on page 4.

You'll start the lesson by viewing the final lesson file to see what you'll accomplish.

1 Start Adobe Photoshop.

If a notice appears asking whether you want to customize your color settings, click No.

2 Choose File > Open, and open the file 09End.psd from the Lessons/Lesson09 folder.

3 When you have finished viewing the file, either leave the 09End.psd file open on your desktop for reference, or close it without saving changes.

 For an illustration of the finished artwork for this lesson, see the gallery at the beginning of the color section.

Now you'll open the start file, which contains an image that has two layers and a background, and you'll work with various layering and masking techniques to complete the image.

4 Choose File > Open, and open the 09Start.psd file, located in the Lessons/Lesson09 folder on your hard drive.

5 If the Layers palette is not already showing, choose Window > Layers to display it.

The Layers palette shows that there are three layers in the file—the Metal Grill layer, the Rust layer, and the background. At this point, you can see only the Metal Grill layer, because the Rust layer and the background are positioned under the image of the metal grill.

Creating a layer clipping path

A layer clipping path creates a sharp-edged mask on a layer. In this part of the lesson, you'll draw a circle and use it as a layer clipping path to knock out the holes in the metal grill image. This will let you see through the holes to the layers below.

You'll begin by drawing the clipping path on the Metal Grill layer.

1 Click the Metal Grill layer in the Layers palette to select it.

2 Select the ellipse tool (○). Then click the Create New Work Path button (▨) in the options bar.

3 Move the pointer to the center of one of the holes in the metal grill.

4 Hold down the Shift and Alt keys (Windows) or the Shift and Option keys (Mac OS) and drag to draw a circle the size of the hole. When the circle is the right size, release the mouse button, and then release the Shift and Alt/Shift and Option keys.

Note: If the circle is not exactly centered when you're done, Command-click the circle and drag it into position.

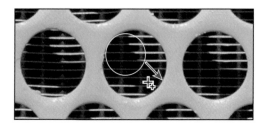

Next you'll make copies for the rest of the metal grill.

5 Select the path component selection tool (▸) and click to select the circle you just created.

6 Alt-drag (Windows) or Option-drag (Mac OS) to place a copy of the circle over another hole in the metal grill. Then repeat this step to place copies over the remaining holes.

Notice that some of the circles go past the edge of the image. This isn't a problem, because they are simply clipping paths.

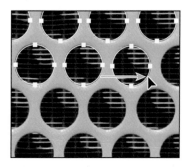

Note: You can adjust the position of a selected circle using the arrow keys on the keyboard.

You're ready to change these circles into a layer clipping path.

7 Shift-click the remaining circles until they are all selected.

8 Click the Subtract from Shape Area (-) button (🖿) in the options bar.

9 Choose Layer > Add Layer Clipping Path > Current Path.

The Rust layer appears through the holes you cut in the Metal Grill layer, and the layer clipping path you just created appears in the Metal Grill layer in the Layers palette.

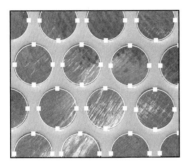

10 Click the Dismiss Target Path button (☑) in the options bar to temporarily hide the circles you made.

11 Choose File > Save to save your work.

Creating layer sets

You can organize and manage individual layers by grouping them into layer sets. You can then expand the layer set to view the layers contained in it or collapse the set to simplify your view. Layer sets let you apply attributes and masks to the layers within the set. In addition, they function like layers, letting you select, duplicate, move, and change the stacking order of layers in the set.

In this section, you'll create two layer sets, one for type and another for the metal grill.

1 In the Layers palette, click the Create a New Set button (▢) twice to create two layer sets.

2 With Set 2 still selected at the top of the Layers palette, choose Layer Set Properties from the palette menu.

3 Enter **Type** for Name and choose Blue from the Color menu. Then click OK. The layer set is renamed "Type" in the Layers palette.

4 Select Set 1 from the Layers palette and again choose Layer Set Properties from the palette menu. This time, enter **Image** for Name and choose Orange from the Color menu. Then click OK.

Now you're going to move the Metal Grill and Rust layers into the Image layer set.

5 Drag the layer Metal Grill in the Layers palette onto the folder icon (▱) for Image, then release the layer to add it to the Image layer set. You can tell Metal Grill is a member of that set, because the thumbnails of the metal grill and clipping mask are now indented under Image in the Layers palette.

6 Drag the Rust layer to add it to the Image layer set, too. Notice that the Rust layer is below the Metal Grill layer in the layer set.

7 Choose File > Save.

Using adjustment layers (Photoshop)

An adjustment layer lets you experiment with color or tonal adjustments to an image without permanently modifying the pixels in the image. The color or tonal changes reside within the adjustment layer, which acts as a veil through which the underlying image layers appear.

Once you create an adjustment layer, you can easily edit the settings, or dynamically replace it with a different adjustment or fill type.

When you create an adjustment layer, its effect appears on all the layers below it. This lets you correct multiple layers by making a single adjustment, rather than making the adjustment to each layer separately. Adjustment layers can be applied and edited only in Photoshop; however, they can be viewed in ImageReady. When you apply an adjustment layer to a layer set, Photoshop adds the new adjustment layer in the layer set above the existing layers.

–From Adobe Photoshop 6.0 online Help

Creating an adjustment layer

Adjustment layers can be added to an image to apply color and tonal adjustments without permanently changing the pixel values in the image. For example, if you add a Color Balance adjustment layer to an image, you can experiment with different colors repeatedly, because the change occurs only on the adjustment layer. If you decide to return to the original pixel values, you can hide or delete the adjustment layer.

Here you'll add a Curves adjustment layer to create a greater contrast between the grill and the rust layer in the background. You'll do this by darkening the entire rust image. An adjustment layer affects all layers below it in the image's stacking order. Because you'll place the Curves adjustment layer below the Metal Grill layer, the adjustment will affect the rust layer and the background but not the metal grill.

1 Select the Rust layer in the Layers palette.

2 Click the Create New Fill or Adjustment Layer button (⬤) at the bottom of the palette and choose Curves from the menu that appears.

3 Click on the middle of the diagonal line in the grid (the color curve) to add a control point on the curve that will adjust the midtones.

4 Drag the control point down and to the right or enter values in the Input and Output text boxes. (We moved the control point so that the value in the Input text box was 150% and the value in the Output text box was 105%.)

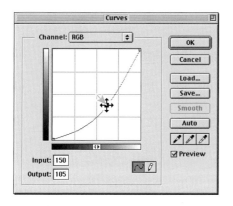

5 Click OK.

An adjustment layer named Curves 1 appears in the Layers palette. The new layer does not include a layer thumbnail; only layer mask thumbnails are displayed for adjustment layers.

6 Choose File > Save.

Creating a knockout gradient layer

Knockout layer options let you specify how one layer reveals other layers. In this section, you'll create a knockout gradient layer so that the lower third of the image reveals the background layer.

You'll begin by creating a new layer in the Image layer set.

1 Select the Image layer set in the Layers palette and click the Create a New Layer button (▣) at the bottom of the palette.

This creates a new layer above the Metal Grill, Curves 1, and Rust layers in the Image layer set.

2 With the new layer selected in the Layers palette, choose Layer Properties from the palette menu. Then enter **Knockout Gradient** for Name and click OK.

Now you'll create a gradient on this layer.

3 Select the gradient tool (▣).

4 Click the Default Foreground and Background Colors icon (▣) in the toolbox to set the foreground color to black and the background color to white.

5 Click the Linear Gradient button (▣) in the options bar to create a linear gradient.

6 Click the arrow (▾) to the right of the gradient display in the options bar to open the gradient picker.

7 Choose Small List from the gradient picker menu. Then choose Foreground to Transparent in the gradient picker.

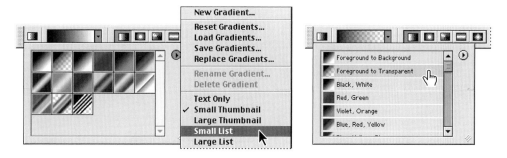

8 Click in the image to close the gradient picker.

9 Shift-drag from the bottom of the image to slightly above the midpoint to create a gradient that goes from black at the bottom to transparent at the top.

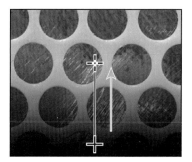

10 Double-click Knockout Gradient in the Layers palette to display the Layer Style dialog box.

11 In the Advanced Blending area, enter **0** for Fill Opacity. Then choose Deep from the Knockout menu to apply this to all of the lower layers in the layer set. Then click OK.

12 Choose File > Save.

Importing a type layer

Text is added to images with the type tool. Each use of the type tool adds a new type layer to the image. Each of these type layers can be moved, edited, or modified independently, giving you virtually unlimited typographic flexibility.

In this part of the lesson, you'll import an existing type layer into your artwork. For information on creating a type layer using the type tool, see Lesson 3, "Layer Basics."

1 Select the Type layer set in the Layers palette.

2 Choose File > Open, select DieselType.psd, and click Open.

3 Drag the Diesel layer from the Layers palette into the 09Start.psd image.

Because the Type layer set was selected in the 09Start.psd image, the Diesel layer is added to that set.

4 Select the move tool (⊹) and drag the word "Diesel" to the bottom center of the image.

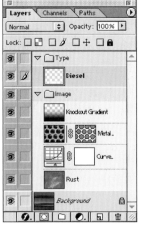

5 Choose File > Save.

6 Close the DieselType.psd file without saving it.

Applying layer styles

Once you have the text arranged on the image, you can add layer styles to enhance the look of the type. Layer styles are automated special effects that you can apply to a layer. For more information on layer styles, see Lesson 3, "Layer Basics."

Now you'll add two different layer styles to the Diesel type layer.

1 Double-click the Diesel layer in the Layers palette to display the Layer Style dialog box.

2 Select Preview on the right side of the dialog box to preview the styles you'll apply.

3 Select Drop Shadow.

4 Select Bevel and Emboss, and then click the name of that option to display individual options for it.

5 In the Structure area, enter **2** for Depth and **2** for Size. Then Click OK.

6 Choose File > Save.

Duplicating and clipping a layer

In this section, you'll learn how to copy the Rust layer and clip it to the shape described by the type layer.

First, you'll copy the Rust layer and move it above the type layer.

1 Select the Rust layer in the Layers palette and drag it onto the Create a New Layer button (▣) at the bottom of the palette.

A new layer called "Rust copy" is created directly above the Rust layer in the palette.

2 In the Layers palette, drag Rust copy just above the Diesel layer inside the Type layer set.

Because Rust copy is the top layer, the rust image is all you can see.

3 Hold down Alt (Windows) or Option (Mac OS) and move the mouse pointer over the line dividing the Rust copy and Diesel layers in the Layers palette. When the pointer changes to two overlapping circles (·◉), click the mouse button.

Rust copy is clipped to the shape of the Diesel text, and you can see the other layers again.

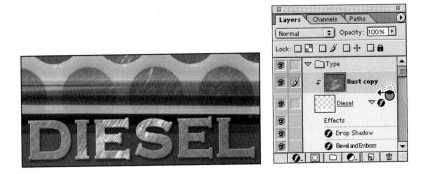

 You can move a clipping path or mask independently of the artwork on the layer by unlinking them. To do so, click the link icon between the layer thumbnail and the mask or clipping path.

4 Choose File > Save.

Using the Liquify command

The Liquify command makes it easy to manipulate areas of an image, as if those areas had been melted. You work with a preview image of the current layer, using special tools to warp, twirl, expand, contract, shift, and reflect areas of the image. An optional warp mesh shows distortions from the original.

You can "freeze" areas of the preview image to protect them from further changes, and "thaw" frozen areas, making them editable. You can also use several reconstruction modes to fully or partially reverse the distortions—or to extend the distortions or redo them in new areas. When you're finished, you can apply the changes to the actual image.

Note: The Liquify command is available only for 8-bit images in RGB Color, CMYK Color, Lab Color, and Grayscale image modes.

–From Adobe Photoshop 6.0 online Help

Liquifying a layer

The Liquify command lets you add a melted look to the image. In this part of the lesson, you'll make the metal grill look as if it has melted from one side to the other.

First you need to rasterize the Metal Grill image and its clipping path into a single image.

1 Select the Metal Grill layer in the Layers palette.

2 Choose Layer > Rasterize > Layer. This converts the clipping path, which is a vector graphic and is resolution-independent, into a mask, which is a raster image and is resolution-dependent.

To view a mask by itself, Alt-click (Windows) or Option-click (Mac OS) the mask thumbnail in the Layers palette. You can then use the painting tools to add to or subtract from the mask. For more information, see Lesson 5, "Masks and Channels."

3 Choose Layer > Remove Layer Mask > Apply to merge the layer with its mask, creating a single rasterized image on that layer.

Now you'll warp the layer with the Liquify command and warp tool.

4 Chose Image > Liquify.

5 Select the warp tool (▨) in the Liquify dialog box. Then enter a brush size that's the same size as the holes in the grill (we used 133) and enter a moderate brush pressure (we used 20).

6 Drag the brush across and down the image in the dialog box. Then click OK.

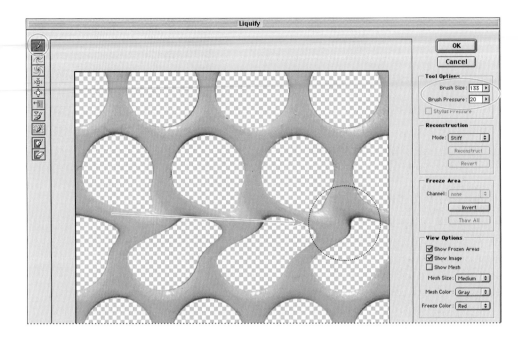

Notice that the metal grill is now warped.

7 Choose File > Save.

Creating a border layer

To give the image a finished look, you'll add a border to it.

1 Click the Create a New Layer button (⬚) in the Layers palette.

2 Choose Layer Properties from the palette menu.

3 Enter **Image Border** for Name and choose Gray from the Color menu. Then click OK.

4 Drag the Image Border layer to the top, until a black line appears immediately above the Type layer set, and then release the mouse button.

The Image Border layer is now the top layer in the image.

5 Choose Select > All to select the entire image.

6 Choose Edit > Stroke. In the Stroke area, enter **5 px** for Width and click OK.
A 5-pixel-wide black stroke is drawn around the entire image.

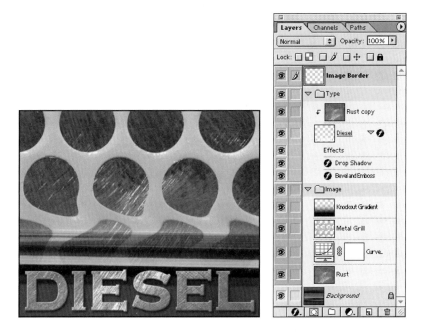

7 Choose Select > Deselect to deselect the entire image.

8 Choose File > Save.

Flattening a layered image

If you plan to send a file out for proofs, it's also a good idea to save two versions of the file—one containing all the layers so that you can edit the file if necessary and one flattened version to send to the print shop. When you flatten a file, all layers are merged into a single background, greatly reducing the size of the file.

1 First, note the file size in the lower-left corner of the 09Start.psd document window. (If the file size isn't displayed, choose File Size from the menu toward the lower-left corner of the document window.)

The number on the left is the printing size of the image, which is about the size of the saved, flattened file in Adobe Photoshop format. The number on the right indicates the file's approximate size including layers and channels.

```
  100%          Doc: 910K/6.18M        ▶
```

2 Choose Image > Duplicate, name the duplicate file **09Final.psd**, and click OK.

3 Choose Flatten Image from the Layers palette menu. The 09Final.psd file is combined onto a single background.

4 Now check the file size of the 09Final.psd image. You'll notice that it is significantly smaller than the 09Start.psd image, because it has been flattened onto the background.

5 Choose File > Save. Then click Save in the Save As dialog box to save the file in Photoshop format.

You've completed the Advanced Layer Techniques lesson. If you like, you can also experiment using layer masks, clipping groups, and adjustment layers with your own work.

Review questions

1 Why would you use layer sets?

2 What is a clipping group? How could you use it in your work?

3 How do adjustment layers work, and what is the benefit of using an adjustment layer?

4 What does an adjustment layer affect when it is added to a clipping group?

5 What are layer styles? Why would you use them?

Review answers

1 Layer sets help you organize and manage layers. For example, you can move all the layers in a layer set as a group and apply attributes or a mask to them as a group.

2 A clipping group consists of at least two layers, where the artwork on the base layer is used as a mask for artwork on the layer or layers above.

3 Adjustment layers are a special type of Photoshop layer that work specifically with color and tonal adjustments. When you apply an adjustment layer, you can edit an image repeatedly without making a permanent change to the colors or tonal range in the image. You can view adjustment layers in ImageReady, but you can create or edit them only in Photoshop.

4 When an adjustment layer is added to a clipping group, only the layers in the clipping group are affected.

5 Layer styles are customizable effects you can apply to layers. They enable you to apply changes to a layer that you can modify or remove at any time.

Lesson 10

10 Creating Special Effects

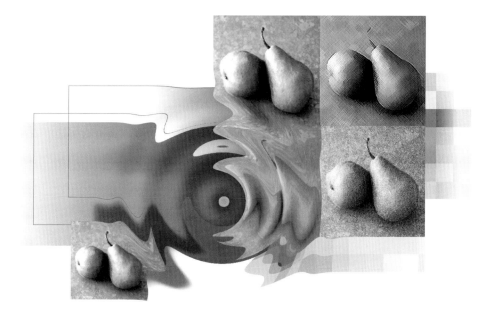

The huge assortment of filters available for Adobe Photoshop lets you transform ordinary images into extraordinary digital artwork. You can select filters that simulate a traditional artistic medium—a watercolor, pastel, or sketched effect—or you can choose from filters that blur, bend, wrap, sharpen, or fragment images. In addition to using filters to alter images, you can use adjustment layers and painting modes to vary the look of your artwork.

In this lesson, you'll learn how to do the following:

• Add a grid to an image to help you make precise selections.

• Desaturate a selection without affecting the color in other parts of the image.

• Paint on a layer above the artwork to color the underlying artwork without changing it permanently.

• Choose colors that are safe to use on the Web.

• Add an adjustment layer to make a color correction to a selection.

• Apply filters to selections to create various effects.

This lesson will take about 30 minutes to complete. The lesson is designed to be done in Adobe Photoshop, but information on using similar functionality in Adobe ImageReady is included where appropriate.

If needed, remove the previous lesson folder from your hard drive, and copy the Lesson10 folder onto it. As you work on this lesson, you'll overwrite the start files. If you need to restore the start files, copy them from the *Adobe Photoshop Classroom in a Book* CD.

Note: *Windows users need to unlock the lesson files before using them. For more information, see "Copying the Classroom in a Book files" on page 3.*

Getting started

Before beginning this lesson, restore the default application settings for Adobe Photoshop. See "Restoring default preferences" on page 4.

You'll start the lesson by viewing the final Lesson file, to see what you'll accomplish.

1 Start Adobe Photoshop.

2 Click Cancel to exit the color management dialog box that appears.

3 Choose File > Open, and open the 10End.psd file, located in the Lessons/Lesson10 folder.

An image containing six sets of pears appears. Some of the pears have been painted, and some have had filters applied to them.

4 When you have finished viewing the file, either leave the end file open on your desktop for reference, or close it without saving changes.

For an illustration of the finished artwork for this lesson, see the gallery at the beginning of the color section.

Now you'll open the start file and begin working.

5 Choose File > Open, and open the 10Start.psd file, located in the Lessons/Lesson10 folder on your hard drive.

Saving and loading a selection

You'll start by making a selection of a set of pears and then saving it. That way you can reuse the selection by reloading it as needed. ImageReady includes the basic marquee selection tools, the lasso and polygon lasso tools, and the magic wand tool familiar to users of Photoshop.

1 Select the zoom tool (🔍), and drag over the set of pears in the upper left corner to magnify your view.

2 Position the pointer on the lasso tool (🔾), and hold down the mouse button to open the hidden tools list. Select the magnetic lasso tool (🔾).

Note: *ImageReady does not include the magnetic lasso tool.*

3 To draw a freehand segment, drag the pointer along the edge you want to trace. Notice that the pointer doesn't have to be exactly on the edge for the segment to snap to it.

As you move the pointer, the active segment snaps to the strongest edge in the image. Periodically, the magnetic lasso tool adds fastening points to the selection border to anchor previous sections. As you move the pointer over the starting point, a hollow circle appears next to the pointer, indicating that you are about to close the segment.

Dragging with magnetic lasso   *Result*
pointer

4 When a circle appears next to the magnetic lasso pointer, release the mouse button to close the segment.

Note: For best results when tracing the pear stem with the magnetic lasso tool, zoom in on your work and decrease the tool's lasso width and frequency values. For example, try tracing the pear using a Lasso Width of 1 or 2 pixels and a Frequency of 40.

5 Save the selection of the right pear by choosing Select > Save Selection. Enter **Alpha 1** in the Name text box, and click OK to save the selection in a new channel. You'll use the selection again for another set of pears. (To learn more about using channels in Photoshop, see Lesson 5, "Masks and Channels.")

6 Choose Select > Deselect to deselect the right pear.

7 Now select the left pear using the magnetic lasso tool.

8 Choose Select > Save Selection, enter **Alpha 2** in the Name text box, and click OK to save the selection of the right pear in a new channel.

9 Choose Select > Deselect to deselect the pear. You'll use this selection again for other sets of pears.

You'll begin this lesson by hand-coloring a set of the pears. You'll begin with the right pear, so you'll need to load the selection you created.

10 Choose Select > Load Selection, and select Alpha 1. Click OK. A selection border appears around the right pear in your image.

Note: You can load a channel in ImageReady using the Select > Load Selection command.

Hand-coloring selections on a layer

First you'll remove the color from the selection so that you can color it by hand. Then you'll add a layer above the pears and apply any new color on the layer. This way, if you don't like the results, you can simply erase the layer and start over.

Desaturating a selection

You'll use the Desaturate command to *desaturate*, or remove the color, from the pear selection. Saturation is the presence or absence of color in a selection. When you desaturate a selection within an image, you create a grayscale-like effect without affecting the colors in other parts of the image. ImageReady has many of the same color correction tools available in Photoshop, including Desaturation.

1 Choose Image > Adjust > Desaturate. The color is removed from the selection.

2 Choose Select > Deselect.

3 Choose File > Save to save your work.

Creating a layer and choosing a blending mode

Now you'll add a layer and specify a layer blending mode. By painting on a layer, you won't permanently alter the image. This makes it easy to change your mind and start again.

You use layer blending modes to determine how the pixels in a layer are blended with underlying pixels on other layers. By applying modes to individual layers, you can create myriad special effects. Blending modes can also be used in ImageReady to blend layers.

1 In the Layers palette, click the New Layer button (⊞) to add Layer 1 to the image. To rename the layer, choose Layer Properties from the Layers palette menu, type **Paint**, and click OK.

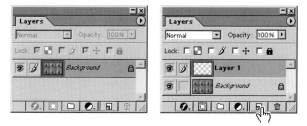

Original

Clicking Create a New Layer button to add layer

Next to the New Layer button, you'll see the Trash button. Any time you want to throw your Painting layer away, you can drag the layer to the trash in the Layers palette.

Now you'll choose a layer blending mode to determine how the pixels in this layer are blended with underlying pixels on the Background layer.

2 In the Layers palette, choose Color from the pop-up mode menu to the left of the Opacity text box.

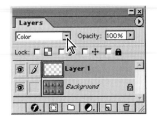

The Color mode lets you change the hue of a selection without affecting the highlights and shadows. This means you can apply a variety of color tints without changing the original highlights and shadows of the pears.

Applying painting effects

To begin painting, you must again load the selection that you created earlier. You will open the Alpha 1 channel. Photoshop and ImageReady share a common set of tools for applying and tracking color.

1 Choose Select > Load Selection > Alpha 1. (Notice in the Load Selection dialog box that the color mode change you just made also was saved as a selection, called "Paint Transparency.")

2 Select the paintbrush tool (✎) to display its tool options bar. Set the Opacity to about **50%**.

💡 *Change the paintbrush opacity by pressing a number on the keypad from 0 to 9 (where 1 is 10%, 9 is 90%, and 0 is 100%).*

3 In the Brush pop-up palette, select a large, soft-edged brush.

4 In the Swatches palette, select a yellow-green color that appeals to you for the foreground color. Paint the entire pear with the light yellow-green color. As you paint, you'll notice that the color of the pear changes to the color you selected. (If you want your colors to be appropriate for use on the Web, first choose Web Color Sliders from the Color palette menu and then choose a color for the pear.)

Selecting yellow-green swatch   Result

5 Next, select a darker green from the Swatches palette. In the Paintbrush Options palette, set the brush opacity to about 30%. Paint around the edges in the pear selection, avoiding the highlight area.

6 To add additional highlights to the pear, select a rose color from the Swatches palette, and select a smaller brush from the Brush pop-up palette. In the Paintbrush Options palette, decrease the paint opacity to about 20%, and paint more highlights on the pear.

7 Choose Select > Deselect.

8 Choose File > Save.

Adding a gradient

Now you'll use the gradient tool to add a gradient to the other pear for a highlight effect. (ImageReady does not have a gradient tool. Instead, gradients are created as ImageReady layer effects.)

First you'll need to load the selection of the left pear you made earlier.

1 Choose Select > Load Selection, and select Alpha 2. Click OK. A selection border appears around the left pear in your image

2 Select red as the foreground color.

3 Click the background color swatch, and select yellow as the background color.

*Selecting red as the
foreground color*

*Selecting yellow as the
background color*

4 Select the gradient tool (), and select Radial Gradient from the tool options bar.

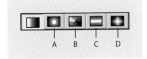

A. *Radial gradient*
B. *Angle gradient*
C. *Reflected gradient*
D. *Diamond gradient*

5 Make sure that Foreground to Background is selected in the Gradient picker, so that the color blends from the foreground color (red) to the background color (yellow). Set the opacity to **40%**.

6 Position the gradient tool near the pear's highlight, and drag toward the stem. (You can select other gradient tools and colors, and then drag to try out different effects.)

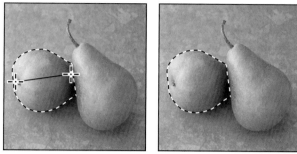

*Applying radial gradient from   Result
pear's highlight to stem*

7 Choose Select > Deselect.

8 When you've finished painting the set of pears, choose Layer > Merge Visible to merge the painting layer with the pear image and to keep the file size small. You'll continue the project by applying effects to the other pears in the image.

9 Choose File > Save.

Combining and moving selections

Before you begin to apply special effects to the next set of pears, you'll combine the earlier selections you made. You'll also move the new combined selection so that you can use it with a different set of pears. Although the process is slightly different, you can combine selections in ImageReady as well.

1 Select the zoom tool. Then hold down Alt (Windows) or Option (Mac OS) to select the zoom-out tool (Q).

2 Click the zoom-out tool as many times as necessary until both the top left pears and top middle pears are visible.

3 Choose Select > Load Selection, and select Alpha 1. Click OK.

4 Choose Select > Load Selection. Select Alpha 2. Click Add to Selection. Click OK. Both pears are now selected.

💡 *To add a channel to an existing selection when using the Select > Load Selection command in ImageReady, hold down the Shift key and keep using the Select > Load Selection command (picking a different channel each time) until all of the channels you want to use have been loaded as one combined selection.*

5 Using the rectangular marquee tool (▢), drag the selection border to the right to position it over the middle pears in the top row.

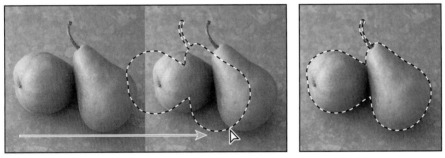

Alpha 1 and Alpha 2 selections combined and then moved using marquee tool

Colorizing a selection

Now you will colorize the selected set of pears. A colorized image has only one hue of color. You colorize a selection or image with the Colorize option in the Hue/Saturation dialog box. You can use the Colorize option to add color to a grayscale image or to reduce the color values in an image to one hue. ImageReady also includes Hue/Saturation.

1 Double-click the hand tool (✋) to fit the image in the window. The top middle pears should still be selected.

2 Choose Image > Adjust > Hue/Saturation.

The Hue/Saturation command lets you adjust the hue, saturation, and lightness of individual color components in an image.

3 Make sure that Preview is selected. Then select the Colorize option.

The upper color bar shows the color before the adjustment; the lower bar shows how the adjustment affects all of the hues at full saturation. The image takes on a reddish tint.

4 Experiment with values in the Hue and Saturation text boxes until you get a desirable color. You can use the sliders to adjust the Hue, Saturation, and Lightness, or you can type in numbers in the text boxes. We used a Hue of 83 and a Saturation of 28 for a greenish color.

Decreasing the saturation lowers the intensity of the color.

5 Click OK to apply the changes.

6 To preview the changes without the selection border, choose View > Show Extras or View > Show > Selection Edges.

7 Choose View > Show Extras or View > Show > Selection Edges, and then choose Select > Deselect to deselect everything.

8 Choose File > Save.

Using a grid

Before you adjust the next set of pears, you'll display a grid and use it to make a precise rectangular selection that you can repeat on the remaining sets of pears. A grid helps you lay out images or elements symmetrically. Selections, selection borders, and tools snap to the grid when they are dragged within 8 screen pixels of it. (Grids are not available in ImageReady.)

1 In Photoshop, choose View > Show > Grid. The grid with the default settings appears in the image window.

2 Choose Edit > Preferences > Guides & Grid.

You adjust the grid settings using the Preferences dialog box. You can set the grid to display as lines or as points, and you can change its spacing or color.

3 In the Grid section of the dialog box, for Color, choose Green. For Gridline Every, enter a value of **2**. For Subdivisions, enter a value of **1**. Click OK to apply the changes to the grid.

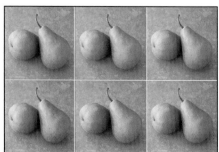

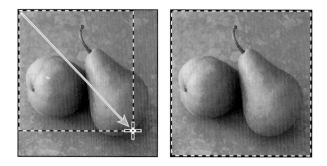

Setting grid option   *Result*

4 In the Navigator palette, zoom in on the pear image, and drag the Navigator marquee to move to the top right corner of the image.

5 Select the rectangular marquee tool (⬚). Then drag a selection border to select the top right set of pears. As you drag, the selection border snaps to the grid.

Next you'll set the rectangular marquee tool to a fixed size to make subsequent selections easier.

6 In the Marquee tool options bar, choose Fixed Size from the Style pop-up menu, and enter the height and width you want to use. We used 200 for both the height and width.

Style: Fixed Size   Width: 200 px   Height: 200 px

7 Choose View > Show Extras or View > Show > Grid to hide the grid.

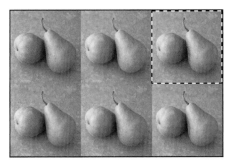

Set of pears selected using fixed-size marquee

Changing the color balance

Now you'll use an adjustment layer to adjust the color balance on this set of pears. You can apply any of the many color correction tools in Adobe Photoshop to an adjustment layer. You can also apply color adjustments to a regular layer or to a channel. ImageReady has many of the same color correction features as Photoshop, but they cannot be applied to adjustment layers or channels, because you cannot create or edit adjustment layers or channels in ImageReady.

Making color adjustments to a channel or a regular layer permanently changes the pixels on that layer. With an adjustment layer, in contrast, your color and tonal changes reside only within the adjustment layer and do not alter any pixels. The effect is as if you were viewing the visible layers through the adjustment layer above them. This lets you try out color and tonal adjustments without permanently changing pixels in the image. (You can also use adjustment layers to affect multiple layers at once.)

1 Choose Layer > New Adjustment Layer > Color Balance. The New Layer dialog box opens; click OK to accept the defaults.

2 The Color Balance dialog box opens, where you can change the mixture of colors in a color image and make general color corrections. When you adjust the color balance, you can keep the same tonal balance, as you'll do here. You can also focus changes on the shadows, midtones, or highlights.

In the Color Balance dialog box, experiment with different Color Levels for the image. When you are happy with the result, click OK. We used +13, –14, and –38.

Notice that the adjustment layer thumbnail in the Layers palette resembles a mask. By making a selection and then adding an adjustment layer, the layer becomes a mask that applies the adjustment only to the selected area.

Adjustment layers act as layer masks, which can be edited repeatedly without permanently affecting the underlying image. You can double-click an adjustment layer to display the last settings used and adjust them repeatedly. Or you can delete an adjustment layer by dragging it to the Trash button at the bottom of the Layers palette.

3 Choose File > Save.

Applying filters

To conclude the project, you'll apply different styles of filters to the remaining pears. Because there are so many different filters for creating special effects, the best way to learn about them is to try out different filters and filter options. ImageReady supports the same filters included with Photoshop.

1 In the Layers palette, select Background.

2 Select the zoom tool ($\mathcal{Q}$), hold down Alt (Windows) or Option (Mac OS), and click the middle of the image to zoom out.

3 Using the rectangular marquee tool ($\square$), click the lower left corner of the image to draw a selection border of the pears. The selection border matches the size of the last border you drew.

4 Choose Filter > Brush Strokes > Crosshatch. Adjust the settings as desired, using the Preview window to see the effect. Click OK.

Previewing and applying filters

To use a filter, choose the appropriate submenu command from the Filter menu. These guidelines can help you in choosing filters:

• *The last filter chosen appears at the top of the menu.*

• *Filters are applied to the active, visible layer.*

• *Filters cannot be applied to Bitmap-mode or indexed-color images.*

• *Some filters only work on RGB images.*

• *Some filters are processed entirely in RAM.*

• *Gaussian Blur, Add Noise, Median, Unsharp Mask, High Pass, Dust & Scratches, and Gradient Map filters can be used with 16-bit-per-channel images.*

–From Adobe Photoshop 6.0 online Help

$\mathcal{Q}$ *To save time when trying various filters, experiment on a small, representative part of your image or a low-resolution copy.*

You can fade the effect of a filter or of a color adjustment using the Fade command. The mode determines how the modified pixels in the selection appear in relation to the original pixels. The blending modes in the Fade dialog box are a subset of those available in the painting and editing tools Options palette.

Using filter shortcuts

Try any of these techniques to help save time when working with filters:

- *To cancel a filter as it is being applied, press Esc or Command-(.) (period) (Mac OS).*

- *To undo a filter, press Ctrl+Z (Windows) or Command+Z (Mac OS).*

- *To reapply the most recently used filter with its last values, press Ctrl+F (Windows) or Command+F (Mac OS).*

- *To display the dialog box for the last filter you applied, press Ctrl+Alt+F (Windows) or Command+Option+F (Mac OS).*

5 Choose Edit > Fade Crosshatch to fade the filter effect. For mode, choose Multiply. Set the Opacity to **50%**, and click OK.

Crosshatch filter applied   *Fade command applied*   *Result*

6 Using the rectangular marquee tool, click the middle set of pears in the bottom row of the image to draw the fixed-size selection border. To adjust the position of the selection border, press the arrow keys to nudge it into place.

7 Choose Filter > Distort > Zigzag. For Amount, enter **4%**; for Ridges, enter **9%**; for style, select Pond Ripples. Click OK. The Zigzag filter distorts an image radially, creating ripples or ridges in an image.

8 Using the rectangular marquee tool, click to select the pears in the lower right corner of the bottom row.

9 Click the Default Colors icon to set the foreground and background colors to their defaults.

10 Choose Filter > Distort > Diffuse Glow. For Graininess, enter **6**; for Glow Amount, enter **6**; and for Clear Amount, enter **15**. Click OK. This filter adds white noise, or pixels, in the same color as the background color to an image.

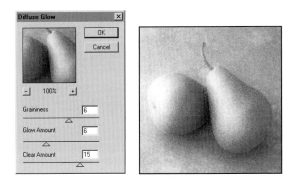

11 Choose File > Save; then close the file.

Tips for creating special effects

Try the following techniques to create special effects with filters. For illustrations of these techniques, see Photoshop 6.0 online Help.

Create edge effects. You can use various techniques to treat the edges of an effect applied to only part of an image. To leave a distinct edge, simply apply the filter. For a soft edge, feather the edge, and then apply the filter. For a transparent effect, apply the filter, and then use the Fade command to adjust the selection's blending mode and opacity. (See Blending filter effects (Photoshop) in Photoshop 6.0 online Help.)

Apply filters to layers. You can apply filters to individual layers or to several layers in succession to build up an effect. For a filter to affect a layer, the layer must be visible and must contain pixels—for example, a neutral fill color. (See Filling a new layer with a neutral color in Photoshop 6.0 online Help.)

Apply filters to individual channels. You can apply a filter to an individual channel, apply a different effect to each color channel, or apply the same filter but with different settings.

Create backgrounds. By applying effects to solid-color or grayscale shapes, you can generate a variety of backgrounds and textures. You might then blur these textures. Although some filters have little or no visible effect when applied to solid colors (for example, Glass), others produce interesting effects. You might try Add Noise, Chalk & Charcoal, Clouds, Conté Crayon, Craquelure, Difference Clouds, Glass, Grain, Graphic Pen, Halftone Pattern, Mezzotint, Mosaic Tiles, Note Paper, Patchwork, Pointillize, Reticulation, Rough Pastels, Sponge, Stained Glass, Texture Fill, Texturizer, and Underpainting.

Combine multiple effects with masks or with duplicate images. Using masks to create selection areas gives you more control over transitions from one effect to another. For example, you can filter the selection created with a mask. You can also use the history brush tool to paint a filter effect onto part of the image. First, apply the filter to an entire image. Next, step back in the History palette to the image state before applying the filter, and set the history brush source to the filtered state. Then, paint the image. (See "Reverting to any state of an image" in Photoshop 6.0 online Help.)

Improve image quality and consistency. You can disguise faults, alter or enhance, or make a series of images look related by applying the same effect to each. Use the Actions palette to record the process of modifying one image, and then use this action on the other images. (See "Using the Actions palette" in Photoshop 6.0 online Help.)

–From Adobe Photoshop 6.0 online Help

Improving performance with filters

Some filter effects can be memory intensive, especially when applied to a high-resolution image. You can use these techniques to improve performance:

• Try out filters and settings on a small portion of an image.

• Apply the effect to individual channels—for example, to each RGB channel—if the image is large and you're having problems with insufficient memory. (With some filters, effects vary if applied to the individual channel rather than the composite channel, especially if the filter randomly modifies pixels.)

• Free up memory before running the filter by using the Purge command. (See "Correcting mistakes" in Photoshop 6.0 online Help.)

• Allocate more RAM to Photoshop or ImageReady. If necessary, exit from other applications to make more memory available to Photoshop or ImageReady.

• Try changing settings to improve the speed of memory-intensive filters such as Lighting Effects, Cutout, Stained Glass, Chrome, Ripple, Spatter, Sprayed Strokes, and Glass filters. (For example, with the Stained Glass filter, increase cell size. With the Cutout filter, increase Edge Simplicity or decrease Edge Fidelity, or both.)

• If you plan to print to a grayscale printer, convert a copy of the image to grayscale before applying filters. However, applying a filter to a color image and then converting to grayscale may not have the same effect as applying the filter to a grayscale version of the image.

This concludes this lesson. Try out other filters to see how you can add different effects to your images.

For detailed information on individual filters and a gallery of examples, see "Using filters" in Photoshop 6.0 online Help.

For the Web: Animated rollover button

Here's a way to quickly create an eye-catching button for your Web pages from an animated rollover that uses layer effects. In this technique, you'll create a button graphic with text that starts animating when the pointer is over it and that changes to a different color when the mouse button is clicked.

This technique requires that you work in ImageReady because you're working with rollovers.

1 In ImageReady, start with a button with type or a contrasting graphic element that will lend itself to an eye-catching gradient. The type or graphic should be on a separate layer from the button. (For the button to work realistically, it should be in a slice of its own, and the slice should be selected.)

Boldfaced fonts with contrasting colors increase legibility. Light or serif fonts with minimal contrast are more difficult to read. For the button background, use simple photos or textures that don't conflict with the text or icon on the button.

2 Click the Rollover palette tab. (If the palette isn't visible, choose Window > Show Rollover.) The palette contains one state, Normal.

3 Choose New State from the Rollover palette pop-up menu to create the Over state.

4 With the Over state selected, in the Layers palette, click the Type layer to select it. Then click the Layer Effect button (❷) at the bottom of the palette. Choose Gradient Overlay from the Layer Effect pop-up menu.

5 In the Gradient/Pattern palette, choose Linear.

6 Choose a gradient from the pop-up menu to the right of the color ramp, or double-click the color stops beneath the color ramp and use the color picker to select your own gradient combinations.

7 Click the Animation palette tab. The button and the type gradient appear as the first frame. From the Delay Frame pop-up menu beneath the frame, choose 0.1 seconds to delay playing the frame.

8 Click the New Frame button (🖻) at the bottom of the Animation palette to create a new frame that duplicates the original frame's settings.

Make sure that the second frame is selected in the Animation palette and the Gradient Overlay effect under the Type layer is still selected in the Layers palette.

9 If necessary, click the double-triangle (⬍) in the Gradient Overlay palette tab to expand the palette, or choose Show Options from the Gradient palette menu. Select Reverse to reverse the direction of the linear gradient.

10 Return to the Rollover palette, and choose New State from the Rollover palette menu to create the Down state.

If desired, you can adjust the type in the Down frame. For example, you can change the type color or remove the gradient to create a different animation when the button is pressed.

11 Choose File > Preview In, and choose a browser to preview the effect.

12 Click the Optimize palette tab. In the Optimize palette, choose GIF, and set other optimization options as desired.

For information on using other optimization options, see Lesson 14, "Optimizing Images for the Web."

13 Choose File > Save Optimized or File > Save Optimized As to save the file as a GIF.

You can repeat this technique to create other eye-catching buttons, using other layer effects applied to graphics or type.

Review questions

1 What is the purpose of saving selections?

2 Name a benefit of using a grid in your image.

3 Describe one way to isolate color adjustments to an image.

4 Describe one way to remove color from a selection or image for a grayscale effect.

Review answers

1 By saving a selection, you can create and reuse time-consuming selections and uniformly select artwork in an image. You can also combine selections or create new selections by adding to or subtracting from existing selections.

2 A grid helps you make precise, rectangular selections and lay out images symmetrically. Selections, selection borders, and tools snap to the grid when they are dragged within 8 screen pixels of it.

3 You can use adjustment layers to try out color changes before applying them permanently to a layer.

4 You can use the Desaturate command to desaturate, or remove the color, from a selection. Or you can use the Hue/Saturation command and adjust only the Saturation component. Photoshop also includes the sponge tool for removing color.

Lesson 11

11 | Setting Up Your Monitor for Color Management

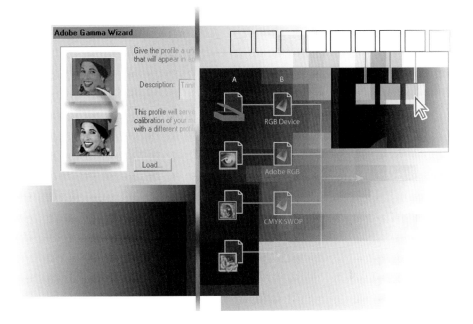

The most basic requirement for color management is to calibrate your monitor and create an ICC profile for it. Applications that support color management will use your monitor's ICC profile to display color graphics consistently. If you don't have a hardware-based calibration and profiling utility, you can get reasonably accurate results using Adobe Gamma.

In this lesson, you'll learn how to do the following:

- Examine the principles associated with color management.

- Calibrate your monitor using Adobe Gamma.

- Create an ICC profile for your monitor using Adobe Gamma.

This lesson will take about 45 minutes to complete.

Note: *You can skip this lesson if you have already calibrated your monitor using a hardware-based tool or an ICC-compliant calibration tool such as the Adobe Gamma utility included with Photoshop 5.0 and later, Illustrator® 8.0 and later, and InDesign® 1.0 and later, and if you haven't changed your video card or monitor settings.*

Getting started

In this lesson, you'll learn some basic color management concepts and terminology. In addition, you'll calibrate your monitor to a known color condition, and then create an ICC profile that describes your monitor's specific color characteristics. For information about setting up RGB and CMYK color spaces in Photoshop, see Lesson 12, "Producing and Printing Consistent Color."

Color management: An overview

Although all color gamuts overlap, they don't match exactly, which is why some colors on your monitor can't be reproduced in print. The colors that can't be reproduced in print are called *out-of-gamut* colors, because they are outside the spectrum of printable colors. For example, you can create a large percentage of colors in the visible spectrum using programs such as Photoshop, Illustrator, and InDesign, but you can reproduce only a subset of those colors on a desktop printer. The printer has a smaller *color space* or *gamut* (the range of colors that can be displayed or printed) than the application that created the color.

Visible spectrum containing millions of colors (far left) compared with color gamuts of various devices and documents

To compensate for these differences and to ensure the closest match between on-screen colors and printed colors, applications use a color management system (CMS). Using a color management engine, the CMS translates colors from the color space of one device into a device-independent color space, such as CIE (Commission Internationale d'Eclairage) LAB. From the device-independent color space, the CMS fits that color information to another device's color space by a process called *color mapping*, or *gamut mapping*. The CMS makes any adjustments necessary to represent the color consistently among devices.

A CMS uses three components to map colors across devices:

• A device-independent (or reference) color space.

• ICC profiles that define the color characteristics of particular devices and documents.

• A color management engine that translates colors from one device's color space to another according to a *rendering intent*, or translation method.

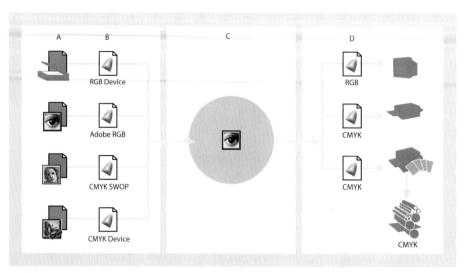

A. *Scanners and software applications create color documents. Users choose document's working color space.* **B.** *ICC source profiles describe document color spaces.* **C.** *A color management engine uses ICC source profiles to map document colors to a device-independent color space through supporting applications.* **D.** *The color management engine maps document colors from the device-independent color space to output device color spaces using destination profiles.*

About the device-independent color space

To successfully compare gamuts and make adjustments, a color management system must use a reference color space—an objective way of defining color. Most CMSs use the CIE LAB color model, which exists independently of any device and is big enough to reproduce any color visible to the human eye. For this reason, CIE LAB is considered *device-independent*.

About ICC profiles

An *ICC profile* describes how a particular device or standard reproduces color using a cross-platform standard defined by the International Color Consortium (ICC). ICC profiles ensure that images appear correctly in any ICC-compliant applications and on color devices. This is accomplished by embedding the profile information in the original file or assigning the profile in your application.

At a minimum, you must have one *source profile* for the device (scanner or digital camera, for example) or standard (SWOP or Adobe RGB, for example) used to create the color, and one *destination profile* for the device (monitor or contract proofing, for example) or standard (SWOP or TOYO, for example) that you will use to reproduce the color.

About color management engines

Sometimes called the color matching module (CMM), the color management engine interprets ICC profiles. Acting as a translator, the color management engine converts the out-of-gamut colors from the source device to the range of colors that can be produced by the destination device. The color management engine may be included with the CMS or may be a separate part of the operating system.

Translating to a gamut—particularly a smaller gamut—usually involves a compromise, so multiple translation methods are available. For example, a color translation method that preserves correct relationships among colors in a photograph will usually alter the colors in a logo. Color management engines provide a choice of translation methods, known as *rendering intents*, so that you can apply a method appropriate to the intended use of a color graphic. Examples of common rendering intents include *Perceptual (Images)* for preserving color relationships the way the eye does, *Saturation (Graphics)* for preserving vivid colors at the expense of color accuracy, *Relative* and *Absolute Colorimetric* for preserving color accuracy at the expense of color relationships.

Color management resources

You can find additional information on color management on the Web and in print. Here are a few resources:

• On the Adobe Web site (www.adobe.com), search for **color management** or go directly to http://www.adobe.com/support/techguides/color/.

• On the Apple® Web site (www.apple.com), search for **ColorSync**.

• On the LinoColor Web site (www.linocolor.com), open the *Color Manager Manual*.

• On the Agfa Web site (www.agfa.com), search for the publication *The Secrets of Color Management*.

• On the ColorBlind Web site (www.color.com), click Color Resources.

• At your local library or bookstore, look for *GATF Practical Guide to Color Management*, by Richard Adams and Joshua Weisberg (May 1998); ISBN 0883622025.

🔲 For information about setting up color management in Photoshop, see Photoshop 6.0 online Help.

Calibrating and characterizing your monitor using Adobe Gamma

The first requirement for color management is to calibrate your monitor and create an accurate ICC profile for it. Although this doesn't address your entire workflow, at least it ensures that your monitor displays colors as precisely as it can. *Calibration* is the process of setting your monitor, or any device, to known color conditions. *Characterization*, or profiling, is the process of creating an ICC profile that describes the unique color characteristics of your device or standard. Always calibrate your monitor, or any device, before creating a profile for it; otherwise, the profile is only valid for the current state of the device.

Although monitor calibration and characterization are best done with specialized software and hardware, you can get reasonably accurate results with the Adobe Gamma utility included with Photoshop 5.0 and later, Illustrator 8.0 and later, and InDesign 1.0 and later. If you have used other calibration utilities to calibrate and characterize your monitor, such as Apple ColorSync, Adobe Gamma will overwrite those settings.

💡 *You may find it helpful to have your monitor's user guide convenient while using Adobe Gamma.*

1 If you have the Mac OS Gamma control panel (included with Adobe Photoshop 4.0 and earlier) or the Monitor Setup utility (included with PageMaker 6.0) for Windows, remove it because it is obsolete. Use the latest Adobe Gamma utility instead.

2 Make sure your monitor has been turned on for at least a half hour. This gives it sufficient time to warm up for a more accurate color reading.

3 Make sure your monitor is displaying thousands of colors or more.

4 Set the room lighting to the level you plan to maintain consistently.

5 Remove colorful background patterns on your monitor desktop. Busy or bright patterns surrounding a document interfere with accurate color perception. Set your desktop to display neutral grays only, using RGB values of 128. For more information, see the manual for your operating system.

6 If your monitor has digital controls for choosing the white point of your monitor from a range of preset values, set those controls before starting Adobe Gamma. Later, in Adobe Gamma, you'll set the white point to match your monitor's current setting. Be sure to set the digital controls before you start Adobe Gamma. If you set them after you begin the calibration process in Adobe Gamma, you'll need to begin the process again.

Starting Adobe Gamma

You'll use the Adobe Gamma utility to calibrate and characterize your monitor. The resulting ICC profile uses the calibration settings to precisely describe how your monitor reproduces color. Depending on your workflow scenario, an ICC monitor profile can be either a source or destination profile. In this section, you'll load an existing monitor profile as a starting point for calibrating your monitor.

Note: Adobe Gamma can characterize, but not calibrate, monitors used with Windows NT®. Its ability to calibrate settings in Windows 98 depends on the video card and video driver software. In such cases, some calibration options documented here may not be available. For example, if you're only characterizing your monitor, you'll choose the default white point and gamma, but not the target calibration settings.

1 Do one of the following to start Adobe Gamma:

• In Windows, choose Start > Settings > Control Panel, and double-click Adobe Gamma.

• In Mac OS, from the Apple menu choose Control Panels > Adobe Gamma.

You can use either the control panel or a step-by-step wizard to make all the adjustments necessary for calibrating your monitor. In this lesson, you will use the Adobe Gamma control panel. At any time while working in the Adobe Gamma control panel, you can click the Wizard (Windows) or Assistant (Mac OS) button to switch to the wizard for instructions that guide you through the same settings as in the control panel, one option at a time.

2 Select Control Panel, and click Next.

The next step is to load an ICC monitor profile that describes your monitor. This profile serves as a starting point for the calibration process by supplying some preset values. You'll adjust these values in Adobe Gamma to characterize the profile to match your monitor's particular characteristics.

3 Do one of the following:

• If your monitor is listed in the Description area at the top of the control panel, select it.

• Click the Load button for a list of other available profiles, and then locate and open the monitor ICC profile that most closely matches your monitor. To see an ICC profile's full name at the bottom of the Open Monitor Profile dialog box, select a file. (Windows profile filenames have the .icm extension, which you may not see if the extension display is off.) Make your choice, and click Open.

• Leave the generic Adobe monitor profile selected in the Description area.

Adobe Gamma utility control panel

Setting the optimum brightness and contrast

Now you'll adjust the monitor's overall level and range of display intensity. These controls work just as they do on a television. Adjusting the monitor's brightness and contrast enables the most accurate screen representation for the gamma adjustment that follows.

1 With Adobe Gamma running, set the contrast control on your monitor to its highest setting. (On many monitors, this control is shown next to a contrast icon (◑).)

2 Adjust the brightness control on your monitor (located next to a brightness icon (☼) on many monitors) as you watch the alternating pattern of black and gray squares across the top half of the Brightness and Contrast rectangle in Adobe Gamma. Make the gray squares in the top bar as dark as possible without matching the black squares, while keeping the bottom area a bright white. (If you can't see a difference between the black and gray squares while keeping the bottom area white, your monitor's screen phosphors may be fading.)

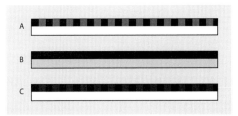

A. Gray squares too light ***B.*** *Gray squares too dark and white area too gray* ***C.*** *Gray squares and white area correctly adjusted*

Do not adjust the brightness and contrast controls on your monitor again unless you are about to update the monitor profile. Adjusting the controls invalidates the monitor profile. You can tape the hardware controls in place if necessary.

Selecting phosphor data

The chemical phosphors in your monitor determine the range of colors you see on your screen.

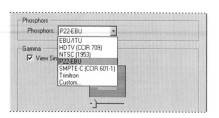

Do one of the following from the Phosphors menu:

• Choose the exact phosphor type used by the monitor you are calibrating. The two most common phosphor types are EBU/ITU and Trinitron.

• If the correct type is not listed but you were provided with chromaticity coordinates with your monitor, choose Custom, and enter the red, green, and blue chromaticity coordinates of the monitor's phosphors.

• If you're not sure which phosphors your monitor uses, see the monitor's documentation; contact the manufacturer; or use a color measuring instrument such as a colorimeter or spectrophotometer to determine them.

Setting the midtones

The gamma setting defines midtone brightness. You can adjust the gamma based on a single combined gamma reading (the View Single Gamma Only option). Or you can individually adjust the midtones for red, green, and blue. The second method produces a more accurate setting, so you will use that method here.

For the Gamma option in the Adobe Gamma utility, deselect the View Single Gamma Only option. Drag the slider under each box until the shape in the center blends in with the background as much as possible. It may help to squint or move back from the monitor.

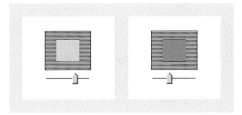

Single gamma not calibrated (left), and calibrated (right)

Make adjustments carefully and in small increments; imprecise adjustments can result in a color cast not visible until you print.

Selecting a target gamma

You may also have an option for specifying a separate gamma for viewing graphics.

Note: *This option is not available in Windows NT due to its hardware protection shield that prevents Adobe Gamma from communicating with the computer's video card.*

If you have this option, choose one of the following from the Desired menu:

• Windows Default for Windows systems. Leave the setting at 2.2.

• Macintosh Default for Mac OS computers. Leave the setting at 1.8.

Setting the monitor's white point

Now you'll adjust the hardware *white point*, the whitest white that a monitor is capable of displaying. The white point is a measurement of color temperature in Kelvin and determines whether you are using a warm or cool white.

First you'll make sure that the white point setting matches the white point of your monitor. Do one of the following:

• If you know the white point of your monitor in its current state, you can select it from the Hardware menu in the White Point section. If your monitor is new, select 9300 Kelvin, the default white point of most monitors and televisions.

• If you started from a manufacturer's profile for your monitor, you can use the default value. However, the older your monitor, the less likely it is that its white point still matches the manufacturer's profile.

• If your monitor is equipped with digital controls for setting the white point, and you already set those controls before starting Adobe Gamma, make sure the Hardware menu matches your monitor's current setting. Remember, though, that if you adjust these hardware controls at this point in the calibration process, you'll need to start over, beginning with the procedure in "Setting the optimum brightness and contrast" on page 297.

• If you don't know the white point and don't know the appropriate values, you can use the Measure option to visually estimate it. If you choose this option, continue to step 1.

♀ *To get a precise value, you need to measure the white point with a desktop colorimeter or spectrophotometer and enter that value directly using the Custom option.*

If you were unable to choose a hardware setting as described, try the following experiment:

1 For best results, turn off all lights in the room.

2 Click Measure, and then click OK (Windows) or Next (Mac OS). Three squares appear.

The goal here is to make the center square as neutral gray as possible. You'll train your eyes to see the contrasts between the extreme cooler (blue) white and warmer (yellow) white, and then adjust the colors in the squares to find the most neutral gray between them.

3 Click the left square several times until it disappears, leaving the middle and right squares. Study the contrast between the bluish square on the right and the center square.

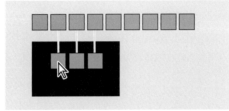

Clicking on the left square will reset all the squares a shade cooler.

4 Click the right square several times until it disappears, and study the contrast between the yellowish square on the left and the center square.

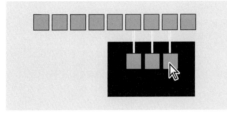

Clicking on the right square will reset all the squares a shade warmer.

5 Click the left or right square until the center square is a neutral gray. When complete, commit the changes by clicking the center square.

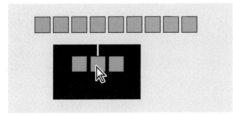

For a color illustration of adjusting the white point, see figure 11-1 of the color section.

Setting an adjusted white point

This option, when available, sets a working white point for monitor display, if that value differs from the hardware white point. For example, if your hardware white point is 6500 Kelvin (daylight), but you want to edit an image at 5000 Kelvin (warm white) because that most closely represents the environment in which the image will be viewed, you can set your adjusted white point to 5000 Kelvin. Adobe Gamma will change the monitor display accordingly.

Do one of the following to specify a separate white point for viewing graphics:

• To use the current white point of your monitor, choose Same as Hardware from the Adjusted menu.

• To specify your monitor's white point to a target value other than the Hardware value, choose the gamma setting you want from the Adjusted menu.

Saving the monitor profile

Now that you have adjusted all settings for your monitor, you will save the ICC profile you have created. Applications that support color management will use this monitor profile to display color graphics.

1 In Adobe Gamma, rename the monitor profile by editing the text in the Description text box. (We named the profile My Monitor.) When you name the monitor here, it appears by default when you start Adobe Gamma.

2 Click OK (Windows) or click the Close button (Mac OS). In Mac OS, click Save when prompted.

3 In the Save As dialog box, type the filename again, and save the file in the Color folder (Windows) or the ColorSync Profiles folder (Mac OS).

Adobe Gamma makes the new monitor profile the default. You can use this profile in any application that supports ICC-compliant color management. In Mac OS, the profile information will be supplied to Apple ColorSync as the default monitor setting.

Review questions

1 What does the color management engine do?

2 What is calibration?

3 What is characterization?

4 What are the four main monitor settings you adjust when you run the Adobe Gamma utility, and why do you adjust them?

Review answers

1 The color management engine translates colors from the color space of one device to another device's color space by a process called color mapping.

2 Calibration is the process of setting a device to known color conditions.

3 Characterization, or profiling, is the process of creating an ICC profile that describes the unique color characteristics of a particular device. You should always calibrate a device before creating a profile for it.

4 Using Adobe Gamma, you adjust the brightness and contrast, phosphors (color characteristics), gamma (color contrast), and white point (extreme highlight) of the monitor. You adjust these settings to calibrate your monitor. Adobe Gamma uses those settings to create an ICC monitor profile that defines your monitor's color space for working on graphics.

Lesson 12

12 | Producing and Printing Consistent Color

The document's embedded color profile does not match the current RGB working space.

To produce consistent color, you define the color space in which to edit and display RGB images, and in which to edit, display, and print CMYK images. This helps ensure a close match between on-screen and printed colors.

In this lesson, you'll learn how to do the following:

• Define RGB, grayscale, and CMYK color spaces for displaying, editing, and printing images.

• Prepare an image for printing on a PostScript® CMYK printer.

• Proof an image for printing.

• Create a color separation, the process by which the colors in an RGB image are distributed to the four process ink colors: cyan, magenta, yellow, and black.

• Understand how images are prepared for printing on presses.

This lesson will take about 60 minutes to complete. The lesson is designed to be done in Adobe Photoshop.

If needed, remove the previous lesson folder from your hard drive, and copy the Lesson12 folder onto it. As you work on this lesson, you'll overwrite the start files. If you need to restore the start files, copy them from the *Adobe Photoshop Classroom in a Book* CD.

Note: *Windows users need to unlock the lesson files before using them. For information, see "Copying the Classroom in a Book files" on page 3.*

Reproducing colors

Colors on a monitor are displayed using combinations of red, green, and blue light (called RGB), while printed colors are typically created using a combination of four ink colors—cyan, magenta, yellow, and black (called CMYK). These four inks are called *process colors* because they are the standard inks used in the four-color printing process.

RGB image with red, green, and blue channels

CMYK image with cyan, magenta, yellow, and black channels

For color samples of channels in both RGB and CMYK images, see figures 12-1 and 12-2 in the color section.

Because the RGB and CMYK color models use very different methods to display colors, they each reproduce a different *gamut*, or range of colors. For example, because RGB uses light to produce color, its gamut includes neon colors, such as those you'd see in a neon sign. In contrast, printing inks excel at reproducing certain colors that can lie outside of the RGB gamut, such as some pastels and pure black. For an illustration of the RGB and CMYK gamuts and color models, see figures 12-3, 12-4, and 12-5 in the color section.

But not all RGB and CMYK gamuts are alike. Each model of monitor and printer is different, and so each displays a slightly different gamut. For example, one brand of monitor may produce slightly brighter blues than another. The *color space* for a device is defined by the gamut it can reproduce.

RGB model

A large percentage of the visible spectrum can be represented by mixing red, green, and blue (RGB) colored light in various proportions and intensities. Where the colors overlap, they create cyan, magenta, yellow, and white.

Because the RGB colors combine to create white, they are also called additive colors. *Adding all colors together creates white—that is, all light is transmitted back to the eye. Additive colors are used for lighting, video, and monitors. Your monitor, for example, creates color by emitting light through red, green, and blue phosphors.*

CMYK model

The CMYK model is based on the light-absorbing quality of ink printed on paper. As white light strikes translucent inks, part of the spectrum is absorbed and part is reflected back to your eyes.

In theory, pure cyan (C), magenta (M), and yellow (Y) pigments should combine to absorb all color and produce black. For this reason these colors are called subtractive colors. *Because all printing inks contain some impurities, these three inks actually produce a muddy brown and must be combined with black (K) ink to produce a true black. (K is used instead of B to avoid confusion with blue.) Combining these inks to reproduce color is called* four-color process printing.

–From Adobe Photoshop 6.0 online Help

An ICC profile is a description of a device's color space, such as the CMYK color space of a particular printer. In this lesson, you'll choose which RGB and CMYK ICC profiles to use. Once you specify the profiles, Photoshop can embed them into your image files. Photoshop (and any other application that can use ICC profiles) can then interpret the ICC profile in the image file to automatically manage color for that image. For general information about color management and about preparing your monitor, see Lesson 11, "Setting Up Your Monitor for Color Management".

For information on embedding ICC profiles, see Photoshop 6.0 online Help.

Getting started

Before beginning this lesson, restore the default application settings for Adobe Photoshop. See "Restoring default preferences" on page 4.

You also need to make sure you have calibrated your monitor as described in Lesson 11. If your monitor does not display colors accurately, the color adjustments you make to an image displayed on that monitor may be wrong.

Specifying color management settings

In the first part of this lesson, you'll learn how to set up a color-managed workflow. To help you with this, the Color Settings dialog box in Photoshop contains most of the color management controls you need. (This dialog box appears the first time you start Photoshop.)

For instance, Photoshop is set up for RGB as part of a Web/online workflow by default. However, if you're preparing artwork for print production, you would likely change the settings to be more appropriate for images that will be printed on paper rather than displayed on a screen.

You'll begin this lesson by starting Photoshop and creating customized color settings.

1 Start Adobe Photoshop.

If you used another application to modify and save the current color settings file, a dialog box appears, prompting you to synchronize the common color settings when you start Photoshop or reopen the Color Settings dialog box in it.

Synchronizing the color settings helps ensure that color is reproduced consistently between Adobe applications that use the Color Settings dialog box. You can also share custom color settings by saving and loading the settings file in the desired applications and providing the settings file to other users. For more information, see Photoshop 6.0 online Help.

2 Choose Edit > Color Settings to display the Color Settings dialog box.

The bottom of the dialog box contains information about the various color-management options in it, which you'll now review.

3 Move the mouse pointer over each part of the dialog box, including the names of areas (such as Working Spaces) and the options you can choose (such as the different menu options), returning the options to their defaults when you're done. As you move the mouse, view the information that appears at the bottom of the dialog box.

Now you'll choose a general set of options that will specify the individual options for you. In this case, you'll pick one designed for a print workflow, rather than an online workflow.

4 Select a prepress default from the Settings menu at the top of the dialog box (we used U.S. Prepress Defaults) and click OK.

Proofing an image

In this part of the lesson, you'll begin working with a typical file of the kind you might scan in from a printed original. You'll open it, convert its color profile, and set it up so that you can see online a close representation of what it will look like when printed. This will enable you to proof the printed image on your screen for printed output.

You'll begin by opening the file.

1 Choose File > Open, and open the file 12Start.tif from the Lessons/Lesson12 folder.

Because 12Start.tif contains a color profile that indicates the image was created in a different color space than the one you set up for Photoshop, the Embedded Profile Mismatch notice appears asking you to resolve this difference.

There are three options in the notice. Selecting Use the Embedded Profile changes the color settings from the ones you defined for Photoshop in the previous section to the ones represented by the profile in the image. Selecting Discard the Embedded Profile displays the document as though it had no profile and can result in inaccurate colors being displayed. Rather than choose either of these, you'll select another option instead.

2 Select Convert Document's Colors to the Working Space and click OK.

An RGB image of a scanned postcard is displayed.

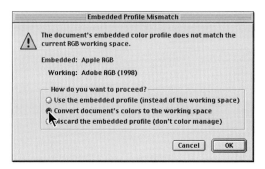

The Convert Document's Color to the Working Space option makes Photoshop compare the color space in 12Start.tif's embedded color profile with the color space you defined in the Color Settings dialog box. Photoshop then converts 12Start.tif's colors as necessary to display the image on-screen as accurately as possible.

Note: Depending on what you've specified in the Color Settings dialog box, if the image did not have a color profile already, the Missing Profile notice would have appeared. This notice lets you choose whether to leave the image without a profile (that is, without color management); apply the current color profile that you specified in the Color Settings dialog box; or assign a profile from a list of possible profiles. Applying the current color profile is generally a good choice.

Before soft-proofing—that is, proofing on-screen—or printing this image, you'll set up a proof profile. A proof profile (also called a *proof setup*) defines how the document is going to be printed, and adds those visual properties to the on-screen version for more accurate soft-proofing. Photoshop provides a variety of settings that can help you proof images for different uses, including print and display on the Web. For this lesson, you'll create a custom proof setup. You can then save the settings for use on other images that will be output the same way.

3 Choose View > Proof Setup > Custom.

4 Select Preview to preview the effects of each option as you choose them.

5 From the Profile menu in the Proof Setup dialog box, choose a profile that represents a final output source color profile, such as the printer you'll use to print the image. If you don't have a specific printer, the profile Working CMYK - U.S. Web Coated (SWOP) v2 is generally a good choice.

6 Make sure Deselect Preserve Color Numbers is not selected. Leaving this option off simulates how the image appears if colors are converted from the document space to their nearest equivalents in the proof profile space.

7 From the Intent menu, choose a rendering intent for the conversion (we chose Relative Colorimetric, a good choice for preserving color relationships without sacrificing color accuracy).

8 If it's available for the profile you chose, select Ink Black. Then choose Paper White.

Notice that the image appears to lose contrast. Ink Black simulates the dynamic range defined by an image's profile. Paper White simulates the specific shade of white for the print medium defined by an image's profile. That is, the whites shown in the image are now simulating the white of paper.

Normal image

Image with Ink Black and Paper White options

9 Click OK.

💡 *To turn the proof settings off and on, choose View > Proof Colors.*

Identifying out-of-gamut colors

Most scanned photographs contain RGB colors within the CMYK gamut, and changing the image to CMYK mode (which you'll do later in order to print the file) converts all the colors with relatively little substitution. Images that are created or altered digitally, however, often contain RGB colors that are outside the CMYK gamut—for example, neon-colored logos and lights.

Note: Out-of-gamut colors are identified by an exclamation point next to the color swatch in the Color palette, the Color Picker, and the Info palette.

Before you convert an image from RGB to CMYK, you can preview the CMYK color values while still in RGB mode.

1 Choose View > Gamut Warning to see out-of-gamut colors. Adobe Photoshop builds a color conversion table and displays a neutral gray where the colors are out-of-gamut.

Because the gray can be hard to spot in the image, you'll now convert it to a stronger gamut warning color.

2 Choose Edit > Preferences > Transparency & Gamut. Then click the Color sample at the bottom of the dialog box.

3 Choose a vivid color, such as pink, and click OK.

4 Click OK again to close the Transparency & Gamut dialog box. The gray is replaced by the new color you chose.

5 Choose View > Gamut Warning to turn off the preview of out-of-gamut colors.

Photoshop will automatically correct these out-of-gamut colors when you save the file in Photoshop EPS format later in this lesson. Photoshop EPS format changes the RGB image to CMYK, adjusting the RGB colors as needed to bring them into the CMYK color gamut.

Adjusting an image and printing a proof

The next step in preparing an image for output is to make any color and tonal adjustments to the image. In this part of the lesson, you'll add some tonal and color adjustments to correct an off-color scan of the original postcard.

So that you can compare the image before and after making corrections, you'll start by making a copy.

1 Choose Image > Duplicate and click OK to duplicate the image.

2 Align the images near each other.

Here you'll adjust the hue and saturation of the image. There are various ways to adjust color, including using the Levels and Curves commands. In this lesson, you'll use the Hue/Saturation command to adjust the artwork.

3 Select 12Start.tif (the original image) and choose Image > Adjust > Hue/Saturation.

4 Adjust the Hue until the colors, especially the fleshtones, look more natural. (We used +20.)

5 Adjust the Saturation until the intensity of the colors looks normal (we used −17), and click OK.

Now you're ready to specify how to print the image.

6 With 12Start.tif still selected, choose File > Print Options.

7 Select Show More Options. Then choose Color Management from the pop-up menu that appears.

8 In the Source Space area, select Proof to use the color profile that describes the way you intend to print the image, rather than the image's embedded color profile.

9 In the Print Space area, choose the profile for the color printer on which you plan to print the image for proofing. If your specific printer isn't listed, choose Working CMYK.

10 Click OK.

11 Choose File > Save to save your work.

12 Print a copy of the image to a color printer and compare it to the online version.

Saving the image as a separation

In this part of the image, you'll learn how to save the image as a separation, so that it can print out in separate cyan, magenta, yellow, and black plates.

1 With 12Start.tif still selected, choose File > Save As.

2 Choose Photoshop EPS from the Format menu.

Saving the file in Encapsulated PostScript (EPS) format changes the file from an RGB image to a CMYK image. This enables you to select the Use Proof Setup option to save the image as CMYK.

Note: *To switch the image and view the difference between the RGB and CMYK versions, you can choose Image > Mode > CMYK Color.*

3 Select Use Proof Setup.

A warning appears, indicating that some data won't be saved. As described earlier in the lesson, this is because some of the colors in the file will be shifted from the RGB gamut of the original file to the CMYK gamut of the Photoshop EPS file.

It is useful to tag an image so that you can preserve the color management settings. This helps maintain color consistency when, for example, you move the image to another application or system.

4 Select Embed Color Profile to save the image as a tagged file.

You can choose Embed Color Profile to save any untagged document with a color profile.

5 Name the file **12Start.eps** and click Save.

6 Click OK on the EPS Options dialog box that appears.

7 Choose File > Open, and open the 12Start.eps file, located in the Lessons/Lesson12 folder.

Notice that 12Start.eps is now a CMYK file. You are done using the TIF and copy versions of the file and can close them now.

8 Choose File > Save to save the changes before closing 12Start.tif and 12Start copy.tif.

Selecting print options

To select printing options, you make choices in the File Info and Page Setup dialog boxes and then choose Options from the Print dialog box. The next sections introduce you to some of the printing options.

For information on all the print options, see Photoshop 6.0 online Help.

Entering file information

Photoshop supports the information standard developed by the Newspaper Association of America and the International Press Telecommunications Council to identify trans-mitted text and images.

In Windows, you can add file information to files saved in Photoshop, TIFF, and JPEG formats. In Mac OS, you can add file information to files saved in any format.

1 Select the 12Start.eps image and choose File > File Info.

2 In the File Info dialog box, type a description of the file in the Caption text box.

Note: To print a caption when you print an image, choose File > Page Setup, and click the Caption option.

3 Enter your name in the Caption Writer text box.

4 Enter any special instructions you may have for printing the image in the Special Instructions text box.

5 For Section, choose Origin. In the origin section, enter information that you or others can refer to later, including an address, date, and other data.

6 Click the Today button to enter today's date in the date box.

Other types of file information you can record include the following:

• Keywords for use with image browser applications.

• Categories for use with the Associated Press regional registry.

• Credits for copyrighted images.

• Copyright & URL for online images.

7 Click OK to attach the information to the file.

For complete information about all the File Info sections, see Photoshop 6.0 online Help.

Specifying settings for different image types

The type of image you're printing and the type of output you or your prepress service provider require determine the selections you make in the Page Setup and Print dialog boxes.

The Page Setup dialog box lets you set up print labels, crop marks, calibration bars, registration marks, and negatives. You can also print emulsion-side down, and use interpolation (for PostScript Language Level 2 printers). The specific options that appear in your Page Setup dialog box depend on the printer you have selected.

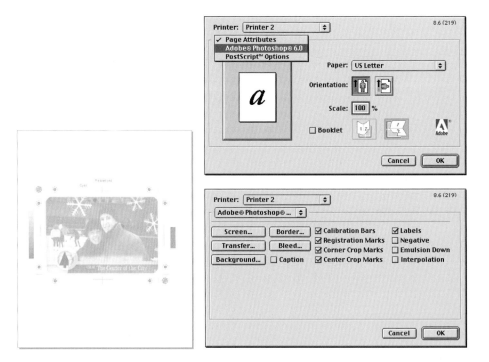

Printing

When you're ready to print your image, use the following guidelines for best results:

• Set the parameters for the halftone screen.

• Print a *color composite*, often called a color *comp*. A color composite is a single print that combines the red, green, and blue channels of an RGB image (or the cyan, magenta, yellow, and black channels of a CMYK image). This indicates what the final printed image will look like.

- Print separations to make sure the image separates correctly.

- Print to film.

Printing a halftone

To specify the halftone screen when you print an image, you use the Screen option in the Page Setup dialog box. The results of using a halftone screen appear only in the printed copy; you cannot see the halftone screen on-screen.

You use one halftone screen to print a grayscale image. You use four halftone screens (one for each process color) to print color separations. In this example, you'll be adjusting the screen frequency and dot shape to produce a halftone screen for a grayscale image.

The *screen frequency* controls the density of dots on the screen. Since the dots are arranged in lines on the screen, the common measurement for screen frequency is lines per inch (lpi). The higher the screen frequency, the finer the image produced (depending on the line screen capability of the printer). Magazines, for example, tend to use fine screens of 133 lpi and higher because they are usually printed on coated paper stock on high-quality presses. Newspapers, which are usually printed on lower-quality paper stock, tend to use lower screen frequencies, such as 85-lpi screens.

The *screen angle* used to create halftones of grayscale images is generally 45°. For best results with color separations, select the Auto option in the Halftone Screens dialog box (choose Page Setup > Screens > Halftone Screens). You can also specify an angle for each of the color screens. Setting the screens at different angles ensures that the dots placed by the four screens blend to look like continuous color and do not produce moiré patterns.

Diamond-shaped dots are most commonly used in halftone screens. In Adobe Photoshop, however, you can also choose round, elliptical, linear, square, and cross-shaped dots.

Note: *By default, an image will use the halftone screen settings of the output device or of the software from which you output the image, such as a page-layout program. You usually don't need to specify halftone screen settings in the following way unless you want to override the default settings.*

1 Select 12Start.eps to make it the active window.

2 Choose Image > Mode > Grayscale; then click OK to discard the color information.

3 Choose File > Page Setup, and choose Adobe® Photoshop® 6.0. (Depending on the printer driver you currently have selected, Photoshop 6 options may already be displayed. The specific options that appear in the dialog box depend on the printer you have selected.)

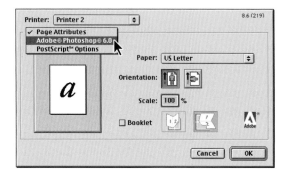

4 Click Screen.

5 In the Halftone Screen dialog box, deselect the Use Printer's Default Screen check box to enter another number.

6 Enter **133** in the Frequency text box, and make sure that the unit of measurement is set to Lines/Inch.

7 For Angle, enter a screen angle of 45°.

8 For Shape, choose Ellipse.

9 Click OK; then click OK again in the Page Setup dialog box.

10 To print the image, choose File > Print. (If you don't have a printer, skip this step.)

11 Look at the printed output to see the shape of the halftone dots (in this case, Ellipse).

12 Choose File > Close, and don't save your changes.

⌨ For more information about printing halftones, see Photoshop 6.0 online help.

Printing separations

By default, a CMYK image prints as a single document. To print the file as four separations, you need to select the Separations option in the Print dialog box. Otherwise the CMYK image prints as a single, composite image.

In this optional part of the lesson, you can print the file as separations.

1 Choose File > Open, and open the12Start.eps file in the Lessons/Lesson12 folder on your hard drive.

2 Choose File > Print.

3 Do one of the following:

• In Windows, for Space, choose Separations (at the bottom of the dialog box).

• In Mac OS, choose Adobe Photoshop 6.0. For Source Space, select Document. For Profile, choose Separations.

4 Click Print. (If you don't have a printer, skip this step.)

5 Choose File > Close, and don't save the changes.

This completes your introduction to producing color separations and printing using Adobe Photoshop.

⌨ For information about all color management and printing options, see Photoshop 6.0 online Help.

Review questions

1 What steps should you follow to reproduce color accurately?

2 What is a gamut?

3 What is an ICC profile?

4 What is a color separation? How does a CMYK image differ from an RGB image?

5 What steps should you follow when preparing an image for color separations?

Review answers

1 Calibrate your monitor, and then use the Color Settings dialog box to specify which color spaces to use. For example, you can specify which RGB color space to use for online images and which CMYK color space to use for images that will be printed. You can then proof the image, check for out-of-gamut colors, adjust colors as needed, and for printed images, create color separations.

2 The range of colors that can be reproduced by a color model or device. For example, the RGB and CMYK color models have different gamuts, as do any two RGB scanners.

3 An ICC profile is a description of a device's color space, such as the CMYK color space of a particular printer. Applications such as Photoshop can interpret ICC profiles in an image to maintain consistent color across different applications, platforms, and devices.

4 A color separation is created when an image is converted to CMYK mode. The colors in the CMYK image are separated in the four process color channels: cyan, magenta, yellow, and black. An RGB image has three color channels: red, green, and blue.

5 You prepare an image for print by following the steps for reproducing color accurately, and then converting the image from RGB mode to CMYK mode to build a color separation.

Lesson 13

13 | Preparing Images for Two-Color Printing

Not every commercially printed publication requires four-color reproduction. Printing in two colors using a grayscale image and spot color can be an effective and inexpensive alternative. In this lesson, you'll learn how to use Adobe Photoshop to prepare full-color images for two-color printing.

In this lesson, you'll learn how to do the following:

- Convert a color image to monochrome, and improve its overall quality.
- Adjust the tonal range of the image by assigning black and white points.
- Sharpen the image.
- Convert a color image to grayscale.
- Add spot color to selected areas of the image.

This lesson will take about 45 minutes to complete. The lesson is designed to be done in Adobe Photoshop. ImageReady does not support channels or spot color.

If needed, remove the previous lesson folder from your hard drive, and copy the Lesson13 folder onto it. As you work on this lesson, you'll overwrite the start files. If you need to restore the start files, copy them from the *Adobe Photoshop Classroom in a Book* CD.

Note: *Windows users need to unlock the lesson files before using them. For more information, see "Copying the Classroom in a Book files" on page 3.*

Printing in color

Color publications are expensive to print commercially because they require four passes through the press—one for each of the four process colors used to create the full-color effect. The colors in the publication must be separated into cyan, magenta, yellow, and black plates for the press, which also adds to the expense.

Printing images in two colors can be a much less costly yet effective approach for many projects, even if they begin with an image in full color. With Photoshop, you can convert color to grayscale without sacrificing image quality. You can also add a second spot color for accent, and Photoshop will create the two-color separations needed for the printing process.

Note: *Spot color is intended for images that will be printed to film during the printing process. The spot color techniques covered in this lesson are not appropriate for color images printed to desktop printers or for images designed for electronic distribution.*

Using channels and the Channels palette

Channels in Adobe Photoshop are used for storing information, and they play an important role in this lesson. *Color channels* store the color information for an image, and *alpha channels* store selections or masks that let you edit specific parts of an image. A third channel type, *spot color channels*, lets you specify color separations for printing an image with spot color inks. For more information about channels, see Lesson 5, "Masks and Channels."

In this lesson, you'll use all three types of channels. You'll learn to mix color channels to improve the quality of an image. You'll select areas of the image by loading a selection from an alpha channel. And you'll use a spot color channel to add a second color to the image.

Getting started

Before beginning this lesson, restore the default application settings for Adobe Photoshop. See "Restoring default preferences" on page 4.

You'll start the lesson by viewing the final Lesson file to see the duotone image that you will create.

1 Start Adobe Photoshop.

2 Choose File > Open, and open the 13End.psd file, located in the Lessons/Lesson13 folder.

3 When you have finished viewing the file, either leave the End file open on your desktop for reference or close it without saving changes.

Now you'll open the start file for the lesson.

4 Choose File > Open, and open the 13Start.psd file in the Lessons/Lesson13 folder on your hard drive.

5 If guides are showing, choose View > Show Extras or View > Show > Guides to hide guides.

Mixing color channels

Sometimes it's possible to improve the quality of an image by blending two or more color channels. For instance, one channel in an image may look particularly strong but would look even better if you could add some detail from another channel. In Photoshop, you can blend color channels with the Channel Mixer command in either RGB mode (for on-screen display) or CMYK mode (for printing). For more information on color modes, see Lesson 11, "Setting Up Your Monitor for Color Management."

In this lesson, you'll use the Channel Mixer command to improve the quality of an RGB image that you'll then convert to Grayscale mode. But first, you'll use the Channels palette to view the different channels in the image.

1 Choose Window > Show Channels, click the Channels tab, and drag the palette from the Layers and Paths palette group. Place the Channels palette on your screen where you can easily access it.

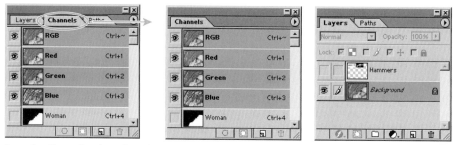

Drag the Channels palette from the Layers palette to make both palettes visible at the same time.

Because the image is in RGB mode, the Channels palette displays the image's red, green, and blue channels. Notice that all the color channels are currently visible, including the RGB channel, which is a composite of the separate red, green, and blue channels. To see the individual channels, you can use the palette's eye icons.

2 Click the eye icons to turn off all color channels in the Channels palette except the red channel. The colors in the document image change to shades of gray.

All channels off except red   *Red channel*

3 Drag the eye icon from the red channel to the green channel and then to the blue channel. Notice how the monochrome image in the document window changes with each channel. The green channel shows the best overall contrast and the best detail in the woman's face, while the blue channel shows good contrast in the framework behind the woman.

Green channel   *Blue channel*

4 In the Channels palette, click the eye icon column for the composite RGB channel to display all the color channels in the image.

All channels displayed   *RGB image*

Now you'll use the Channel Mixer command to improve the image in this lesson. Specifically, you'll divide the image into two areas, the woman and the framework, and mix different amounts of source channels in each selection.

Mixing the woman's image

First you'll select the woman's image by loading a premade selection.

1 In the Layers palette, make sure that the background is selected.

2 Choose Select > Load Selection. In the dialog box, select Woman from the Channel menu to load a selection that outlines the image of the woman. Click OK.

Now you'll mix the green and blue channels to improve the selection's contrast. You'll use green as the base channel because it has the best overall contrast for the image.

3 Choose Image > Adjust > Channel Mixer.

4 In the Channel Mixer dialog box, choose Green for the Output Channel. The Source Channel for Green changes to 100%.

5 Select Monochrome to change the image to shades of gray. This option gives you an idea of how the selection will look in Grayscale mode, so that you can more accurately adjust the selection's tonal range.

The resulting image is a little flat. You can bring out the contrast and improve the highlights by blending in some of the blue channel.

6 Drag the slider for the Blue Source Channel to 10%. Click OK.

Selection loaded   *Channel Mixer dialog box with 10% blue*

Mixing the framework's image

Next you'll select the framework, convert this part of the image to monochrome, and again mix channels to improve the contrast and detail.

1 Choose Select > Inverse to select the framework behind the woman.

2 Choose Image > Adjust > Channel Mixer.

3 In the Channel Mixer dialog box, choose Green for the Output Channel, and select Monochrome.

This time the resulting image is dark and lacks contrast. You can improve the image again by blending in some of the blue channel to increase the contrast.

4 Drag the slider for the Blue Source Channel to 26%. Click OK.

Inverse of selection   *Channel Mixer dialog box with 26% blue*

5 Choose Select > Deselect.

Both the woman and the framework now show better contrast and detail. But the image is still an RGB color image (one that contains only gray values). To convert the image to Grayscale mode, you will use the Grayscale command.

6 Choose Image > Mode > Grayscale. When prompted, select Don't Flatten to keep the image's two layers intact. (You'll use the second layer later in this lesson.) The image converts to Grayscale mode, and the color channels in the Channels palette are replaced by a single Gray channel.

7 Choose File > Save to save your work.

Assigning values to the black and white points

You can further improve the quality of the image by adjusting the black and white limits of its tonal range. In Lesson 6, "Photo Retouching," you learned to use the sliders on the Levels command histogram to adjust the range. In this lesson, you'll control the range more accurately by using the Levels command eyedropper to assign specific values to the darkest and lightest points.

1 Choose Image > Adjust > Levels.

2 In the Levels dialog box, double-click the white eyedropper tool (🖊) to open the color picker for the white point.

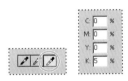

3 Enter **0, 0, 0,** and **5** in the CMYK text boxes, and click OK. These values generally produce the best results when printing the white points (highlights) of a grayscale image onto white paper.

4 Next double-click the black eyedropper tool (🖊) in the Levels dialog box to open the color picker for the black point.

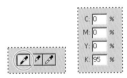

5 Enter **0, 0, 0,** and **95** in the CMYK text boxes, and click OK. These values generally produce the best results when printing the black points (shadows) of a grayscale image onto white paper.

Now that you've defined the values for the black and white points, you'll use the Levels command eyedropper to assign the values to the darkest and lightest areas in the image.

6 Make sure that the black eyedropper tool is selected, and position it in the darkest area of the framework behind the woman's elbow. Click to assign this area the values you set in step 5.

7 Next select the white eyedropper tool in the Levels dialog box, position the tool in the lightest area of the woman's collar, and click to assign this area the values you set in step 3.

Black eyedropper selecting darkest area behind elbow

White eyedropper selecting lightest area in collar

8 Click OK to close the dialog box and apply the changes.

Assigning the black and white points shifts the image's histogram to produce a more evenly distributed tonal range.

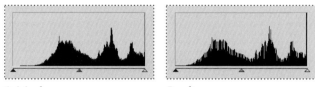

Original   *Result*

9 Choose File > Save.

Sharpening the image

By applying the Unsharp Mask filter to the image, you can create the illusion of a more focused image.

1 Choose Filter > Sharpen > Unsharp Mask. Make sure that the Preview option is selected so that you can view the effect before you apply it. To get a better view, you can place the pointer within the preview window and drag to see different parts of the image (we focused on the woman's face). You can also change the magnification of the preview image with the plus and minus buttons located below the window.

2 Drag the Amount slider until the image is as sharp as you want (we used 57%), and make sure that the Radius is set to 1 pixel.

3 Click OK to apply the Unsharp Mask filter to the image.

Setting up for spot color

Spot colors, also called *custom colors*, are premixed inks that are used instead of, or in addition to, the cyan, magenta, yellow, and black process color inks. Each spot color requires its own color separation or printing plate. Graphic designers use spot colors to specify colors that would be difficult or impossible to achieve by combining the four process inks.

You'll now add spot color to the image in this lesson by creating a spot color channel.

1 In the Channels palette, choose New Spot Channel from the palette menu.

2 In the New Spot Channel dialog box, click the color box, and select Custom in the color picker.

3 In the Custom Colors dialog box, type **124** for the Pantone® custom color 124. (Because there is no text box for the number, you must type it quickly.) Then click OK.

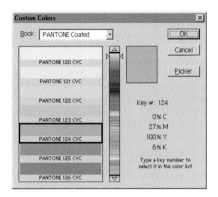

4 In the New Spot Channel dialog box, enter **100**% for Solidity. The solidity setting lets you simulate on-screen the ink solidity of the printed spot color. Inks range from transparent (0% solidity) to opaque (100% solidity). The Solidity option affects the on-screen preview only and has no effect on the printed output.

5 Click OK to create the spot color channel. A new spot color channel named PANTONE 124 CVC is added to the Channels palette.

6 Choose File > Save.

About spot colors

Note the following when working with spot colors:

• *For spot color graphics that have crisp edges and knock out the underlying image, consider creating the additional artwork in a page-layout or illustration application.*

• *To apply spot color as a tint throughout an image, convert the image to Duotone mode and apply the spot color to one of the duotone plates. You can use up to four spot colors, one per plate. (See "Printing color separations" in the Photoshop 6.0 User Guide, Chapter 14, "Printing."*

• *The names of the spot colors print on the separations.*

• *Spot colors are overprinted on top of the fully composited image. Each spot channel is overprinted in the order in which it appears in the Channels palette.*

• *You cannot move spot colors above a default channel in the Channels palette except in Multichannel mode.*

• *Spot colors can't be applied to individual layers.*

• *If you print an image that includes spot color channels to a composite printer, the spot colors print as extra pages.*

• *You can merge spot channels with color channels, splitting the spot color into its color channel components. Merging spot channels lets you print a single-page proof of your spot color image on a desktop printer.*

• *You can create new spot channels or convert an existing alpha channel to a spot channel.*

• *Like alpha channels, spot channels can be edited or deleted at any time.*

–From Adobe Photoshop 6.0 online Help

Adding spot color

You can add spot color to selected areas of an image in different ways with varying effects. For instance, you can apply spot color to part of a grayscale image so that the selection prints in the spot color rather than in the base ink. Because spot colors in Photoshop print over the top of a fully composited image, you may also need to remove the base color in an image when adding spot color to it. If you do not remove the base color, it may show through the semitransparent spot color ink used in the printing process.

You can also use spot color to add solid and screened blocks of color to an image. By screening the spot color, you can create the illusion of adding an extra, lighter color to the printed piece.

Removing a grayscale area and adding spot color

You'll begin your work in spot color by changing the framework behind the woman to the color. You must first select the framework, remove it from the grayscale image, and then add the selection to the spot color channel.

1 In the Channels palette, select the Gray channel.

2 Choose Select > Load Selection. In the dialog box, choose Woman from the Channel menu and select Invert. Click OK to load a selection of the framework behind the woman.

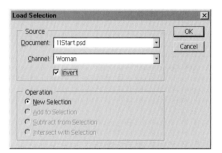

3 Choose Edit > Cut to cut the selection from the image. Make sure that black is set as the foreground color.

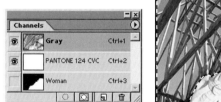 

Gray channel active   *Selection made in Gray channel*   *Selection cut from Gray channel*

4 In the Channels palette, select the PANTONE 124 CVC channel.

5 Choose Edit > Paste to paste the framework selection into the spot color channel. In the 13Start window, the framework reappears in the Pantone color.

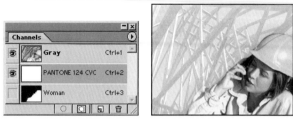

Selection pasted into spot color channel

6 Choose Select > Deselect.

7 Choose File > Save.

Removing spot color from a grayscale area

Now you'll remove some spot color where it overlaps the grayscale area of a second layer of the image.

1 In the Layers palette, click the eye icon column next to the Hammers layer to make it visible. (Click just the eye icon column. Do not select the layer.)

Notice that the spot color of the framework overlaps part of the Hammers layer. You'll remove this overlap by making a new selection and cutting it from the spot color channel.

2 Choose View > Show Extras. If guides do not appear over the image, choose View > Show > Guides.

3 Select the rectangular marquee tool ( ), and drag a selection from the top left edge of the image to the right horizontal guide and top vertical guide. Normal should be chosen for Style in the Marquee tool options bar.

4 Make sure that the spot channel in the Channels palette is still active, and press Delete to remove the rectangular selection from the channel. In the document window, the spot color disappears from the hammers image.

Making selection   *Selection cut from spot color channel*

5 Choose Select > Deselect.

6 Choose File > Save.

Adding solid and screened areas of spot color

Next you'll vary the effect of adding spot color by adding a solid block of the color and then a block of the color screened to 50%. The two areas will appear to be different colors even though you have used the same Pantone custom color on the same color separation.

First you'll make a selection for the solid block of color and fill the selection using a keyboard shortcut.

1 With the rectangular marquee tool still selected, make a selection in the upper right corner of the image bounded by the two guides.

2 Hold down Alt (Windows) or Option (Mac OS), and press Delete to fill the selection with the foreground color. Because you are in the PANTONE 124 CVC channel, the foreground color is PANTONE 124 and fills the square with solid color.

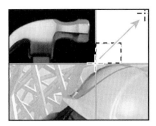

Making selection for spot color   *Selection filled with solid color*

Now you can add a lighter block of spot color to the image.

3 Make a rectangular selection directly below the left hammer and bounded by the guides.

4 In the Color palette, drag the color slider to 20% to set the value for the new block of color.

5 Hold down Alt/Option and press Delete to fill the selection with a 20% screen of PANTONE 124.

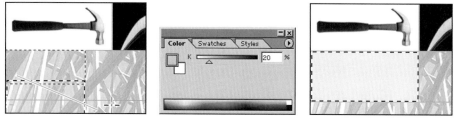

Making selection   *Color value set to 20%*   *Selection filled with 20% color*

6 Choose Select > Deselect.

7 Choose View > Show Extras or View > Show > Guides to hide guides.

8 Choose File > Save.

Adding spot color to text

Text in an image can also appear in spot color. There are different methods for creating this effect, but the most straightforward is to add the text directly to the spot color channel. Note that text in a spot channel behaves differently from text created on a type layer. Spot channel text is uneditable. Once you create the type, you cannot change its specifications, and once you deselect the type, you cannot reposition it.

Now you'll add text to the spot color channel and place the text in the light block of spot color.

1 In the Color palette, return the color slider to 100%.

2 Select the type tool (T), and click the image in the light block of color. A red mask appears over the artwork, and an insertion point for the text flashes.

3 In the Type tool options bar, choose a sans serif bold typeface from the Font menus, and enter **66** for the point size in the Size text box. We chose Helvetica*.

4 Type **work** in the image window.

5 Select the move tool (✛), and drag the text so that it is centered in the light block of color.

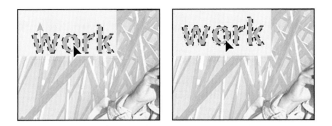

6 Choose Select > Deselect.

7 Choose File > Save.

You have finished preparing the image for two-color printing. To see how the color separations for the printed piece will look, try alternately hiding and displaying the two color channels in the Channels palette.

8 Click the eye icon for the Gray channel in the Channels palette. The Gray channel is hidden, and the image window changes to just the areas of the image that will print in the spot color.

9 Redisplay the Gray channel by clicking its eye icon column. Then hide the PANTONE 124 CVC channel by clicking its eye icon. Just the grayscale areas of the image appear in the image window.

10 Click the eye icon column for the PANTONE 124 CVC channel to display both channels.

  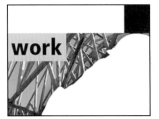

Final image   *Black channel*   *PANTONE 124 CVC channel*

If you have a printer available, you can also try printing the image. You'll find that it prints on two sheets of paper—one representing the color separation for the spot color and one representing the grayscale areas of the image.

For the Web: Creating two-color Web graphics

Two-color images are used in print to keep costs down and expand the tonal range of grayscale images. Even when printing costs aren't an issue, you can use two-color images for effect. Try this technique in ImageReady for creating effective two-color graphics for the Web that give maximum impact without increasing the file size. You can start with an image in Photoshop, or you can work exclusively in ImageReady.

1 For a duotone effect, start by creating a grayscale image in Photoshop or by desaturating an ImageReady image. To convert your color Photoshop image to grayscale, choose Image > Mode > Grayscale.

In ImageReady, it's not possible to create a grayscale image, but you can use the Image > Adjust > Desaturate command. ImageReady only supports RGB files. Even an image that may appear to be grayscale in ImageReady is actually an RGB file.

2 In Photoshop, to convert your grayscale image to RGB mode, choose Image > Mode > RGB Color.

3 Create a new layer and position it beneath the grayscale image in the Layers palette.

In Photoshop, if the grayscale image is the Background, you must convert the Background to a layer by double-clicking the Background in the Layers palette and naming it in the Make Layer window.

4 In the image, fill the new layer with the second color of choice.

5 Select the top layer of the image and choose Multiply from the Layers palette mode menu.

Multiply mode looks at the color information in each layer and multiplies the base color by the blend color. The result color is always a darker color. Multiplying any color with a color produces progressively darker colors.

6 Duplicate the top layer by dragging it to the New Layer button at the bottom of the Layers palette.

Grayscale image with color layer beneath

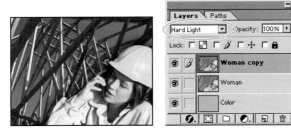
Duplicating the top layer

7 With the new layer selected, choose Hard Light from the Layers palette mode menu. This mode brings out the color underneath.

Hard Light filter applied

This technique works most effectively on the top layer of an image with the Hard Light mode applied. Hard Light mode multiplies or screens the colors, depending on the blend color. The effect is similar to shining a harsh spotlight on the image. If the blend color (light source) is lighter than 50% gray, the image is lightened, as if it were screened. This is useful for adding highlights to an image. If the blend color is darker than 50% gray, the image is darkened as if it were multiplied. This is useful for adding shadows to an image.

8 Select the middle layer. Choose Image > Adjust > Levels, and adjust the histogram using the sliders to let more or less color from the bottom layer show through.

9 If desired, decrease the opacity of the different layers and note the effect.

10 Save the file in the GIF file format for the Web, optimizing the file as needed.

As a variation, select the dodge or burn tool and adjust one detail or object in your image at a time.

Review questions

1 What are the three types of channels in Photoshop, and how are they used?

2 How can you improve the quality of a color image that has been converted to grayscale?

3 How do you assign specific values to the black and white points in an image?

4 How do you set up a spot color channel?

5 How do you add spot color to a specific area in a grayscale image?

6 How can you apply spot color to text?

Review answers

1 Channels in Photoshop are used for storing information. Color channels store the color information for an image; alpha channels store selections or masks for editing specific parts of an image; and spot color channels create color separations for printing an image with spot color inks.

2 You can use the Color Mixer command to blend color channels to bring out the contrast and detail in an image. You can extend the tonal range of the image by adjusting its black and white points. You can also sharpen the image by applying the Unsharp Mask filter.

3 You assign specific values with the Levels command black and white eyedropper tools.

4 You set up a spot color channel by choosing New Spot Channel from the pop-up menu on the Channels palette and by specifying a color from the Custom color picker in the New Spot Channel dialog box.

5 With the Gray channel active, you select the area, cut it from the Gray channel, and paste it into the spot color channel.

6 You can add the text to the spot color channel. However, text created in this way is not editable and cannot be repositioned once it is deselected.

Lesson 14

14 | Optimizing Images for the Web

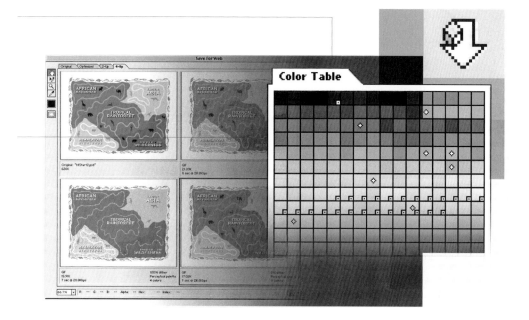

Adobe Photoshop and Adobe ImageReady let you optimize the display and file size of your images for effective Web publishing results. In general, the file size of an image should be small enough to allow reasonable download times from a Web server but large enough to represent desired colors and details in the image. ImageReady also lets you turn an image into an image map, creating Web-ready navigation elements from your art.

In this lesson, you'll learn how to do the following:

• Optimize JPEG and GIF files, and adjust the optimization settings to achieve the desired balance between file size and image quality.

• Adjust the amount of dithering applied to an image.

• Define a transparent background for an image.

• Create a hypertext image map.

• Batch-process files to automate the optimization process.

This lesson will take about 45 minutes to complete. The lesson is designed to be done in Adobe Photoshop and Adobe ImageReady.

If needed, remove the previous lesson folder from your hard drive, and copy the Lesson14 folder onto it. As you work on this lesson, you'll overwrite the start files. If you need to restore the start files, copy them from the *Adobe Photoshop Classroom in a Book* CD.

Note: *Windows users need to unlock the lesson files before using them. For information, see "Copying the Classroom in a Book files" on page 3.*

Optimizing images using Photoshop or ImageReady

Adobe Photoshop and Adobe ImageReady give you an effective range of controls for compressing the file size of an image while optimizing its on-screen display quality. Compression options vary according to the file format used to save the image.

• The JPEG format is designed to preserve the broad color range and subtle brightness variations of continuous-tone images (photographs, images with gradients). This format can represent images using millions of colors.

• The GIF format is effective at compressing solid-color images and images with areas of repetitive color (line art, logos, illustrations with type). This format uses a palette of 256 colors to represent the image, and supports background transparency.

• The PNG format is effective at compressing solid-color images and preserving sharp detail. The PNG-8 format uses a 256-color palette to represent an image; the PNG-24 format supports 24-bit color (millions of colors). However, many older browser applications do not support PNG files.

In this lesson, you'll learn how to use Photoshop and ImageReady to optimize and save images in JPEG and GIF format for distribution on the World Wide Web. You'll work with a set of images designed to be used on a fictitious Web site for a virtual zoo.

It is important to note that Photoshop and ImageReady share many of the same capabilities when it comes to image optimization. Both Photoshop (through its Save For Web dialog box) and ImageReady let you view and compare different optimized versions of a file, select from a wide array of file formats and settings, and work with color palettes and individual colors to preserve color integrity as much as possible while creating small, efficient files.

For the Web: Compressing images

Because file size is important in electronic publishing, file compression is an absolute must. Two graphics formats in HTML—GIF and JPEG—include automatic compression. The Adobe Acrobat® family of PDF creation products also automatically apply compression. Uncompressed files have redundant information. For example, with 35 white pixels in a row, an uncompressed file repeats the "white pixel" command 35 times. Each pixel contains one instruction.

The two basic types of compression are lossy *and* nonlossy *(or lossless). Lossy compression loses data to make the file smaller. For example, if there are 30 white pixels followed by one gray pixel, and four more white pixels, a lossy compression converts the gray pixel to white and writes a code saying "35 white pixels here." Nonlossy compression never eliminates detail but instead looks for more efficient ways to define the image (for example, "32 white pixels here, one gray pixel next, four white pixels after that").*

Common compression types are LZW, ZIP, CCITT, and JPEG. Your electronic publishing software will use whatever type is best for the image at hand. Only JPEG supports lossy compression, and lets you choose the level of compression so you can regulate fidelity versus image size. Low JPEG compression results in files that are almost identical to the original. Medium JPEG compression eliminates detail that may or may not be evident on-screen. High JPEG compression tends to blur images and degrade some of the detail, but on many images the result is still perfectly acceptable and worth the small file size you get in return.

Compression does not decrease resolution; it simply makes the file smaller. Compression lets you have high-resolution images that can be printed at decent quality without becoming too large. But compression is never a substitute for keeping resolution to the maximum needed. For online-only publications, keep the resolution of your images to 72 ppi. For dual-use publications, consider whether a higher image resolution of 150–200 ppi is necessary if you want the images to look good in print too.

–From the *Official Adobe Electronic Publishing Guide*, Chapter 3, "Preparing Text and Graphics."

Getting started

Before beginning this lesson, restore the default application settings for Adobe Photoshop and Adobe ImageReady. See "Restoring default preferences" on page 4.

Optimizing a JPEG image

In this lesson, you will optimize files in both JPEG and GIF format. You will use Photoshop to perform the JPEG compression and ImageReady for the GIF compression, although either application works equally well for either type of compression.

Optimizing and saving a file in Photoshop

With the Save For Web dialog box, Photoshop has all of the optimization capabilities of ImageReady built right in. You can compare two or more versions of a file as you work, allowing you to adjust optimization settings until you have the optimal combination of file size and image quality.

Now you'll open the start file and begin the lesson by optimizing an image containing photographs in JPEG format and compare the results of different palette and dither settings.

1 Start Adobe Photoshop.

If a notice appears asking whether you want to customize your color settings, click No.

2 Choose File > Open, and open the file 14Start1.psd from the Lessons/Lesson14 folder.

This file is a modified version of the zoo map you will be using later in this lesson. It has been enhanced with scanned photographs of animals, which have been further manipulated in Photoshop. Currently, the file size is far too large for use on a Web site. You'll compare different file compression formats to see which one gives you the most compression without sacrificing too much image quality.

3 Choose File > Save for Web.

4 In the Save For Web dialog box, click the 4-Up tab to view four versions of the image.

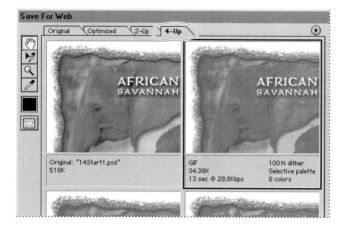

By looking at four different file settings, you can get a good idea of which settings will best suit your purpose. Using either the 4-Up or 2-Up view, you can adjust optimization settings for each version of the image to select the best combination of settings.

5 In the lower-left corner of the Save For Web dialog box, choose 200% or greater from the Zoom Level menu so that you can see the details of the image.

6 Move the pointer over the version of the image in the upper-right corner of the dialog box. (This is the active version, as indicated by a dark border.)

The pointer becomes a hand, indicating that you can drag to move the image.

7 Drag to reposition the image so that the Tropical Rainforest text (in the center of the image, over the green parrot) is visible.

8 Choose GIF 128 Dithered from the Settings menu.

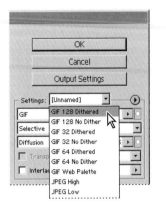

Notice the dark group of pixels around the text and on the parrot's beak. (You may need to scroll to the left to see the beak.)

You'll use the two bottom versions of the image to see how it would look as either a JPEG or a PNG file.

9 Click the lower-left version of the image to select it.

10 Choose JPEG Low from the Settings menu.

The image looks pretty choppy and the quality is unacceptably poor around the text. Now you will attempt to increase the image quality without an unacceptable increase in file size.

11 Choose JPEG High from the Settings menu.

JPEG Low   *JPEG High*

This improves image quality but also results in a significant increase in the size of the file.

12 Choose JPEG Medium from the Settings menu.

The image quality is now acceptable, while the file size is still significantly smaller than either the JPEG High version or the GIF version.

13 If you want, experiment with different values in the Quality text box (click the triangle to display the Quality slider) and compare image quality to file size. (We used a value of 45 for the Quality.)

14 Select the lower-right version of the image.

15 Choose PNG-8 128 Dithered from the Settings menu.

Although this results in a smaller file size than the original image, the image quality is not as good as the JPEG Medium version, which also has a smaller file size. Furthermore, many older browsers cannot read the PNG format. To make this image compatible with older browsers, you will use the JPEG Medium version.

16 Select the JPEG version in the lower-left corner of the dialog box.

17 Select the Progressive option, and click OK.

The Progressive option causes the image to download in several passes, each of which increases the image quality.

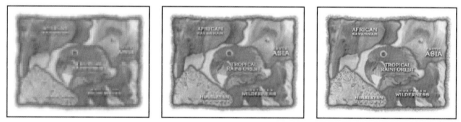

The Progressive JPEG download

18 In the Save Optimized As dialog box, use the default name **14Start1.jpg**, and save the file in the same folder as the original Photoshop file.

19 Close the original Photoshop file 14Start1.psd without saving changes.

Using channels to modify JPEG quality

When you use an alpha channel to optimize the range of quality in a JPEG image, white areas of the mask yield the highest quality and black areas of the mask yield the lowest quality. You can adjust the maximum and minimum level of quality in the Modify Quality Setting dialog box.

To use a channel to modify JPEG quality:

1. In the Optimize panel/palette, choose a JPEG setting from the Settings menu, or choose JPEG from the file format menu.

2. Click the channel button to the right of the Quality text box.

3. In the Modify Quality Setting dialog box, choose the desired channel from the Channel menu. In ImageReady, you can choose Save Selection to create a new alpha channel based on the current selection.

4. To preview the results of the weighted optimization, select the Preview option.

5. Define the quality range:

• To set the highest level of quality, drag the right (white) tab on the slider, enter a value in the Maximum text box, or use the arrows to change the current value.

• To set the lowest level of quality, drag the left (black) tab on the slider, enter a value in the Minimum text box, or use the arrows to change the current value.

6. Click OK.

–From Adobe Photoshop 6.0 online Help

Optimizing a GIF image

Now you'll optimize a flat-color image in GIF format in ImageReady and compare the results of different palette and dither settings.

Choosing optimization settings in ImageReady

The Optimize palette lets you specify the file format and compression settings for the optimized image. The optimized image is updated as you edit, letting you interactively preview the effects of different settings.

1 In Photoshop, click the Jump To ImageReady button () at the bottom of the toolbox to switch from Photoshop to ImageReady.

Note: *If you do not have enough memory to run both applications simultaneously, quit Photoshop and then start ImageReady.*

2 In ImageReady, choose File > Open, and open the file 14Start2.psd from the Lessons/Lesson14 folder.

This image was created in Adobe Illustrator, and then rasterized into Photoshop format. The image contains many areas of solid color.

3 Click the 2-Up tab in the document window.

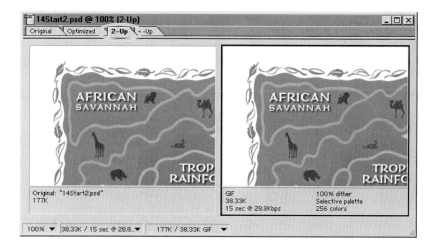

The optimized version of the image is selected on the right side of the window.

4 In the Optimize palette, choose GIF 128 No Dither from the Settings menu. (If the Optimize palette is not visible, choose Window > Show Optimize to display it.)

5 Choose Perceptual from the Color Reduction Algorithm menu.

• Perceptual gives priority to colors that appear most commonly in the image and are more sensitive to the human eye. This palette usually produces images with the greatest color integrity.

• Selective creates a color table similar to the Perceptual color table, but favors broad areas of color and the preservation of Web colors.

• Adaptive samples colors from the portion of the RGB spectrum that appears most commonly in the image. For example, an image containing predominantly blue hues produces a palette consisting mostly of shades of blue.

• Web consists of the 216 colors that are shared in common by the Windows and Mac OS system palettes. When displaying images, a browser application will use a 16-bit or 24-bit color table (thousands or millions of colors) if the system display is set to one of these modes; otherwise, the browser will use the default 8-bit system palette. Although few Web designers use 8-bit color systems, many Web users do.

• Custom preserves the current perceptual, selective, or adaptive color table as a fixed palette that does not update with changes to the image.

• Mac OS or Windows uses the computer system's default 8-bit (256-color) palette, which is based on a uniform sampling of RGB colors.

The status bar at the bottom of the image window displays the view magnification and other useful information about the original and optimized versions of the image. You can display two sets of file values simultaneously.

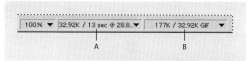

A. *File size and download time of optimized image*
B. *File sizes of original and optimized images*

6 In the status bar, choose Image Dimensions from the second pop-up menu.

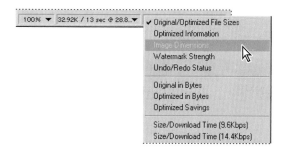

This option displays the size of the image in pixels, which is important when planning how to fit an image into a predesigned Web-page template.

7 If the Color Table palette is not displaying, choose Window > Show Color Table to display it.

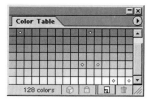

White diamonds indicate
Web-safe colors.

This palette shows the colors that make up the Perceptual palette for the zoo map image. The white diamonds on certain colors indicate that those colors are Web-safe. The total number of colors appears at the bottom of the palette. You can resize the palette or use the scroll bar to view all the colors. You can also change how the colors are arranged in the palette.

8 Choose Sort By Hue from the Color Table palette menu.

Now you'll observe how a different palette option affects the image.

9 In the Optimize palette, choose Web from the Color Reduction Algorithm menu.

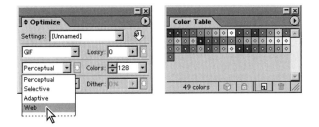

Notice that the color changes in the image and in the Color Table palette, which updates to reflect the Web palette.

10 Experiment with different optimize options and notice the effects on the image and on the Color Table palette.

For the Web: Viewing hexadecimal values for colors in the Info palette

In Photoshop, hexadecimal values for colors are displayed in the Info palette when you select Web Color mode for one or both color readouts. In ImageReady, hexadecimal values for colors are displayed automatically in the right side of the Info palette, next to RGB color values. The Photoshop and ImageReady Info palettes also display other information, depending on the tool being used.

To view hexadecimal color values in the Photoshop Info palette:

1. *Choose Window > Show Info or click the Info palette tab to view the palette.*

2. *Choose Palette Options from the Palette menu.*

3. *Under First Color Readout, Second Color Readout, or both, choose Web Color from the Mode menu.*

4. *Click OK.*

The Info palette displays the hexadecimal equivalents for the RGB values of the color beneath the pointer in the image.

–From Adobe Photoshop 6.0 online Help

Reducing the color palette

To compress the file size further, you can decrease the total number of colors included in the Color Table palette. A reduced range of colors will often preserve good image quality while dramatically reducing the file space required to store extra colors.

1 In the Optimize palette, choose the Perceptual option.

2 In the document window, change the magnification to 200% or more so that you can see details in the image.

3 Select the optimized version of the image, hold down the spacebar, and drag the image to place the Tropical Rainforest text at the bottom center of the display.

4 Note the current file size of the optimized image. Then, in the Optimize palette, enter **32** in the Colors text box.

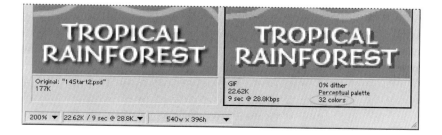

Notice that the new value represents a significant reduction in file size, but the quality of the image is lower. Specifically, the animal silhouettes have changed colors. For the African Savannah silhouettes, they have changed to a green-brown, and for the Northern Wilderness, the animal silhouettes have changed to the background color, making them invisible.

5 Hold down the spacebar and drag within the active panel to move the image so that you can see the Northern Wilderness area, or simply change the magnification back to **100%**.

6 Change the number of colors back to **128**.

This time, before reducing the color palette, you'll lock several colors to ensure that these colors do not drop from the reduced palette.

7 Select the eyedropper tool ( ), and click in the camel silhouette in the African Savannah area to sample its color.

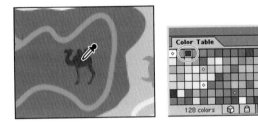

The dark brown color is selected in the Color Table palette.

8 Click the Lock button ( ) at the bottom of the Color Table palette to lock the selected color.

A small square appears in the lower-right corner of the color swatch, indicating that the color is locked. (To unlock a color, select the locked color swatch and click again on the Lock button.)

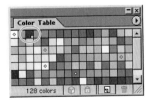

9 Repeat the procedure to lock the dark blue bear silhouette in the Northern Wilderness area. (You'll probably need to hold down the spacebar and move the image up to see the Northern Wilderness portion.)

10 In the Optimize palette, reduce the number of colors to **32**.

Notice that the locked colors remain in the palette after the reduction. However, new color-shift problems appear.

11 Change the number of colors back to **128**.

12 Continue to select and lock the colors of all the animal silhouettes and the three shades of blue in the Northern Wilderness area. However, don't lock the green background color of the Tropical Rainforest area for now. You will be working with that color later in this lesson.

Note that significant image degradation can occur when the palette is reduced below 32 colors. In fact, for all but the simplest images, even 32 colors may be too drastic a reduction. For the best file compression of a GIF image, try to use the fewest number of colors that will still display the quality you need.

For an illustration of the image set to different palette values, see figure 14-1 in the color section.

13 When you have finished experimenting, set the colors to **32** in the Optimize palette and choose File > Save to save the file.

Controlling dither

You may have noticed that certain areas of the image appear mottled or spotty when optimized with different color palettes and numbers of colors. This spotty appearance results from *dithering*, the technique used to simulate the appearance of colors that are not included in the color palette. For example, a blue color and a yellow color may dither in a mosaic pattern to produce the illusion of a green color that does not appear in the color palette. You can select from three predefined dither patterns.

Note: To fine-tune and improve the appearance of dithered colors, you can create your own dither patterns using the Dither Box filter.

⸬ For information on creating custom dither patterns, see "Creating and Applying Custom Dither Patterns" and "Optimizing Images for the Web" in Adobe Photoshop 6.0 online Help.

When optimizing images, keep in mind the two kinds of dithering that can occur:

• *Application dither* occurs when ImageReady or Photoshop attempts to simulate colors that appear in the original image but not in the optimized color palette you specify. You can control the amount of application dither by dragging the Dither slider in the Optimize palette.

• *Browser dither* occurs when a Web browser using an 8-bit (256-color) display simulates colors that appear in the optimized image's color palette but not in the system palette used by the browser. Browser dither can occur in addition to application dither. You can control the amount of browser dither by shifting selected colors to Web-safe colors in the Color Table palette.

In ImageReady, you can view application dither directly in an optimized image. You can also preview the additional browser dither that will appear in the final image when viewed in a browser using an 8-bit display.

Controlling application dither

The Dither slider lets you control the range of colors that ImageReady simulates by dithering. Dithering creates the appearance of more colors and detail, but it can also increase the file size of the image. For optimal compression, use the lowest percentage of application dither that provides the color detail you require.

1 Open the file 14Start2.psd file if it's not already open.

2 Make sure that the optimized version of the image is selected, and that the Optimize palette is set to GIF format, Perceptual, and 32 colors.

3 In the Optimize palette, change the dithering algorithm from No Dither to Diffusion.

4 Enter **100%** in the Dither text box.

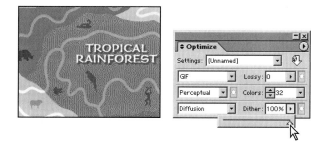

Using a combination of different colors, ImageReady tries to simulate the colors and tonalities that appear in the original image but not in the 32-color palette. Notice the speckled pattern that replaces the blocky drop shadows below the text. While not ideal, this pattern is a significant improvement and is acceptable. The dithered green background color for the Tropical Rainforest, however, is not acceptable.

5 Drag the Dither slider to **50%**. Experiment with different dither amounts.

ImageReady minimizes the amount of dither in the image, but no percentage of dither will preserve the drop shadows without ruining the green background.

For an illustration of the effects of different dither percentages on an image, see figure 14-2 in the color section.

6 Set the dither back to **100%**.

7 Change the number of colors back to **128**, lock the Tropical Rainforest green background color, and then switch back to **32** colors.

8 In the document window, change the magnification back to **100%**.

The image is now acceptable.

Previewing and minimizing browser dither

As you learned earlier, images that include non-Web-safe colors undergo a process of dithering when displayed in a Web browser using an 8-bit display because the browser simulates colors that do not occur in the 8-bit system palette. ImageReady lets you preview how an optimized image will look when dithered in a Web browser.

To protect a color from browser dither, you can Web-shift the color, converting the color to its nearest equivalent in the Web palette. Because the Web palette includes the subset of colors that appear in both the Windows and the Mac OS system palettes, Web palette colors will display without dithering in browsers on either platform.

1 With the optimized 14Start2.psd image open, choose View > Preview > Browser Dither. A check mark appears in the menu next to the command when it is active, letting you preview the effects of browser dithering on the optimized image.

Notice that browser dither occurs in the brown African Savannah background. If you don't see the dithering right away, turn off the browser dither preview and then turn it back on to observe the effects. You can quickly toggle the browser dither preview off and on by pressing Ctrl+Shift+Y (Windows) or Command+Shift+Y (Mac OS).

Next you'll Web-shift one of the colors to reduce the amount of browser dither in the image.

2 Using the eyedropper tool ( ), click in the dithered brown area. The sampled color appears selected in the Color Table palette.

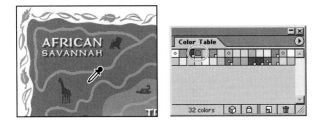

3 Click the Web-shift button ( ) at the bottom of the Color Table palette.

The swatch adjusts its position in the palette and a small diamond appears in the center of the swatch, indicating that it has been shifted to its nearest Web-palette equivalent.

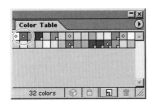

By Web-shifting the brown background, you change its color to one that can be displayed without dithering by a Web browser on a 256-color system.

4 Choose File > Save.

Specifying background transparency

Background transparency lets you place a nonrectangular graphic object against the background of a Web page; the areas outside the borders of the object are defined as transparent, letting the Web page background color show through. You can specify background transparency for GIF and PNG images.

> **For the Web: Making transparent and matted images**
>
> *Transparency makes it possible to place a nonrectangular graphic object against the background of a Web page. Background transparency, supported by GIF and PNG formats, preserves transparent pixels in the image. These pixels blend with the Web page background in a browser.*
>
> *Background matting, supported by GIF, PNG, and JPEG formats, simulates transparency by filling or blending transparent pixels with a matte color that you choose to match the Web page background on which the image will be placed. Background matting works only if the Web page background will be a solid color, and if you know what that color will be.*
>
> *The original image must contain transparent pixels in order for you to create background transparency or background matting in the optimized image. You can create transparency when you create a new layer.*
>
> –From Adobe Photoshop 6.0 online Help

Creating transparency

An image must contain transparent pixels before you can create background transparency. In this part of the lesson, you'll use the magic eraser tool to quickly convert the background color of the zoo map to transparent pixels.

1 Select the Original tab at the top of the document window.

2 Choose Fit on Screen from the Zoom Level menu in the lower-left corner of the document window.

Before you can use the GIF file format's ability to preserve transparency, you must create some transparency in your image. To do this, you'll first convert the image background to a layer and then you'll remove the white background pixels using the magic eraser tool.

3 In the Layers palette, double-click the Background to open the Layer Options dialog box. Use the default settings, including the name Layer 0, and click OK.

The magic eraser tool erases all pixels of a particular color with a single click. You'll use this tool to erase all of the white pixels in the layer. However, you only want to erase the white pixels outside of the zoo map (not the white of the lettering), so you will first create a selection that excludes the interior portion of the image.

4 Select the marquee tool (⬚).

5 Draw a rectangular selection marquee around the five regions of the zoo map, as shown.

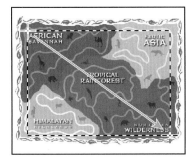

6 Choose Select > Inverse to select everything outside of the rectangular selection marquee.

7 Select the magic eraser tool (✎) hidden under the eraser tool (✐).

8 In the tool options bar, deselect the Contiguous option so that all white pixels in the selection will be erased, including each isolated white section within the leaves.

9 Click the white background outside of the zoo map.

Now you will ensure that the transparent areas in the image are included as transparent pixels in the optimized GIF file.

10 In the Optimize palette, choose Show Options from the palette menu.

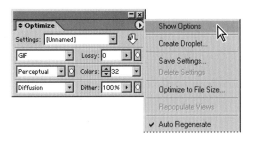

11 Make sure the Transparency option is selected in the palette (a check mark must appear in the box).

Selecting Transparency converts areas in the original image with less than 50% opacity to background transparency in the optimized image.

12 Choose Select > Deselect.

13 Choose File > Save.

Creating background matting in GIF and PNG images

When you know the Web page background color on which an image will be displayed, you can use the matting feature to fill or blend transparent pixels with a matte color that matches the Web page background. The Web page background must be a solid color, not a pattern.

The results of matting GIF and PNG-8 images depend on the Transparency option. If you select Transparency, only the partially transparent pixels, such as those at the edge of an anti-aliased image, are matted. When the image is placed on a Web page, the Web background shows through the transparent pixels, and the edges of the image blend with the background. This feature prevents the halo effect that results when an anti-aliased image is placed on a background color that differs from the image's original background. This feature also prevents the jagged edges that result with GIF hard-edged transparency.

If you deselect Transparency, fully transparent pixels are filled with the matte color, and partially transparent pixels are blended with the matte color.

–From Adobe Photoshop 6.0 online Help

To view the transparency you've just defined, you'll use ImageReady to preview the GIF image in a Web browser. Because ImageReady displays the image on a Web page with a white background, you'll change the matte color of the image so you can see the transparency you created.

14 Click the Matte text box in the Optimize palette to open the Color Picker dialog box. Select a color other than white, and click OK.

15 Choose File > Preview In, and choose the desired Web browser from the submenu.

Note: *To use the Preview In command, you must have a Web browser installed on your system.*

If it is not already open, the browser first starts and then displays the optimized image in the upper-left corner of the browser window. In addition, the browser displays the pixel dimensions, file size, file format, and optimization settings for the image, along with the HTML code used to create the preview.

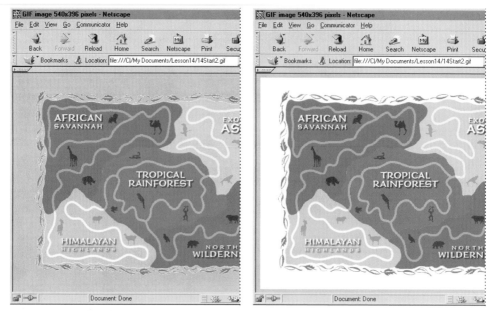

Transparency option selected   Transparency option deselected

16 Quit your browser when you're done previewing the image.

Trimming extra background areas

Although the background of the zoo map image now contains transparent pixels that do not display, these pixels still take up file space, adding to the size of the image. You can trim away unneeded background areas to improve the layout of the image and optimize the file size.

1 In ImageReady, choose Image > Trim.

The Trim command lets you crop your image, according to the transparency or pixel color of the extra border area.

2 In the Trim dialog box, select Transparent Pixels, and click OK.

ImageReady trims the extra transparent areas from the image.

3 Choose File > Save Optimized As.

4 In the Save Optimized As dialog box, use the default name (**14Start2.gif**), and click Save.

5 In the Replace Files dialog box, click Replace.

6 Choose File > Close.

You will be prompted to save the 14Start2.psd file before closing. Since you are finished with this file for the lesson, there is no need to save the last changes.

Creating an image map

An *image map* is an image that contains multiple hypertext links to other files on the Web. Different areas, or *hotspots*, of the image map link to different files. Adobe ImageReady creates client-side image maps and server-side image maps.

Note: For information about slicing an image into multiple image files and linking each slice to another Web page, see Lesson 15, "Creating Web Graphics Using Slices and Rollovers."

Creating and viewing image maps (ImageReady)

Image maps enable you to link an area of an image to a URL. You can set up multiple linked areas—called image map areas—in an image, with links to text files; other images; audio, video, or multimedia files; other pages in the Web site; or other Web sites. You can also create rollover effects in image map areas.

The main difference between using image maps and using slices to create links is in how the source image is exported as a Web page. Using image maps keeps the exported image intact as a single file, while using slices causes the image to be exported as a separate file. Another difference between image maps and slices is that image maps enable you to link circular, polygonal, or rectangular areas in an image, while slices enable you to link only rectangular areas. If you need to link only rectangular areas, using slices may be preferable to using an image map.

Note: To avoid unexpected results, do not create image map areas in slices that contain URL links— either the image map links or the slice links may be ignored in some browsers.

–From Adobe Photoshop 6.0 online Help

In this part of the lesson, you'll create an image map in an existing image. You define hotspots using layers or one of the image map tools. You'll use a version of the zoo map that has each geographic region on its own layer and convert each layer to an image map hotspot. By using layers to define the hotspots, you have more control over the shapes of the areas than you do with the rectangle, circle, or polygon image map tools.

1 In ImageReady, choose File > Open, and open the file 14Start3.psd from the Lessons/Lesson14 folder.

Although this image looks similar to the previous zoo map, it is actually composed of several different layers. You'll make this map image into a graphical table of contents linking to different areas of the zoo's Web site.

2 In the Optimize palette, choose GIF 64 Dithered from the Settings menu.

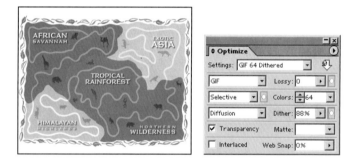

3 If the Layers palette is not already showing, choose Window > Show Layers.

Notice that the map pieces representing different sections of the zoo reside on separate layers.

4 In the Layers palette, select the African Savannah layer.

5 Choose Layer > New Layer Based Image Map Area.

6 Choose Window > Show Image Map to display the Image Map palette.

7 In the Image Map palette, choose Polygon from the Shape menu, and enter **90** in the Quality text box.

The Shape option determines the boundary of the hotspot area. The Quality value determines how closely the boundary line follows the shape of the area.

The URL option lets you specify the target file for the hotspot link. You can link to another file in your Web site, or to a different location on the Web. For the purposes of this lesson, you'll link your hotspots to fictitious URLs for the zoo.

8 Type **http://www.adobe.com/african_savannah.html** in the URL text box, and press Enter.

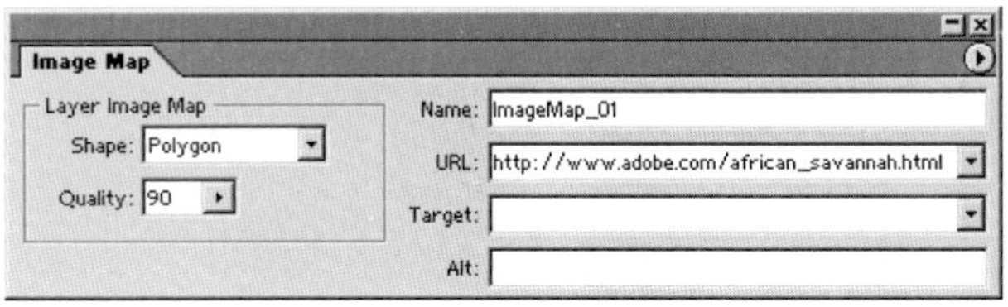

The URL you entered appears below the African Savannah layer name in the Layers palette.

9 Repeat steps 4 through 8 to create hotspots for the Exotic Asia, Tropical Rainforest, Himalayan Highlands, and Northern Wilderness layers. Use the same settings, but change the URL so that the last word matches the name of the layer you are working with.

10 Choose File > Save.

Previewing and adjusting the cross-platform gamma range

Now you'll check to see if the brightness of your image is compatible across monitors on different platforms. Windows systems generally display a darker midtone brightness, or *gamma*, than do Mac OS systems. Be sure to preview and, if necessary, adjust the cross-platform brightness of your image before publishing it on the Web.

Note: *Before starting this part of the lesson, be sure to calibrate your monitor so that it displays color accurately. For information, see Lesson 11, "Setting Up Your Monitor for Color Management."*

1 In the toolbox, click the Toggle Image Maps Visibility button (🖳) to hide the polygon boundary lines of the image map areas.

2 Choose View > Preview > Standard Macintosh® Color or View > Preview > Standard Windows Color to preview the image as it will appear on the designated platform.

An image created on a Windows system will appear lighter on a Mac OS system. An image created on a Mac OS system will appear darker on a Windows system.

3 Choose Image > Adjust > Gamma.

The Gamma dialog box appears, letting you automatically correct the image's gamma for cross-platform viewing.

Gamma	
Gamma: [1]	OK
darker lighter	Cancel
Windows to Macintosh	☑ Preview
Macintosh to Windows	

4 Click the Windows to Macintosh button if you are working on the Windows platform and want to preview how the image would appear on the Mac OS platform. If you are working on the Mac OS platform, click the Macintosh to Windows button to preview the change from Mac OS to Windows. Then, click OK.

5 Choose File > Save Optimized As.

6 In the Save Optimized As dialog box, choose Images Only from the Format menu, use the default name **14Start3.gif**, and click Save.

Now you'll preview your image map in a Web browser.

7 Choose File > Preview In, and choose a browser application from the submenu.

8 In the browser window, move the pointer over the different zoo regions, and notice that these elements contain hypertext links. If you had a modem and an Internet connection and if these were authentic URLs, you could click the hotspots to jump to the specified page of the zoo site.

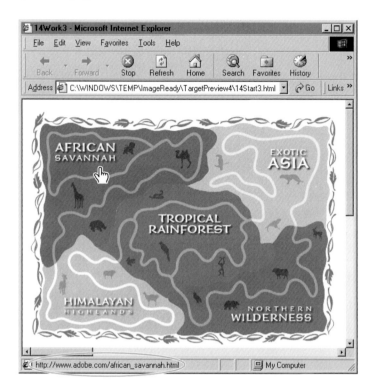

9 Quit your browser to return to Adobe ImageReady.

Creating the HTML file

When you save an image map in an HTML file, the basic HTML tags needed to display the image on a Web page are generated automatically. The easiest way to do this is simply to choose the HTML and Images Format option when you save the optimized image.

Once you have created the HTML file, it can be easily updated to reflect any changes, such as new or modified image map areas or URLs.

1 In ImageReady, choose File > Save Optimized As.

Note: In Photoshop, you create an HTML file in the Save Optimized As dialog box that appears after optimizing the image and clicking OK in the Save For Web dialog box.

2 In the Save Optimized As dialog box, choose HTML and Images from the Format menu (Mac OS) or from the Save As Type menu (Windows), use the default name **14Start3.html**, and click Save.

When you select the HTML and Images option, an HTML page containing the image is saved automatically, in addition to the graphic file. This HTML file will have the same name as the image, but with the .html extension.

3 In the Replace Files dialog box, click Replace.

Now you'll use ImageReady to change one of the URL links and update the HTML file.

4 In the toolbox, select the Image Map Select tool (⬚) hidden under the Rectangle Image Map tool (⬚).

5 Click in the document window to select the African Savannah image map area.

6 In the Image Map palette, change the URL to **http://www.adobe.com/newafrica.html**.

7 Choose File > Update HTML.

8 In the Update HTML dialog box, select the 14Start3.html file, and click Open.

9 In the Replace Files dialog box, click Replace.

10 Click OK to dismiss the update message.

11 Choose File > Close to close the image. Don't save changes, if prompted.

If desired, you can use your Web browser to open and view 14Start3.html. You can also open the file in a text editor, word-processing, or HTML editing program to make your own revisions to the HTML code

---

For the Web: HTML File Naming Conventions

Use the UNIX® file-naming convention, because many network programs truncate (shorten) long filenames. This convention requires a filename of up to eight characters, followed by an extension. Use the .html or .htm extension.

Do not use special characters such as question marks (?) or asterisks (*), or spaces between the letters in your filename—some browsers may not recognize the pathname. If you must use special characters or spaces in the filename, check with an HTML editing guide for the correct code to use. For example, to create spaces between letters you will need to replace the space with "%20".

Batch-processing file optimization

ImageReady supports batch-processing through the use of *droplets*—icons that contain actions for ImageReady to perform on one or more files. Droplets are easy to create and use. To create a droplet, you drag the droplet icon out of the Optimization palette and onto the desktop. To use a droplet, you drag a file or folder over the droplet icon on the desktop.

1 In ImageReady, choose File > Open, and open any file in the Lessons/Lesson14/Photos folder.

2 Experiment with different file formats and other settings in the Optimize palette as desired until you are satisfied with the result.

3 Drag the droplet icon (🖱) out of the Optimize palette and drop it anywhere on your desktop. (If you are using Windows, you may have to resize the ImageReady window to make your desktop visible.)

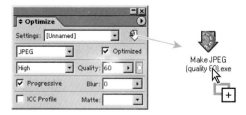

4 Close the file (without saving it), and quit ImageReady.

5 From your desktop, drag the Photos folder from the Lessons/Lesson14 folder and drop it onto the droplet to batch-process the photographic images within the folder.

ImageReady optimizes each file and adds the Web image to the Photos folder.

6 Open any of the Web image files in the Photos folder.

Notice that they have all been optimized according to the settings specified when the droplet was created.

7 Quit ImageReady when you are done.

Review questions

1 For image optimization, what are the advantages of using ImageReady rather than Photoshop?

2 What is a color table?

3 When does browser dither occur, and how can you minimize the amount of browser dither in an image?

4 What is the purpose of assigning matte color to a GIF image?

5 Summarize the procedure for creating an image map.

Review answers

1 There aren't really any advantages to using one application over the other for optimization. Both Photoshop and ImageReady can perform a wide range of image optimization tasks. ImageReady has many Web-specific features that you won't find in Photoshop, but image optimization is not one of them.

2 A color table is a table that contains the colors used in an 8-bit image. You can select a color table for GIF and PNG-8 images, and add, delete, and modify colors in the color table.

3 Browser dither occurs when a Web browser simulates colors that appear in the image's color palette but not in the browser's display system. To protect a color from browser dither, you can select the color in the Color Table palette, and then click the Web-shift button at the bottom of the palette to shift the color to its closest equivalent in the Web palette.

4 By specifying a matte color, you can blend partially transparent pixels in an image with the background color of your Web page. Matting lets you create GIF images with feathered or anti-aliased edges that blend smoothly into the background color of your Web page.

5 To create an image map, you define hotspot areas of the image using the image map tools or by selecting layers and choosing Layer > New Layer Based Image Map Area. Then you use the Image Map palette to define the shape of the hotspot and link each hotspot to a URL address.

Lesson 15

15 | Creating Web Graphics Using Slices and Rollovers

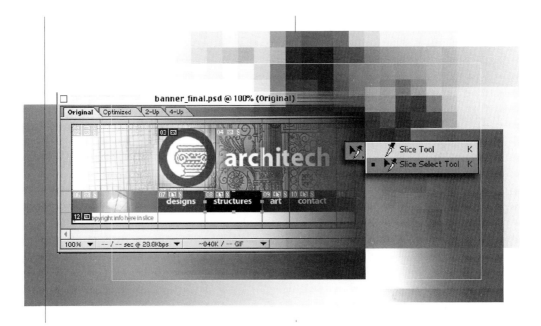

Adobe Photoshop and Adobe ImageReady let you divide your image into individual slices so you can optimize each slice in different Web image formats. Slices can be animated, linked to URL addresses, and used for rollover buttons.

In this lesson, you'll learn how to do the following:

• Slice an image using four different methods.

• Optimize each image slice using various settings and file formats.

• Create "no image" slices to contain text and HTML.

• Create rollover buttons in a banner.

• Apply a warped text style to the image that appears only when the rollover button is in its Over state.

• Show or hide certain layers in the image when a rollover button is in its Over state or Down state.

• Generate an HTML page that contains the sliced image in a table.

This lesson will take about 70 minutes to complete. The lesson is designed to be done in Adobe Photoshop and Adobe ImageReady.

If needed, remove the previous lesson folder from your hard drive, and copy the Lesson15 folder onto it. As you work on this lesson, you'll overwrite the start files. If you need to restore the start files, copy them from the *Adobe Photoshop Classroom in a Book* CD.

Note: *Windows users need to unlock the lesson files before using them. For information, see "Copying the Classroom in a Book files" on page 3.*

Getting started

Before beginning this lesson, restore the default application settings for Adobe Photoshop and Adobe ImageReady. See "Restoring default preferences" on page 4.

You'll start the lesson by viewing an example of the finished HTML banner that you'll create.

1 Start a Web browser, and open the end file Banner.html from the Lessons/Lesson15/ 15End/Architech Pages folder.

The file contains an HTML table that links to several Web images all created from Photoshop and ImageReady slices. Each of the words "designs," "structures," "art," and "contact" is a rollover button with different Over and Down states—when you move or "roll" the mouse pointer over a button, the image changes; when you hold the mouse down on the button, the image changes again.

2 Move the mouse pointer over the buttons in the banner.

Notice the different images that appear to the left of the buttons and the change to the word "Architech" when a button is in its Over state.

You'll create secondary rollovers like these that change the appearance of the image when the mouse pointer is over a button and when the mouse is held down on a button. You'll also add URL links to each button that go to another page when you click the button.

3 Hold the mouse pointer down on the Designs, Structures, or Art button, and notice how the word "Architech" changes.

4 Click a button to go to another page.

5 When you're done viewing the end file, close it and quit the browser.

For an illustration of the finished artwork for this lesson, see the gallery at the beginning of the color section.

About slices

Slices are areas in an image that you define based on layers, guides, or precise selections in the image, or by using the slice tool. When you define slices in an image, Photoshop or ImageReady creates an HTML table or cascading style sheet to contain and align the slices. If you want, you can generate an HTML file that contains the sliced image along with the table or cascading style sheet.

You can optimize slices as individual Web images, add HTML and text to slices, and link slices to URL addresses. In ImageReady, you can animate slices and create rollovers with them.

In this lesson, you'll explore different ways to slice an image in Photoshop and ImageReady, optimize the slices, and create four rollover buttons for the banner.

To learn how to animate slices, see Lesson 17, "Creating Animated Images for the Web."

Slicing the image in Photoshop

Adobe Photoshop lets you define slices using the slice tool or by converting layers into slices. You'll begin the lesson by slicing parts of a banner image for buttons using the slice tool in Photoshop. You'll name the slices and link them to URL addresses, and then optimize the slices. Then you'll continue slicing the banner image in ImageReady and create rollovers for the button slices.

About designing Web pages with Photoshop and ImageReady

When designing Web pages using Adobe Photoshop and Adobe ImageReady, keep in mind the tools and features that are available in each application.

• *Photoshop provides tools for creating and manipulating static images for use on the Web. You can divide an image into slices, add links and HTML text, optimize the slices, and save the image as a Web page.*

• *ImageReady provides many of the same image-editing tools as Photoshop. In addition, it includes tools and palettes for advanced Web processing and creating dynamic Web images like animations and rollovers.*

–From Adobe Photoshop 6.0 online Help

Using the slice tool to create slices

You use the slice tool to define rectangular areas in your image as slices. Slices created by the slice tool are called *user-slices*. When you define a user-slice in an image, Photoshop or ImageReady creates *auto-slices* for all the undefined areas surrounding the user-slice. Using the slice tool, you'll define four user-slices for buttons in the banner.

1 Start Adobe Photoshop.

If a notice appears asking whether you want to customize your color settings, click No.

2 Choose File > Open, and open the file 15start.psd from the Lessons/Lesson15/15Start folder.

If a notice appears asking whether you want to update the text layers for vector based output, click Update.

Horizontal and vertical guidelines were added to the lesson file to help you as you define sliced areas in the banner.

3 If you don't see the guidelines, choose View > Show > Guides.

You'll slice text areas in the image to create four buttons.

4 Choose View > Show > Slices.

A number (01) and a slice icon (▣) appear in the upper-left corner of the image indicating that currently the entire image is a slice.

5 Select the slice tool ( ).

Notice that slice style, size, and line color options appear in the tool options bar when you select the slice tool.

To help you as you draw marquees with the slice tool, you'll use the Snap To Guides and Snap To Slices commands.

6 If it's not already selected, choose View > Snap To > Guides.

This will help you define a slice area by snapping to the guides as you draw.

7 If it's not already selected, choose View > Snap To > Slices.

Snapping to slices that already exist will help ensure that a new sliced area doesn't overlap the other slices.

8 Using the slice tool, draw a marquee around the rectangular area containing the "Designs" text so that it lines up with the guides. When you release the mouse, Photoshop creates a slice and assigns a number to the upper-left corner of the slice.

Areas to the left, right, and below the new slice become new auto-slices. Slices 01, 02, 04, and 05 are auto-slices; slice 03 is your new user-slice.

The entire image is slice 01 by default.   The new "Designs" slice becomes slice 03.

9 Using the slice tool and the guides, draw marquees around the text "Structures," "Art," and "Contact" to create slices for three more buttons.

Make sure there are no gaps between the slices because gaps will become auto-slices. (If necessary, use the zoom tool (🔍) to get a closer view, and then double-click the zoom tool to return to 100%.)

Notice that the auto-slices are renumbered each time you create a new user-slice.

💡 *You can change the way the pointer appears on-screen for the slice tool by changing your Photoshop preferences. To change the slice tool's standard pointer (✐) to the precise pointer (⊹), choose Edit > Preferences > Display & Cursors, select Precise for Other Cursors, and click OK.*

Auto-slices are renumbered each time you define a new user-slice.

10 To resize a slice, select the slice select tool (⚡) hidden behind the slice tool, select the slice, and drag the selection handles.

11 Choose File > Save to save your work.

Types of slices

Slices you create using the slice tool are called user-slices; *slices you create from a layer are called* layer-based slices. *When you create a new user-slice or layer-based slice, additional auto-slices are generated to account for the remaining areas of the image. In other words, auto-slices fill the space in the image that is not defined by user-slices or layer-based slices. Auto-slices are regenerated every time you add or edit user-slices or layer-based slices. User-slices, layer-based slices, and auto-slices look different—user-slices and layer-based slices are defined by a solid line, while auto-slices are defined by a dotted line.*

A subslice is a type of auto-slice that is generated when you create overlapping slices. Subslices indicate how the image will be divided when you save the optimized file. Although subslices are numbered and display a slice symbol, you cannot select or edit them separately from the underlying slice. Subslices are regenerated every time you arrange the stacking order of slices.

–From Adobe Photoshop 6.0 online Help

Setting options for slices in Photoshop

Before optimizing slices as Web images, you can set options for them, such as naming the slices or assigning URL links to them. The names you assign to the slices will determine the filenames of the optimized images.

In this part of the lesson, you'll name the four user-slices that you defined, link them to Web pages, specify blank target frames so each linked page will appear in a separate browser window, and specify alternative text to appear in place of the images if they don't appear in a browser.

Note: Setting options for auto-slices automatically promotes them to user-slices.

1 Select the slice select tool (⚡), and use it to select the Designs slice.

The tool options bar changes to display options for the slice select tool.

2 Click the Slice Options button in the tool options bar.

By default, Photoshop names each slice based on the filename and the slice number.

3 In the Slice Options dialog box, enter **Designs_button** in the Name text box, **Designs.html** in the URL text box, **_blank** in the Target text box, and **Designs** in the Alt Tag text box. Then click OK.

Setting options for the selected Designs slice in Photoshop

4 Repeat steps 1 through 3 to rename and link the other three slices you made. Using the slice select tool, double-click a slice to open the Slice Options dialog box. Enter **Structures_button**, **Art_button**, and **Contact_button** for the names; **Structures.html**, **Art.html**, and **Contacts.html** for the URLs; and **Structures**, **Art**, and **Contact** for the alternative text.

In the Slice Options dialog box, you can also specify message text to appear in the browser's status area, specify dimensions to move or resize a slice, and change a slice to a No Image slice that contains HTML and text. Additional output settings for changing the background color of a slice are available when you open the Slice Options dialog box from the Save For Web dialog box or Save Optimized dialog box.

5 Choose File > Save.

Optimizing slices in Photoshop

You optimize slices in Photoshop by selecting them in the Save For Web dialog box, choosing optimization settings for each selection, and saving optimized files for either the selected slices or all slices. Photoshop creates an Images folder to contain the optimized files.

Here you'll optimize the four user-slices you defined.

1 Choose File > Save for Web.

2 Select the slice select tool (⭢) in the Save For Web dialog box.

3 Shift-click in the optimized version of the image to select the four slices you created.

4 Choose GIF Web Palette from the Settings menu, and click OK.

5 In the Save Optimized As dialog box, choose Images Only from the Format menu, choose Selected Slices from the bottom pop-up menu, leave the Name setting as it is, locate the Lessons/Lesson15/15Start/Architech Pages folder, and click Save.

Photoshop saves the optimized images in an Images folder within the Architech Pages folder and uses the names you specified in the Slice Options dialog box for the filenames. If there are any gaps in the table, Photoshop creates a Spacer.gif file.

6 Choose File > Save.

Slicing the image in ImageReady

Similar to Adobe Photoshop, Adobe ImageReady lets you define slices using the slice tool or by converting layers into slices. In addition, you can define all the slices in an image by converting guides into slices and you can define the precise shapes of slices by converting selections into slices. In this part of the lesson, you'll convert a layer into a slice, create a No Image slice, and create a precisely shaped slice from a selection.

Creating slices from guides

In ImageReady, you can convert all the areas between guides into user-slices. When you convert guides into slices, the entire image is sliced and you lose any preexisting slices.

1 In Photoshop, click the Jump to ImageReady button (⬚⬚).

The 15Start.psd file opens in ImageReady.

2 Choose View > Show > Slices.

3 Choose Window > Show Slice to display the Slice palette. Then choose Show Options from the palette menu to expand the Slice palette.

Notice that the Slice palette is similar to the Slice Options dialog box in Photoshop.

4 Select the slice select tool (⬚), and select the Designs_button slice.

Setting options for slices in ImageReady

Notice that the slice's name, URL, Target, and Alt text that you entered in Photoshop appear in the Slice palette.

5 If the guides aren't showing, choose View > Show > Guides.

6 Choose Slices > Create Slices from Guides.

This is a quick method for creating slices for every rectangular area between the guides.

7 Use the slice select tool to select the Designs slice again.

Notice that the options in the Slice palette for the Designs slice have changed to a default name based on the filename and slice number, and you've lost the options you set in Photoshop.

8 Choose Edit > Undo Create Slices from Guides.

Creating slices from layers

Another method for defining slices in Photoshop and ImageReady is to convert layers into slices. A layer-based slice includes all the pixel data in the layer. When you edit the layer, move it, or apply a layer effect to it, the layer-based slice adjusts to encompass the new pixels. To unlink a layer-based slice from its layer, you can convert it to a user-slice.

You'll create a slice based on the Copyright Strip layer, and then apply a layer effect to it so you can see how the slice adjusts to the new effect.

1 In the Layers palette, expand the Copyright Strip layer set and select the Strip Background layer.

The Strip Background layer contains the white strip that goes across the bottom of the banner.

2 Choose Layer > New Layer Based Slice.

ImageReady replaces the auto-slices with one layer-based slice for the entire layer. Notice the icon (▣) in the upper-left corner of the slice that indicates the slice is based on a layer. Now you'll apply a layer effect to see how the slice resizes to accommodate it.

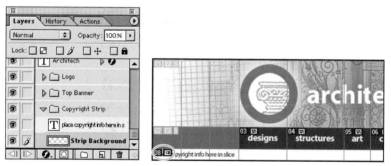

An icon next to the slice number indicates that the layer-based slice is linked to its layer.

3 With the Strip Background layer selected, choose Layer > Layer Style > Outer Glow.

Notice that the selection line around the layer-based slice expands to include the new layer effect.

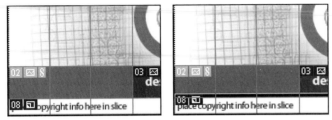

Before applying a layer effect   *After applying a layer effect*

4 Choose Edit > Undo Outer Glow to cancel the new layer effect.

5 Choose File > Save to save your work in ImageReady.

Creating No Image slices

In ImageReady and Photoshop, you can create *No Image* slices and add text or HTML source code to them. No Image slices can have a background color and are saved like any other table cell or DIV element as part of the HTML file.

The primary advantage of using No Image slices for text is that the text can be edited in any HTML editor, saving you the trouble of having to go back to Photoshop or ImageReady to edit it. The disadvantage is that if the text grows too large for the slice, it will break the HTML table and introduce unwanted gaps.

Now you'll convert the Copyright Strip slice into a No Image slice and add text to it.

1 Make sure the layer-based slice that you created for the copyright information is selected.

2 In the Slice palette, choose No Image from the Type menu.

3 Enter the copyright information for your banner in the Text box.

The text that you type here in the Slice palette will appear in the Web page; however, it will not appear in your sliced image in ImageReady or Photoshop.

You can add a copyright symbol by pressing Alt+0169 on the numeric keypad (Windows) or Option+G (Mac OS).

Because you chose No Image for the slice type, the layer of placeholder text ("place copyright info here in slice") that you do see in ImageReady will not appear in the Web page.

4 Choose File > Save.

Previewing in a Web browser

To make sure the text that you type will fit in the table cell, you'll preview the image in a Web browser.

1 In the toolbox, click the Preview in Default Browser button (☞ or ▓) or choose a browser from the button's pop-up menu.

The image appears in the browser window, and the HTML source for the preview appears in a table below the image.

Note: *To add your browser to the Preview in Default Browser button, drag its shortcut (Windows) or alias (Mac OS) into the Preview In folder located inside the Helpers folder in the Photoshop 6.0 folder.*

2 When you're done previewing the copyright text, quit the browser to return to ImageReady.

Creating slices from selections

In ImageReady, the easiest way to create a slice for a small or unusually shaped graphic element is to select the element with the magic wand tool and use the selection as the basis for the slice. This is also a useful technique for slicing objects that are crowded closely together.

You'll use the magic wand tool to select the blue logo and convert it to a slice.

1 In the Layers palette, expand the Logo layer set and select the Big Circle layer.

2 Select the magic wand tool (✳).

3 Click the blue area of the logo in the image to select the outer edge of the circle.

Slices are created based on the outer boundary of the selection. This means that every pixel within the circle will be part of the slice.

4 Choose Slices > Create Slice from Selection.

Notice the additional auto-slices that are created around the logo to complete the table.

Select the graphic element with the magic wand tool.   *Convert the selection to a slice.*

5 In the Slice palette, enter **Logo** in the Name text box, **Home.html** in the URL text box, and **Home** in the Alt text box. Enter **_blank** in the Target text box by choosing it from the Target pop-up menu.

💡 *You can choose URLs that you've already entered previously from the URL pop-up menu in the Slice palette.*

6 With the magic wand tool (✳) selected, choose Select > Deselect to remove the magic wand selection lines from the logo.

7 Choose File > Save.

Optimizing slices in ImageReady

ImageReady records separate optimization settings for every slice in the image. You specify optimization settings for a slice by selecting it and entering values in the Optimize palette. Then you can save an optimized image file for the selected slice.

In this part of the lesson, you'll explore how to set the optimization for slices in ImageReady, and then you'll link the slices together to share the optimization settings.

Setting the optimization for selected slices

Slices use the optimization settings of the entire image until you select them and specify new settings.

1 Select the slice select tool (🢖).

2 Select the number 02 auto-slice in the image.

3 Click the 2-UP tab in the document window to display the original image next to the optimized image.

4 Choose 200% from the Zoom Level menu in the lower-left corner of the document window.

Notice that the quality of the optimized image at its default setting (GIF Web Palette) is poor compared to the original image.

5 If you don't see the Optimize palette, choose Window > Show Optimize to display it.

6 In the Optimize palette, choose GIF 32 Dithered from the Settings menu.

Notice that the quality of the selected slice is better than it was with the default GIF Web Palette setting.

GIF Web Palette setting   GIF 32 Dithered setting

7 Choose 100% from the Zoom Level menu in the lower-left corner of the document window.

8 If you want, click the Toggle Slices Visibility button (▥) in the toolbox to hide the slice numbers while you're viewing the optimized image.

9 In the image, select another auto-slice.

Notice in the Optimize palette that the selected slice has the same GIF 32 Dithered setting. This is because all auto-slices are linked together, and any optimization setting that you choose for one auto-slice is automatically applied to the others.

Linking slices together

In ImageReady, you can link slices together to share the same optimization settings. Then, in ImageReady or Photoshop, you can change the settings for a linked slice and the new settings are instantly applied to the entire set of linked slices. Linked sets are color-coded to help identify slices in a set.

1 Using the slice select tool (✎), Shift-click in the optimized version of the image to select the four button slices. Then Shift-click to select the auto-slice to the right of the Contact button.

The order in which you select slices for linking makes a difference. If the first slice you select is a user-slice, any auto-slices you link to that slice also become user-slices. Similarly, if the first slice you select is an auto-slice, any user-slices you select are linked to the auto-slice set.

2 Choose Slices > Link Slices.

A link icon (⊠) appears in the upper-left corner of every linked slice and the slice color changes to red. The next set of slices that you link will have a different color.

Unlinked slices   Linked slices

3 Click away from the selection and then select the slice to the right of the Contact button.

Notice in the Optimize palette that the auto-slice setting of GIF 32 Dithered has changed to the GIF Web Palette setting shared by the other linked slices.

4 Click the Original tab in the document window to return to a single view of the image.

5 Choose File > Save.

You'll save the optimized slices later, after you create some rollovers. For information about the optimization settings and available Web formats for your image slices, see Lesson 14, "Optimizing Images for the Web."

Creating rollovers

ImageReady lets you create rollovers and secondary rollovers from slices or image map areas. (To learn how to create an image map, see "Creating an image map" on page 373.) Rollovers are multistate buttons that change their appearance or behavior when you roll the mouse pointer over them or click them. Secondary rollovers affect the appearance or behavior of other areas of the image when you perform the mouse action on the rollover button.

You can create different effects when a rollover is in a Normal, Over, Down, Click, Out, or Up state. If you know JavaScript, you can also create Custom states. You can also preserve the current state of an image for later use as a rollover state. (A rollover state designated as None will not be displayed on the Web page.)

You can animate user-slices in different rollover states in the same way that you animate an image in its normal state. To promote an auto-slice to a user-slice so you can animate it, select the slice, and choose Slices > Promote to User-Slice. To learn how to animate the image, see Lesson 17, "Creating Animated Images for the Web."

In this part of the lesson, you'll create secondary rollovers for the text buttons to display different layers of the banner image when the mouse pointer rolls over or is held down on the buttons. You'll also display a special warped text effect for one of the rollover states.

Displaying warped text in the Over state

You'll create an effect that makes the word "Architech" appear warped when the mouse pointer is rolled over the Contact button.

1 Choose Window > Show Rollover to display the Rollover palette.

2 Using the slice select tool (🖠), select the Contact_button slice in the image.

3 In the Rollover palette, click the Creates New Rollover State button (🔲) to create a new Over state for the selected slice.

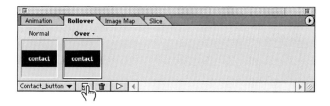

You can create these types of rollover states in this order: Over, Down, Click, Out, Up, Custom, and None.

Rollover states in ImageReady

Over—when the Web viewer rolls over the slice or image map area with the mouse while the mouse button is not pressed. (Over is automatically selected for the second rollover state.)

Down—when the Web viewer presses the mouse button on the slice or image map area. (This state appears as long as the viewer keeps the mouse button pressed down on the area.)

Click—when the Web viewer clicks the mouse on the slice or image map area. (This state appears after the viewer clicks the mouse and remains until the viewer activates another rollover state.)

Out—when the Web viewer rolls the mouse out of the slice or image map area. (The Normal state usually serves this purpose.)

Up—when the Web viewer releases the mouse button over the slice or image map area. (The Over state usually serves this purpose.)

Custom—a new rollover state. (You must create JavaScript code and add it to the HTML file for the Web page in order for the Custom rollover option to function. See a JavaScript manual for more information.)

None—current state of the image preserved for later use as a rollover state. (A state designated as None will not be displayed on the Web page.)

Note: *Different Web browsers, or different versions of a browser, may process clicks and double-clicks differently. For example, some browsers leave the slice in the Click state after a click, and in the Up state after a double-click; other browsers use the Up state only as a transition into the Click state, regardless of single- or double-clicking. To ensure your Web page will function correctly, be sure to preview rollovers in various Web browsers.*

–From Adobe Photoshop 6.0 online Help

4 In the Layers palette, select the Architech type layer.

5 Select the type tool (T).

Notice that the tool options bar now displays options that are specific for type.

6 In the tool options bar, click the Create Warped Text button (𝒯) to apply an effect to the selected Architech layer.

7 In the Warp Text dialog box, choose an option (such as Bulge) from the Style menu. Select Preview and wait a moment to see the affect applied to the type. (You may need to move the dialog box so you can see the type in the image.) Try other styles and drag the sliders to achieve different effects. When you're satisfied with a style, click OK.

The Warped Text effect is applied only to the Over state of the button.

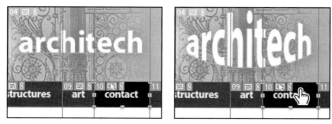

Normal state of the Contact button   Over state of the Contact button

8 In the Rollover palette, click the Normal state.

9 Choose File > Save.

Previewing rollovers in ImageReady

ImageReady provides a quick way to preview rollovers in the document window without the need to use a Web browser. This rollover preview mode in ImageReady is consistent with Internet Explorer 5.0 for Windows.

1 Choose View > Show > Guides to deselect and hide the guides.

2 Select the Toggles Slices Visibility button (⊟) in the toolbox to hide the slices.

3 Select the Rollover Preview button (👆) in the toolbox.

4 Move the pointer over the Contact button in the image and notice how the Architech text changes.

5 Click the Rollover Preview button again to deselect it.

6 Click the Toggles Slices Visibility button to show the slices.

Showing or hiding layers in a rollover state

You'll create Down rollover states for the Designs, Structures, and Art buttons to hide various letters in the Architech text when the mouse is held down on the buttons. Then you'll create Over rollover states that show a special image when the mouse is rolled over each button.

1 Select the slice select tool (✹).

2 Select the Designs_button slice in the image.

3 In the Rollover palette, click the Creates New Rollover State button (⊡) twice to create an Over state and a Down state for the slice.

4 Select the Down state.

5 In the Layers palette, select the Architech Highlights layer set.

Notice the blue text that appears over the word "Architech" in the image. You'll hide parts of the blue text to draw attention to other parts of the word.

6 Expand the Architech Highlights layer set and click the eye icons (●) next to the top four layers to hide the last four letters of the blue word, "t-e-c-h."

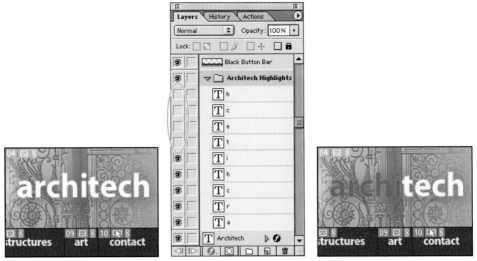

Normal state of the Designs button   Layers hidden in the Down state of the Designs button

The Down state of the Designs button now shows the letters "archi" in blue and "tech" in white.

Now you'll show a special image for the Designs button when it's in the Over state.

7 In the Rollover palette, select the Over state.

8 In the Layers palette, select and expand the Image Rollovers layer set.

9 Click the eye icons ( ) to hide two of the layers so that only the For Designs layer is showing.

10 Repeat steps 2 through 9 for the Structures_button slice and the Art_button slice, showing the layer set, and hiding and showing the appropriate layers as described in this table.

For this slice	Hide these layers in the Down state	Show these layers in the Over state
Designs_button	Top four layers (h, c, e, t) in the Architech Highlights folder	For Designs in the Image Rollovers folder
Structures_button	Bottom four layers (h, c, r, a) in the Architech Highlights folder	For Structures in the Image Rollovers folder
Art_button	Three layers (t, r, a) in the Architech Highlights folder	For Art in the Image Rollovers folder

11 Choose File > Save.

Previewing the completed banner in a browser

Before you save the optimized image slices, you'll preview the completed rollovers for the banner in a Web browser. However, the URL links that you assigned to the slices won't work in Preview in Browser mode, so you'll test them later when you generate the final HTML file and open the file from the browser.

1 In the toolbox, click the Preview in Default Browser button ( ) ( ) or choose a browser from the button's pop-up menu.

2 Move the pointer over each rollover button in the banner.

A different image appears for each of the first three buttons, and the warped text effect appears for the last button.

3 Hold the mouse button down when the pointer is over each button.

When you hold down the mouse button, on the Designs button, the white letters "tech" are visible; on the Structures button, the white letters "arch" are visible; and on the Art button, the white letters "art" are visible.

4 When you're finished previewing the rollovers, quit the browser and return to ImageReady.

Saving the sliced images in ImageReady

Now that the banner is complete, you'll save the optimized image slices and generate an HTML file that contains an HTML table of the sliced image.

💡 *ImageReady also lets you save slices in a cascading style sheet rather than a table. To set up the file for cascading style sheets, choose File > Output Settings > HTML. For Slice Output, select Generate CSS, and click OK. You can also change the output settings from the Save Optimized dialog box.*

1 Choose File > Save Optimized.

2 In the Save Optimized dialog box, enter **Banner.html** in the Name text box, choose HTML and Images from the Format menu, choose All Slices from the pop-up menu, locate the Lesson/Lesson15/15Start/Architech Pages folder, and click Save.

The Replace Files dialog box appears for the four button images you saved earlier in Photoshop.

3 Click Replace to save the new versions of the images.

ImageReady saves the HTML table of the entire sliced image in an HTML file and saves the optimized images for all of the auto-slices, user-slices, layer-based slices, and rollover states inside the Images folder. The filenames of the images are based on either the names you specified for the slices or the default names and numbers for the slices.

4 To test the URL links that you assigned to the slices, start a Web browser and use it to open the Banner.html file.

Now that you've learned how to create slices and rollovers, try animating them. For example, you could animate an image to move across a section of the banner when the pointer is over a rollover button. For information, see Lesson 17, "Creating Animated Images for the Web."

Review questions

1 What are slices?

2 Describe the five ways that image slices are created.

3 What is the advantage of linking slices together?

4 Describe the method for creating a slice with boundaries that exactly encompass a small or unusually shaped object.

5 How do you create a slice that contains no image? What purpose would such a slice serve?

6 Name two common rollover states and the mouse actions that trigger them. How many states can a slice have?

7 Describe a simple way to create rollover states for an image.

Review answers

1 Slices are rectangular areas of an image that you can define in Photoshop or ImageReady for individual Web optimization. With slices, you can create animated GIFs, URL links, and rollovers.

2 Image slices are created when you define areas in the image using the slice tool, or when you convert guides, layers, or selections into slices. They are also created automatically for areas in the sliced image that you leave undefined.

3 The advantage of linking slices together is that they'll share optimization settings— if you change the settings for one linked slice, the optimization settings automatically change for the other slices in the set.

4 Using the magic wand tool (or another appropriate selection tool) in ImageReady, select the object, and choose Slices > Create Slice from Selection.

5 Select the slice with the slice selection tool. In the Slice Options dialog box (Photoshop) or Slice palette (ImageReady), choose No Image from the Type menu. No Image slices can contain a background color, text, and HTML source code, or they can serve as a place-holder for graphics to be added later.

6 Normal and Over. Normal is active in the absence of any mouse action, and Over is triggered by moving the pointer over the slice. Down is another state, which is triggered by holding down the mouse button while the pointer is within a slice. There are seven predefined states, including Custom and None. But because you can create your own Custom states, there really is no limit to the number of states a slice can have.

7 Using a multilayer image, hide and reveal layers to create different versions of the image for each rollover state.

Lesson 16

16 | Designing Web Pages Using Multiple Adobe Programs

Adobe Photoshop works well with other Adobe programs to help you create your Web site. You can design the content for your Web pages in Photoshop, review the designs and share review comments in Adobe Acrobat, add rollovers or animations in Adobe ImageReady, and import the designs into Adobe GoLive® to create the Web pages.

In this lesson, you'll learn how to do the following:

• Create and annotate a PDF (Portable Document Format) file in Photoshop.

• Annotate the Photoshop PDF file in Acrobat and reopen it in Photoshop with all its layers intact.

• Import a layered Photoshop file into a GoLive document as separate DHTML layers.

• Use a Photoshop file as a tracing image in GoLive.

• Link your Web page to an ImageReady file using a GoLive Smart Object.

This lesson will take about 60 minutes to complete. The lesson is designed to be done in Adobe Photoshop, Adobe Acrobat, and Adobe GoLive 5.0.

If needed, remove the previous lesson folder from your hard drive, and copy the Lesson16 folder onto it. As you work on this lesson, you'll overwrite the start files. If you need to restore the start files, copy them from the *Adobe Photoshop Classroom in a Book* CD.

Note: *Windows users need to unlock the lesson files before using them. For information, see "Copying the Classroom in a Book files" on page 3.*

Getting started

Before beginning the lesson, restore the default application settings for Adobe Photoshop. See "Restoring default preferences" on page 4.

In this lesson, you'll explore ways to use Adobe Acrobat and Adobe GoLive with two Photoshop files and an ImageReady file to create a Web page. You'll start the lesson by viewing an example of the finished Web page.

1 Start a Web browser that can display DHTML layers, such as Netscape Communicator or Microsoft® Internet Explorer.

2 Use the browser to open the end file Index.html from the Lessons/Lesson16/16End/ Architech Folder/Architech folder.

You'll create this Web page based on two Photoshop designs and a banner with rollovers that was created in ImageReady. To learn how to create the rollovers in the banner, see Lesson 15, "Creating Web Graphics Using Slices and Rollovers."

3 Roll the mouse pointer over the buttons in the banner, and notice that the image changes.

4 Click a button to go to another page.

5 When you're done viewing the end file, close it and quit the browser.

For illustrations of the finished artwork for this lesson, see the gallery at the beginning of the color section.

Using Adobe Acrobat for design reviews

Adobe Photoshop lets you save your image files including all their layers in PDF format. Others can review your work in Adobe Acrobat, and add notes to the files, and then you can reopen the annotated files in Photoshop with the layers still intact.

You'll review a Web page design made in Photoshop, and learn how to annotate the file both in Photoshop and in Acrobat. Later, you'll use a part of the design in the Web page you create.

PDF

Portable Document Format (PDF) is a flexible, cross-platform, cross-application file format. Based on the PostScript imaging model, PDF files accurately display and preserve fonts, page layouts, and both vector and bitmap graphics. In addition, PDF files can contain electronic document search and navigation features such as electronic links.

Photoshop and ImageReady recognize two types of PDF files: Photoshop PDF files and Generic PDF files. You can open both types of PDF files; however, you can only save images to Photoshop PDF format.

• Photoshop PDF files are created using the Photoshop Save As command. Photoshop PDF files can contain only a single image. Photoshop PDF format supports all of the color modes and features that are supported in standard Photoshop format. Photoshop PDF also supports JPEG and ZIP compression, except for Bitmap-mode images, which use CCITT Group 4 compression.

• Generic PDF files are created using applications other than Photoshop, such as Adobe Acrobat and Adobe Illustrator, and can contain multiple pages and images. When you open a Generic PDF file, Photoshop rasterizes the image.

–From Adobe Photoshop 6.0 online Help

Annotating your design in Photoshop

Adobe Photoshop provides a complete annotation system that includes attaching notes and audio annotations to images, and importing annotations from other PDF documents. Notes are displayed in resizeable windows and can be identified by author. In this part of the lesson, you'll attach a note to the first Photoshop design for the Web page.

1 Start Adobe Photoshop.

If a notice appears asking whether you want to customize your color settings, click No.

2 Choose File > Open, and open the file Design1.psd from the Lessons/Lesson16/ 16Start/Designs folder.

Two annotated notes appear in the document that were made by the designer in Photoshop.

3 If you don't see the notes, choose View > Show > Annotations.

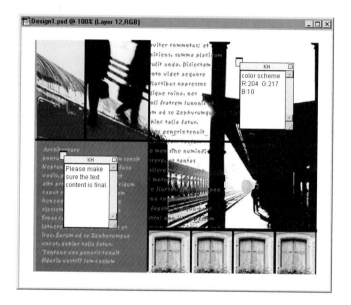

4 Select the notes tool (□) in the toolbox.

Options you can set for notes appear in the tool options bar, including the name of the note's author, the font and size for the note text, and the color of the note icon and title bar of the note window.

5 In the tool options bar, enter your name in the Author text box.

6 In the document window, drag the notes tool pointer to draw a rectangular marquee. (You can also click with the notes tool to create a note.)

When you release the mouse, a note window appears with your Author name in the title bar.

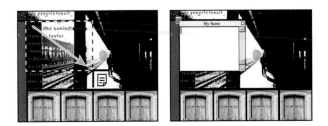

7 Enter some text in the window.

You can resize the window by dragging the lower-right corner and close the window by clicking the close box in the title bar.

Saving a Photoshop PDF file

Photoshop lets you save RGB, indexed-color, CMYK, grayscale, Bitmap-mode, Lab color, and duotone images in PDF format. You'll save the Design1 image with your annotation in Photoshop PDF format so you or others can open the file in Adobe Acrobat. You'll include the image layers with the PDF file so you can continue to work with them after the file has been reviewed.

1 Choose File > Save As.

2 In the Save As dialog box, choose Photoshop PDF from the Format menu and make sure Layers and Annotations are selected.

Photoshop PDF files saved with their layers are significantly larger than those saved without them. For example, a 164K Photoshop PDF file saved without layers might be 568K when it's saved with the layers.

3 Navigate to the Designs folder (Lessons/Lesson16/16Start/Designs) and click Save to save the Design1.pdf file.

The PDF Options dialog box appears with different options depending on the type of image you're saving (for example, an image containing vector graphics or type includes options for embedding fonts and using outlines for text). The dialog box does not appear for bitmap-mode images, which are automatically encoded using CCITT compression. For information on PDF options, see "Setting file saving options (Photoshop)" in Photoshop 6.0 online Help.

4 In the PDF Options dialog box, enter **5** in the Quality text box, and click OK.

5 Choose File > Close and save and close the new Design1.pdf file.

Reviewing the Photoshop PDF file in Acrobat

Although you can read your PDF file in Adobe Acrobat Reader, you must use Adobe Acrobat or Photoshop to annotate the PDF file. Now you'll use Acrobat to review the Design1.pdf file you created, add an annotation, and reopen the file in Photoshop.

About annotations in Adobe Acrobat

There are three types of annotation and markup tools available on the tool bar—annotation, graphic markup, and text markup. Each has a hidden tool menu.

The annotation tools—notes tool, text annotation tool, audio annotation tool, stamp tool, and file annotation tool—allow you to attach comments to a PDF document on a variety of formats. Each tool provides a unique method for conveying annotation information. For information on how to use these tools, see "Using the annotation tools."

The graphic markup tools—pencil tool, rectangle tool, ellipse tool, and line tool—allow you to visually mark an area of a PDF document with a graphic symbol and associate a note with the markup for additional comments. For information on how to use these tools, see "Marking up documents with graphic markup tools."

Text markup tools—highlight text tool, strikethrough text tool, and underline text tool—allow you to visually mark up text on a PDF document page and associate a text note with the markup for further comments. For information on how to use these tools, see "Marking up documents."

You can change the properties of the current annotation with the annotation's Properties dialog box; however, you must use the Preferences dialog box to change the properties globally for all subsequent annotations.

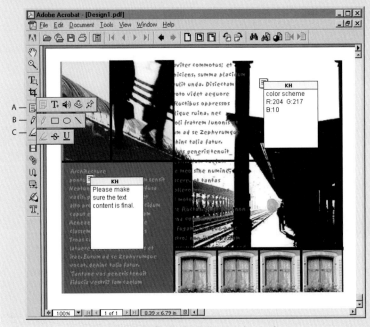

A. Annotation tools B. Graphic markup tools C. Text markup tools

–From Adobe Acrobat 4.0 online Help

1 Start Adobe Acrobat.

2 Choose File > Open and open the Design1.pdf file you saved in the Lessons/Lesson16/ 16Start/Designs folder.

You'll see the note you made in Photoshop along with the other two designer notes. Now you'll annotate the file in Acrobat.

3 Choose File > Preferences > Annotations, enter your name in the Author text box, and click OK.

4 Select the notes tool (▤).

5 Drag to draw a notes window and enter your comments.

6 In Acrobat, choose File > Save to save your work.

7 Close the Design1.pdf file and quit Adobe Acrobat.

Note: The file must be closed in Acrobat before you can save changes to the file in Photoshop.

8 In Photoshop, choose File > Open Recent > Design1.pdf.

Notice that the comments you entered in Acrobat now appear in Photoshop. Because you originally saved the PDF file with all its layers, you can continue working on the image and then save the file in Photoshop (PSD) format when you're done. To hide your notes while working on the image in Photoshop, choose View > Show > Annotations.

9 Close the Design1.pdf file and quit Adobe Photoshop.

Creating the Web page in Adobe GoLive

In this part of the lesson, you'll explore three ways that Adobe GoLive lets you use Photoshop images in your Web pages: You'll open a Photoshop file directly in GoLive by importing the file as HTML. Then you'll use a Photoshop file as a tracing image in GoLive. Finally, you'll use a Smart Object to link the banner image between GoLive and ImageReady, so changes you make to the image in the original source application will always be updated in the optimized Web image.

As you explore these GoLive features, you'll create the index page for the Architech Web site based on two designs made in Photoshop and a banner made in ImageReady.

Importing layered Photoshop files as DHTML layers

The Import Photoshop as HTML feature in GoLive lets you import layers from a Photoshop file and save them as individual Web images. When you import a Photoshop file as HTML, the Save For Web dialog box appears for each layer in the file so you can choose optimization settings for each Web image. GoLive saves each optimized image inside a floating box (a DHTML layer) on the page.

A Web site has been set up for this lesson in GoLive. You'll open the site file and import the second Photoshop design into the blank index page.

1 Start Adobe GoLive 5.0.

2 Choose File > Open and open the file Architech.site from the Lessons/Lesson16/ 16Start/Architech Folder.

3 In the Files tab of the site window, double-click Index.html to open the page.

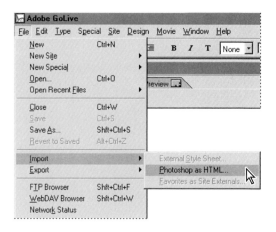

4 Drag the site window to the lower-left corner of your screen so that you can see it and the document window at the same time.

5 Select the document window, choose File > Import > Photoshop as HTML, and open the file Design2.psd from the Lessons/Lesson16/16Start/Designs folder.

GoLive asks you to choose a location for the optimized layers. You'll save them in the Images folder of the Architech site.

6 In the Browser for Folder (Windows) or Choose a Folder (Mac OS) dialog box, navigate to the Architech site folder (Lessons/Lesson16/16Start/Architech Folder/Architech), select the Images folder, and click OK (Windows) or Choose (Mac OS).

The Save For Web dialog box will open seven times for each layer in the Design2.psd file.

7 In the Save For Web dialog box, choose a Web image format from the Settings menu (such as GIF 32 Dithered), choose any other optimization settings that you want for the first layer, and click OK.

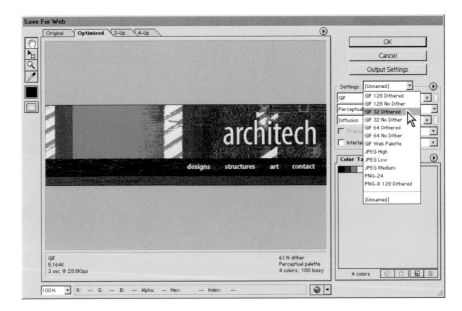

8 Repeat step 7 for all seven layers. The optimization settings can be different for each layer.

Each layer in the Design2.psd file is saved as a Web image inside a floating box on the page. GoLive names each Web image file based on the names of the Photoshop file ("Design2") and the layer.

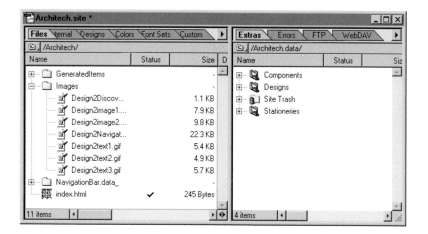

9 Choose File > Save.

Using a Photoshop file as a tracing image

Adobe GoLive lets you use Photoshop files that contain RGB or Grayscale 8-bit images as tracing images for your Web page. You can cut out areas of the tracing images and save the cutouts as individual Web images within floating boxes in their original positions on the page.

Note: In addition to Photoshop (PSD) images, you can import JPEG, GIF, PNG, BMP, TARGA, PCX, PICT (Mac OS), PIXAR, TIFF, and Amiga IFF image files as tracing images.

Your clients have decided that they like an image in the first design better than one of the images in this design. No problem. You'll use the Photoshop file as a tracing image and replace the unwanted image with the new one. First you'll delete the unwanted image and its floating box.

1 In the document window, use the hand pointer (✋) to select the floating box that contains the image below the banner on the right side of the page. (You'll know that you've selected the floating box rather than the image inside it because the Image Inspector changes to the Floating Box Inspector.)

The hand pointer and the Inspector indicate that the floating box is selected.

The arrow pointer and the Inspector indicate that the image is selected.

2 Choose Window > Reset Palettes to restore the palettes to their default positions.

3 If you don't see the Floating Boxes palette, choose Window > Floating Boxes to display it, and then resize the palette so you can see all of the floating boxes in the list.

Notice that the Image2 floating box is selected in the Floating Boxes palette.

4 Choose Edit > Cut or press Delete to remove the selected floating box and its image from the page.

5 In the Floating Boxes palette, click the eye icons (👁) to hide the six remaining floating boxes and their images.

6 Choose Window > Tracing Image or click the palette's tab to display the Tracing Image palette.

7 In the Tracing Image palette, select the Source check box, click the Browse button (🔲), and open the Design1.psd file from the Lessons/Lesson16/16Start/ Designs folder.

The Design1.psd file appears as a tracing image in the document window.

You can position the tracing image anywhere on the page by using the move tool (🖐) in the Tracing Image palette or by entering *X* and *Y* coordinates in the palette.

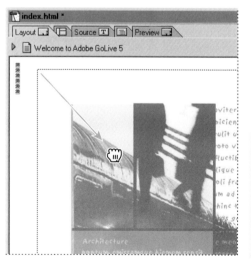

Slicing the tracing image with the cut out tool

The cut out tool in the Tracing Image palette is similar to the crop tool—it lets you crop the tracing image into rectangular areas that you save as separate optimized images. Next, you'll cut out the area in the tracing image that your clients want and save it as a new Web image.

1 In the Tracing Image palette, select the cut out tool (⊠).

2 In the document window, draw a rectangular marquee around the second image in the upper-left corner of the composition. After releasing the mouse, you can move or resize the marquee as desired.

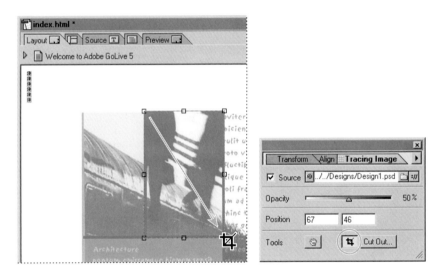

3 In the Tracing Image palette, click the Cut Out button.

4 In the Save For Web dialog box, choose the optimization settings that you want (such as GIF 32 Dithered) and click OK.

5 In the Specify Target File dialog box, name the file, and save it in the Images folder of the site folder (Lessons/Lesson16/16Start/Architech Folder/Architech/Images).

GoLive places the new image in a floating box that's in the same position as the cut-out area of the tracing image.

6 In the Tracing Image palette, deselect Source to hide the tracing image.

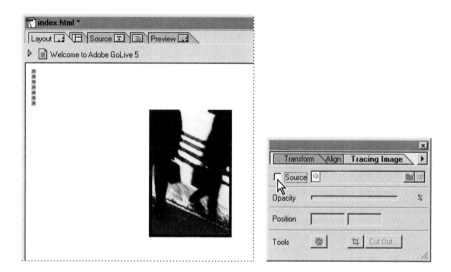

7 Choose File > Save.

Renaming and moving the floating box

By default, floating boxes are named as layers and numbered consecutively in the order that they are created (Layer1, Layer2, and so forth). The names of the floating boxes in this lesson file were renamed using the Floating Box Inspector. You'll rename the floating box for your new image and move it to the position where the unwanted image was on the page.

1 In the Floating Boxes palette, select the new Layer1 floating box.

2 In the Floating Box Inspector, enter **NewImage** in the Name text box.

GoLive won't allow spaces in the name because browsers will not recognize floating box names (DIV element IDs) with spaces in them.

Floating boxes can be dragged to any position you want on the page. They can also be moved by entering X and Y coordinates in the Floating Box Inspector. You'll move the new floating box and its image to the precise X and Y coordinates that the unwanted image was in.

3 In the Floating Box Inspector, enter **370** in the Left text box and enter **200** in the Top text box.

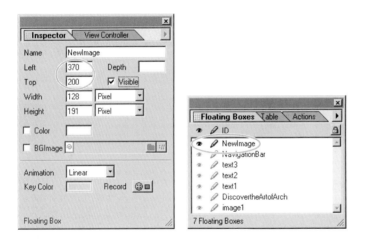

Notice the NewImage name that you entered in the Floating Box Inspector appears in the Floating Boxes palette.

4 In the Floating Boxes palette, click the eye icons again to show all of the floating boxes and their images.

5 Choose File > Save.

About floating boxes

Floating boxes let you position any object on a page absolutely, so you can use transparent floating boxes to position and animate objects, for example, and to create layered effects. You can also convert floating boxes to text frames.

Floating boxes are based on the DIV element, which has been available since HTML 3.2. HTML 4.0 substantially enhances the DIV element's functionality, allowing it to be absolutely positioned and stacked to accept a background image or background color. The DIV element is also a core element of Dynamic HTML and a major building block for absolute positioning with cascading style sheets.

Note: *To display properly, floating boxes require Web browsers version 4.0 or later. Although floating boxes may soon be used as commonly as HTML tables, viewers with older browsers may have trouble viewing pages that contain floating boxes.*

Technically, a floating box is a visual representation of a DIV element, usually formatted with a CSS ID style. The ID style specifies the width, visibility, and absolute position of the floating box, instructing the browser to create a subdivision that is not part of the normal flow of HTML code within the page. This property of being absolutely positioned allows floating boxes to be moved.

–From Adobe GoLive 5.0 online Help

Using Smart Photoshop Objects

In GoLive, you can use Smart Photoshop Objects to link to Photoshop and ImageReady files on your Web page. GoLive optimizes the images for the Web and creates a smart link between the optimized images and the Photoshop or ImageReady files. Changes you make to the linked source file are automatically updated in the optimized image.

To use PSD files with Smart Photoshop Objects, the PSD files must be RGB 8-bit images, and the images can be sliced. You can also use Smart Photoshop Objects with files in BMP, PICT (Mac OS only), PCX, Pixar, Amiga IFF, TIFF, and TARGA image formats.

The banner image in the Design2.psd file is a placeholder for the real banner that was designed in ImageReady. You'll use a Smart Photoshop Object to link to the ImageReady file so you'll always be able to update the original file in ImageReady or Photoshop.

1 In the document window, click in the middle of the Architech banner with the arrow pointer icon ( ) to select only the image and not the floating box. Then delete the image.

2 Select the empty floating box with the hand pointer icon ( ).

3 In the Objects palette, click the Smart tab ( ) and drag the Smart Photoshop icon into the selected floating box in the document window.

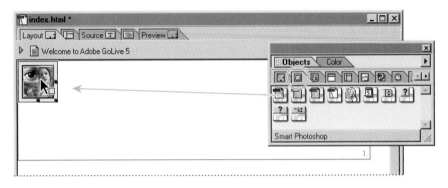

A Smart Object placeholder appears in the floating box, and the Inspector changes to the Live Image Inspector.

Linking the Smart Photoshop Object to an ImageReady file

The banner for the Architech site in this lesson is a sliced ImageReady image with rollover buttons (similar to the banner you created in Lesson 15). Optimization settings for all of the slices have already been set in ImageReady.

When you link a Smart Photoshop Object to a sliced ImageReady image, GoLive uses the optimization settings from ImageReady, so you won't see the Save For Web dialog box as you do for Photoshop sliced images. GoLive creates an images folder for the optimized slices inside a data folder you specify for the linked image file. The Photoshop or ImageReady source file of the sliced image must also be in the data folder you specified.

1 With the Smart Object placeholder selected in the document window, drag a line from the Source Point and Shoot button (⬚) in the Live Image Inspector to the file NavigationBar.psd inside the NavigationBar.data folder in the Files tab of the site window.

When you release the mouse, GoLive displays a Specify Target File (Windows) or Save (Mac OS) dialog box so you can specify the data folder that will contain all of the HTML and sliced Web image files for the banner.

2 In the Specify Target File (Windows) or Save (Mac OS) dialog box, locate and open the Architech folder (Lessons/Lesson16/16Start/Architech Folder/Architech). Use the default name **NavigationBar.data** in the Name text box and click Save.

GoLive starts ImageReady in the background, converts all the slices in the banner into Web image files, and saves them in an Images folder inside the folder you specified. If the name you enter in the Name text box matches an existing data folder, GoLive saves the files inside that folder. Otherwise, GoLive will create a data folder with the name you specify (and an images folder inside it) to contain the files.

Next you'll update the site window so you can see the new images from the sliced banner file.

3 Select the site window, click inside the Files tab to select it, and then click the Update button (✔) in the toolbar.

4 In the site window, expand the Images folder inside the NavigationBar.data folder to see all its files.

5 In the document window, position the banner where you want it in the page. (Make sure the pointer is a hand (🖑) so you'll select both the image and the floating box.)

Whenever you want to edit the banner, you can double-click the Smart Object image and the original source file will open in ImageReady. To select the entire image, not just one of the slices, click the top border of the image when the pointer becomes an arrow with a solid square (🔲), rather than a sliced square (🔳). The path to the Source file appears in the Live Grid Inspector.

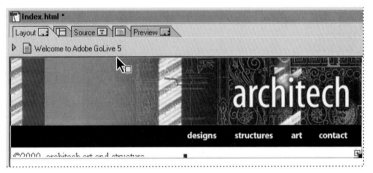

Position the pointer at the top of the banner and double-click to go to the source file.

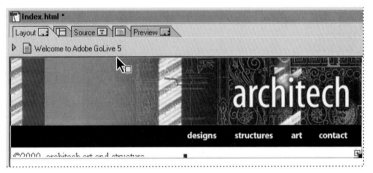

The original source file opens in ImageReady.

If desired, you can use the Image Slice Inspector in GoLive to change the URL page links in the sliced banner, by selecting each slice and entering a new URL address in the Image Slice Inspector.

Select a slice in the GoLive document window and enter a new URL in the Image Slice Inspector.

6 Choose File > Save.

Now you'll preview the Web page in a browser.

7 Select the document window, and click the Show in Browser button (🌐) in the toolbar, or choose a browser from the pop-up menu.

To set up a browser in GoLive for previewing, choose Edit > Preferences, click the Browsers icon (🌐), click Add, select the browser, click Add again, and click Done. Then click OK to close the Preferences dialog box.

Review questions

1 What is the advantage of saving your Photoshop designs in PDF format?

2 Describe a quick way that you can save Photoshop layers as individual Web images.

3 What is the cut out tool used for and where is it located?

4 What is the difference between the Floating Box Inspector and the Floating Boxes palette?

5 How does an image placed on your Web page using the Image icon differ from an image placed using the Smart Object icon?

6 How do you link an image slice to a Web page in GoLive?

Review answers

1 The advantage of saving Photoshop designs in PDF format is that others can review the designs and add their comments without having Photoshop, special fonts, or the same operating system on their computers. By saving a design in Photoshop PDF format including the image layers, you can continue your work on the design in the same PDF file after it has been reviewed. Keep in mind, however, that PDF files saved with all the layers will be larger than those saved without.

2 In GoLive, you can save Photoshop layers as individual Web images by importing the Photoshop file as HTML (choose File > Import > Photoshop as HTML).

3 The cut out tool is used for saving individual Web images that are cut out from a tracing image. The tool is located in the Tracing Image palette in Adobe GoLive.

4 In GoLive, the Floating Box Inspector contains options for a selected floating box, including name, dimensions, and background color for the floating box. The Floating Boxes palette lists all of the floating boxes on the page, and includes options for showing and hiding each floating box, and for using a grid with them.

5 In GoLive, an image placed on the page using the Image icon must be in a Web format such as GIF, JPEG, or PNG. An image placed on the page using the Smart Object icon can be in a variety of non-Web bitmapped or vector-based formats created by Photoshop, Illustrator, or LiveMotion.

6 To link an image slice to a page in GoLive, select the slice in the document window and enter the relative URL in the Image Slice Inspector. If the page you're linking to the slice is located inside another folder within the data folder for the slices, include the folder's name in the URL. For example, you might enter **../Architech Pages/Designs.html** to link a slice to the Designs.html page located in the Architech Pages folder within the NavigationBar.data folder.

Lesson 17

17 | Creating Animated Images for the Web

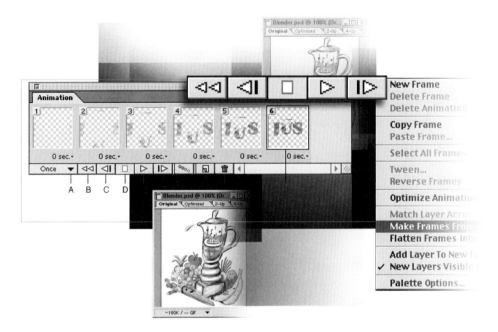

To add dynamic content to your Web page, use Adobe ImageReady to create animated GIF images from a single image. Compact in file size, animated GIFs display and play in most Web browsers. ImageReady provides an easy and convenient way to create imaginative animations.

In this lesson, you'll learn how to do the following:

• Open a multilayered image to use as the basis for the animation.

• Use the Layers palette in conjunction with the Animation palette to create animation sequences.

• Make changes to single frames, multiple frames, and an entire animation.

• Use the Tween command to automatically vary layer opacity and position across frames.

• Preview animations in Adobe ImageReady and in a Web browser.

• Open and edit an existing animated GIF image.

• Optimize the animation using the Optimize palette.

This lesson will take about 90 minutes to complete. The lesson is designed to be done in Adobe ImageReady.

If needed, remove the previous lesson folder from your hard drive, and copy the Lesson17 folder onto it. As you work on this lesson, you'll overwrite the start files. If you need to restore the start files, copy them from the *Adobe Photoshop Classroom in a Book* CD.

Note: Windows users need to unlock the lesson files before using them. For information, see "Copying the Classroom in a Book files" on page 3.

Creating animations in Adobe ImageReady

In Adobe ImageReady, you create animation from a single image using animated GIF files. An *animated GIF* is a sequence of images, or frames. Each frame varies slightly from the preceding frame, creating the illusion of movement when the frames are viewed in quick succession. You can create animation in several ways:

• By using the New Frame button in the Animation palette to create animation frames and the Layers palette to define the image state associated with each frame.

• By using the Tween feature to quickly create new frames that warp text or vary a layer's opacity, position, or effects, to create the illusion of a single element in a frame moving or fading in and out.

• By opening a multilayer Adobe Photoshop or Adobe Illustrator file for an animation, with each layer becoming a frame.

When creating an animation sequence, it's best to remain in Original image view—this saves ImageReady from having to reoptimize the image as you edit the frame contents. Animation files are output as either GIF files or QuickTime movies. You cannot create a JPEG or PNG animation.

For the Web: About layer-based animation

Working with layers is the key to creating animations in ImageReady. Each new frame starts out as a duplicate of the preceding frame—you edit the frame by adjusting its layers. You can apply layer changes to a single frame, a group of frames, or the entire animation.

When you work with layers in a frame, you can create or copy selections in the layer; adjust color and tone; change the layer's opacity, blending mode, or position; add layer effects; and perform editing tasks as you would with layers in any image.

Using layer attributes to create animation effects is very simple and allows you to save an animation file in Photoshop format for later re-editing.

Keep in mind that some changes you make to layers affect only the active frame, while others affect all frames:

Frame-specific changes *Affect only the selected frames in the Animation palette. Changes you make to a layer using Layers palette commands and options—including a layer's opacity, blending mode, visibility, position, and layer effects—are frame-specific.*

Global changes *Affect all frames in an animation. Changes you make to the layer's pixel values, using painting and editing tools, color and tone adjustment commands, filters, type, and other image-editing commands, affect every frame in which the layer is included.*

When you work with layer masks and layer clipping paths, changes in position, state (enabled or disabled), and link state are frame-specific, whereas changes in pixel or vector content affect all frames.

–From Adobe Photoshop 6.0 online Help

Getting started

Before beginning this lesson, restore the default application settings for Adobe Photoshop and Adobe ImageReady. See "Restoring default preferences" on page 4.

In this lesson, you'll work with a set of images designed to appear on the Web page of a fresh juice company. If you have a browser application installed on your computer, you can preview the finished animations.

1 Start your browser application.

2 From your browser, choose File > Open, and open the file Jus.html from the Lessons/Lesson17/Jus folder.

3 When you have finished viewing the file, quit the browser.

Creating simple motion

You'll start by animating the construction of a text logo, using a multilayered Photoshop image.

Using layers to create animation frames

In this part of the lesson, you'll adjust the position and opacity of layers in an image to create the starting and ending frames of an animation sequence.

1 Start ImageReady.

2 Choose File > Open, and open the file Logo1.psd from the Lessons/Lesson17 folder on your hard drive.

The logo consists of four different components that reside on separate layers.

3 If the Layers palette is not showing, choose Window > Show Layers to display it.

In the Layers palette, notice that all the layers are currently visible. Visible layers appear with an eye icon (👁) in the palette.

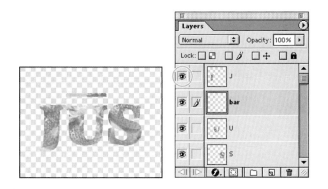

To define an animation, you use the Layers palette in conjunction with the Animation palette. The Animation palette lets you add new frames, update existing frames, change the order of frames, and preview the animation.

4 If the Animation palette is not showing, choose Window > Show Animation to display it.

The Animation palette opens with a single default frame that reflects the current state of the image. The frame is selected (outlined with a border), indicating that you can change its content by editing the image.

You'll compose animation frames that show the letters of the logo appearing and moving into their final position from different areas. The current image state reflects how you want the logo to appear at the end of the animation.

5 In the Animation palette, click the New Frame button (⧉) to create a new animation frame.

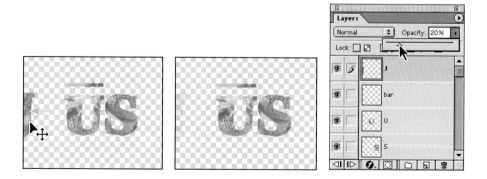

Each new frame you add starts as a duplicate of the preceding frame. Now you'll show the components of the logo text in different starting positions.

6 In the Layers palette, select the J layer.

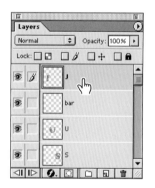

7 With frame 2 selected in the Animation palette, select the move tool (▸₊). Hold down Shift to constrain the movement, and in the image, drag the "J" to the left, repositioning it at the left edge of the image. In the Layers palette, reduce the opacity of the J layer to 20%.

8 In the Layers palette, select the S layer.

9 In the image, press Shift as you drag the "S" to the right edge of the image.

10 In the Layers palette, reduce the opacity of the S layer to 20%.

11 Use the procedures you've learned in steps 7 through 10 to select, move, and change the opacity of the bar layer and the U layer as follows:

• Move the bar to the upper edge of the image, and reduce the opacity to 20%.

• Move the "U" to the lower edge of the image, and reduce the opacity to 20%.

In the Animation palette, notice that frame 2 has updated to reflect the current image state. To make frame 2 the starting state of your animation, you'll switch the order of the two frames.

12 In the Animation palette, drag frame 2 to the left, releasing the mouse when the black bar appears to the left of frame 1.

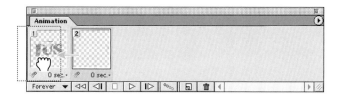

13 Choose File > Save to save your work.

Tweening the position and opacity of layers

To finish the animation sequence, you'll add frames that represent transitional image states between the two existing frames. When you change the position, opacity, or effects of any layer between two animation frames, you can instruct ImageReady to *tween*, or automatically create intermediate frames.

1 In the Animation palette, make sure that frame 1 is selected; then choose Tween from the palette menu.

You can vary just selected layers in the selected frames, or you can vary all layers in the selection.

2 In the Tween dialog box, select All Layers, Position, and Opacity. (You can also select Effects to vary the settings of layer effects evenly between the beginning and ending frames. You won't choose this option here.)

3 Choose Tween with Next Frame to add frames between the selected frame and the following frame. Enter **4** in the Frames to Add text box. Click OK.

ImageReady creates four new transitional frames based on the opacity and position settings of the layers in the original two frames.

4 At the lower left of the Animation palette, position the pointer on the inverted triangle and press to display the Select Looping Options pop-up menu. Then choose Once from the menu that appears.

In the Animation palette, click the Play button (▷) to preview your animation in ImageReady.

For the Web: Tweening frames

You use the Tween command to automatically add or modify a series of frames between two existing frames—varying the layer attributes (position, opacity, or effect parameters) evenly between the new frames to create the appearance of movement. For example, if you want to fade out a layer, set the opacity of the layer in the starting frame to 100%; then set the opacity of the same layer in the ending frame to 0%. When you tween between the two frames, the opacity of the layer is reduced evenly across the new frames.

The term "tweening" is derived from "in betweening," the traditional animation term used to describe this process. Tweening significantly reduces the time required to create animation effects such as fading in or fading out, or moving an element across a frame. You can edit tweened frames individually after you create them.

If you select a single frame when tweening, you choose whether to tween the frame with the previous frame or the next frame. If you select two contiguous frames, new frames are added between the frames. If you select more than two frames, existing frames between the first and last selected frames are altered by the tweening operation. If you select the first and last frames in an animation, these frames are treated as contiguous, and tweened frames are added after the last frame. (This tweening method is useful when the animation is set to loop multiple times.)

Note: *You cannot select discontiguous frames for tweening.*

–From Adobe Photoshop 6.0 online Help

Preserving transparency and optimizing animations

Next you'll optimize the image in GIF format with background transparency and preview your animation in a Web browser. Remember that only the GIF format supports animated images.

1 In the Optimize palette, choose GIF for the format, Perceptual for the palette, and then choose the number of colors. (We chose 256.)

2 Choose Show Options from the palette menu or click the Show Options button on the Optimize tab to display all of the options.

Show Options button in
Optimize palette

3 Select Transparency to preserve the background transparency of the original image, and choose White from the matte menu.

💡 *An easy way to set the color to white is to click the Default Colors icon, and then choose Background Color from the Matte pop-up menu in the Optimize palette.*

4 From the Animation palette menu, choose Select All Frames. Then right-click (Windows) or Control-click (Mac OS) one of the frames to display the Disposal Method context menu.

5 Make sure that the Automatic option is selected.

The disposal options (Restore to Background ( ) and Automatic) clear the selected frame before the next frame is played, eliminating the danger of displaying remnant pixels from the previous frame. The Do Not Dispose ( ) option retains the frames. The Automatic option is suitable for most animations. This option selects a disposal method based on the presence or absence of transparency in the next frame and discards the selected frame if the next frame contains layer transparency.

Now you'll set options to optimize the animation.

6 Choose Optimize Animation from the Animation palette menu.

In addition to the optimization tasks applied to standard GIF files, several other tasks are performed for animated GIF files. If you optimize the animated GIF using an adaptive, perceptual, or selective palette, ImageReady generates a palette for the file based on all of the frames in the animation. A special dithering technique is applied to ensure that dither patterns are consistent across all frames, to prevent flickering during playback. Also, frames are optimized so that only areas that change from frame to frame are included, greatly reducing the file size of the animated GIF. As a result, ImageReady requires more time to optimize an animated GIF than to optimize a standard GIF.

7 Choose Optimize by Bounding Box to direct ImageReady to crop each frame to preserve only the area that has changed from the preceding frame. Animation files created using this option are smaller but are incompatible with GIF editors, which do not support the option. (This option is selected by default and is recommended.)

8 Choose Optimize by Redundant Pixel Removal to make all pixels in a frame that are unchanged from the preceding frame transparent. (This option is selected by default and is recommended.) Click OK.

When you choose the Redundant Pixel Removal option, the Disposal Method must be set to Automatic, as in step 5.

9 In the image window, click the Optimized tab to build the optimized image. Then click the 2-Up tab to compare the original image on the left with the optimized image on the right.

Notice the Optimized file size in the image information box at the bottom of the document window. Adding animation frames to an image also adds to the file size. To reduce the file size of your animated GIF images, experiment with different palette and color settings.

For complete information, see "Optimizing Images for the Web" in Photoshop 6.0 online Help.

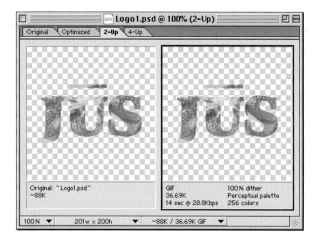

10 Choose File > Preview In, and choose a browser application from the submenu. This command plays back an animation accurately, according to the timing you've set.

Note: To use the Preview In command, you must have a browser application installed on your system. For more information, see "Previewing an image in a browser" in Photoshop 6.0 online Help.

11 Return to the ImageReady application.

12 Choose File > Save Optimized As, name the image **Logo1.gif**, and click Save.

For the Web: Setting the frame disposal method

The frame disposal method specifies whether to discard the current frame before displaying the next frame. You select a disposal method when working with animations that include background transparency in order to specify whether the current frame will appear through the transparent areas of the next frame.

The Disposal Method icon below each frame in the Animation palette indicates whether the frame is set to Do Not Dispose or Restore to Background. No icon appears when the disposal method is set to Automatic.

Choose the Automatic option to determine a disposal method for the current frame automatically, discarding the current frame if the next frame contains layer transparency. For most animations, the Automatic option yields the desired results and is, therefore, the default option.

***Note:** Choose the Automatic disposal option when using the Redundant Pixel Removal optimization option, to enable ImageReady to preserve frames that include transparency.*

Choose the Do Not Dispose option to preserve the current frame as the next frame is added to the display. The current frame (and preceding frames) may show through transparent areas of the next frame. To accurately preview an animation using the Do Not Dispose option, preview the animation in a browser.

Choose the Restore to Background option to discard the current frame from the display before the next frame is displayed. Only a single frame is displayed at any time (and the current frame will not appear through the transparent areas of the next frame).

–From Adobe Photoshop 6.0 online Help

Navigating animation frames

You can use a number of techniques to preview and scroll through your animation frames.

1 Use the following navigation controls to practice moving through the frames of the logo text animation.

- You can select a frame by clicking its thumbnail in the Animation palette. The image and the Layers palette update to reflect the state of the selected frame.

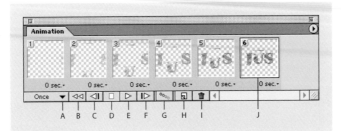

A. Looping pop-up menu B. First Frame button C. Backward button
D. Stop button E. Play button F. Forward button G. Tween button
H. New Frame button I. Trash J. Selected frame

- In the Animation palette, the Forward and Backward buttons let you move forward and backward through the frame sequence. The First Frame button lets you select the first frame in the sequence.

- In the Layers palette, the Forward and Backward buttons let you move forward and backward through the frame sequence. (These buttons are especially convenient when you want to quickly edit the layers for a succession of frames.)

A. Backward button
B. Forward button

2 When you have finished practicing, choose File > Close, and close the original image without saving changes.

Creating a transition between image states

Now you'll animate layer opacity to create the illusion of an image fading gradually into a different state.

1 Choose File > Open, and open the file Logo2.psd from the Lessons/Lesson17 folder.

The logo image contains two layers that represent different background styles. A photographic background of an orange tree currently appears in the image.

2 In the Layers palette, click in the eye icon (◉) column next to the Photo layer to hide the layer. The Illustration layer is now visible in the image and shows a version of the background tree that looks more hand-drawn.

You'll create an animation that shows the background changing from the photo style into the illustration style.

3 In the Layers palette, click in the eye icon column to make the Photo layer visible. Eye icons should appear next to both the Photo and Illustration layers.

The photo background appears in the image, defining the starting state of the animation. Notice that the first frame in the Animation palette appears with the photo visible. Now you'll define the ending state of the animation.

4 In the Animation palette, click the New Frame button(▣).

5 In the Layers palette, click in the eye icon (👁) column to hide the Photo layer.

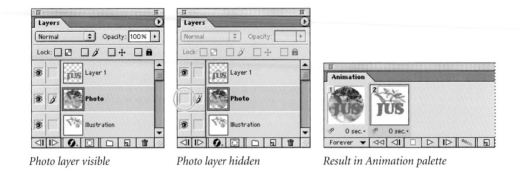

Photo layer visible   *Photo layer hidden*   *Result in Animation palette*

6 Choose Tween from the Animation palette menu. In the Tween dialog box, select All Layers. Deselect Position and Effects; select Opacity; for Tween With, choose Previous Frame; and for Frames to Add, enter **4**. Click OK.

ImageReady adds four transitional frames with intermediate opacities. When tweening the frames, ImageReady treats the hidden photo layer as a 1% opaque layer.

7 In the Animation palette, choose Once from the Looping pop-up menu.

8 Click the Play button (▷) to play the animation sequence.

Although you can preview animations in ImageReady, the timing of this preview may not be accurate. This is because ImageReady takes a moment to build the composition of each frame during playback. For a more accurate preview, play your animation in a Web browser.

9 Choose File > Preview In, and choose a browser application from the submenu.

10 When you have finished previewing the animation, quit the browser and return to ImageReady.

11 Choose File > Save Optimized As, name the image **Logo2.gif**, and click Save. ImageReady saves the animation as a GIF using the settings in the Optimize palette.

Remember that you can change the palette and color settings in the Optimize palette to reduce file size.

12 Choose File > Close to close the original image without saving changes.

Creating a two-step animation

You can create a simple two-step animation by toggling the visibility of two layers. For example, you can make an animated character alternate between different expressions or make an object move back and forth in a simple pattern. In this part of the lesson, you'll animate the shaking of a cartoon juice blender.

1 Choose File > Open, and open the file Blender.psd from the Lessons/Lesson17 folder.

The blender image consists of several layers. You'll create animation frames that alternate between hiding and showing two layers representing different positions of the blender pitcher.

In the Layers palette, an eye icon (👁) appears next to Layer 1, indicating that this is the only visible layer in the image.

2 In the Animation palette, click the New Frame button (🔲) to create frame 2.

3 In the Layers palette, click in the eye icon column next to Layer 2 to display this layer in the image. Because Layer 2 sits above Layer 1 in the stacking order, it's not necessary to hide Layer 1.

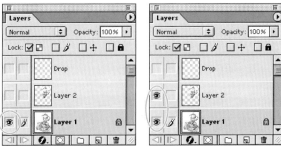

Layer 1 visible   *Layers 1 and 2 visible*

4 In the Animation palette, choose Forever (the default) from the Looping pop-up menu.

5 Click the Play button (▷) in the Animation palette to preview the animation. Click the Stop button (□) to stop the animation.

Now you'll preview the animation in a Web browser.

6 Choose File > Preview In, and choose a browser application from the submenu. (You can also press Ctrl+Alt+P (Windows) or Command+Option+P (Mac OS) to launch a browser preview quickly.)

When you have finished previewing the animation, quit the browser window, and return to Adobe ImageReady.

7 Choose File > Save Optimized As, name the image **Blender.gif**, and click Save.

Rotating and moving an object

Now you'll animate a different element in the blender image, adding to the existing animation. By successively copying and transforming a layer, you can make an object move or fall in a realistic trajectory.

Creating transformed layers

You'll start by creating layers that simulate the path of a juice drop falling from the top of the blender as the blender shakes.

Before adding layers to an image that already contains an animation, it's a good idea to create a new frame. This step helps protect your existing frames from unwanted changes.

1 In the Animation palette, select frame 2. Then click the New Frame button (⬛) to create a new frame (frame 3) after frame 2.

2 In the Layers palette, make the Drop layer visible.

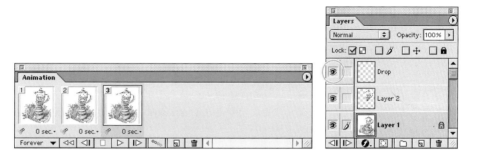

Notice the small juice drop that appears at the top left edge of the blender in the image.

3 In the Animation palette, make sure New Layers Visible in All Frames is deselected in the options menu.

4 Select the Drop layer in the Layers palette. Drag the layer name to the New Layer button (⬛) to duplicate the layer.

Note: *The duplicate layer would be visible in all three frames in the Animation palette if New Layers Visible in All Frames was not deselected in the options menu.*

5 With the Drop Copy layer selected, choose Edit > Free Transform.

The transformation bounding box appears around the Drop Copy layer.

6 Position the pointer outside the bounding box (the pointer becomes a curved double arrow (↰)), and drag to rotate the drop counterclockwise. Then position the pointer inside the bounding box (the pointer becomes an arrowhead (▸)), and drag to reposition the drop as shown in the illustration. Zoom in on the drop to see the pointer change to an arrow. Press Enter (Windows) or Return (Mac OS) to apply the transformation.

Drop Copy selected

Rotating Drop Copy layer

Dragging Drop Copy layer

7 Now drag the Drop Copy layer to the New Layer button (▣) to duplicate the layer.

8 With the Drop Copy 2 layer selected, choose Edit > Free Transform. Rotate and reposition the layer as shown in the illustration. Press Enter or Return to apply the transformation.

You should now have two copied and transformed Drop layers.

9 Choose File > Save to save a copy of the original image with the layers you've just created. In ImageReady, the Save command saves the layered Photoshop file, including all of the animation and optimization information.

Creating simultaneous animations

Now you'll define the falling drop animation by successively hiding and showing the layers you've just created. You'll also build in the shaking blender animation as the drop falls.

1 In the Animation palette, make sure that frame 3 is selected. In the Layers palette, select Layer 1 and make the Drop layer visible; then hide all other layers.

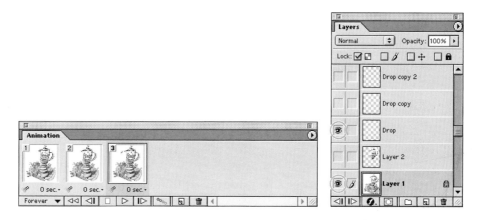

When you hide or show a layer in a frame, the visibility of the layer changes for that frame only.

Now you'll add a frame that continues the shaking of the blender while the drop falls.

2 Click the New Frame button (▣) in the Animation palette to create frame 4.

3 In the Layers palette, make Layer 2 visible, along with Drop Copy and Layer 1.

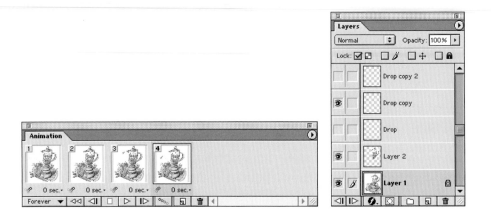

4 Continue to click the New Frame button in the Animation palette to create new frames, and then use the Layers palette to change the layer visibility as follows:

• For frame 5, make Drop Copy 2 and Layer 1 the visible layers.

• For frame 6, make Layer 2 and Layer 1 the visible layers.

Now you'll set a delay for playing each frame in the animation.

5 From the Animation palette menu, choose Select All Frames. In the palette, position the pointer on the time beneath frame 1, and press the mouse button to display the Frame Delay pop-up menu. Choose Other. In the Set Frame Delay dialog box, enter **0.05** in the Set Delay for All Frames text box. (0 seconds is the default.) Click OK.

Frame Delay pop-up menu   Set Frame Delay dialog box

The value appears below each frame thumbnail, indicating that the time delay applies to all the frames in the palette. You can also vary the time delay for individual frames.

6 Click the Play button (▷) in the Animation palette to view your animation.

The juice drop should fall as the blender shakes.

7 Click the Stop button (□) to stop the animation.

8 Choose File > Preview In, and choose a browser application from the submenu to play the animation with accurate timing.

9 Choose File > Save Optimized As. Make sure that the image is named **Blender.gif**, click Save, and replace the existing file.

The Save Optimized As command saves a file in the GIF, JPEG, or PNG format, for use in you Web pages.

10 Choose File > Close to close your original image without saving changes.

Creating a montage sequence

In this part of the lesson, you'll create a quickly changing sequence, or *montage*, of fruit images. You create montage effects by hiding and showing layers in succession.

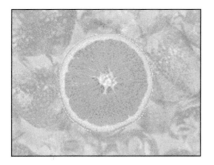

Setting the montage order

You'll work with an image that contains a number of layers showing different fruit images.

1 Choose File > Open, and open the file Fruit.psd from the Lessons/Lesson17 folder.

2 In the Animation palette, choose Make Frames From Layers from the palette menu.

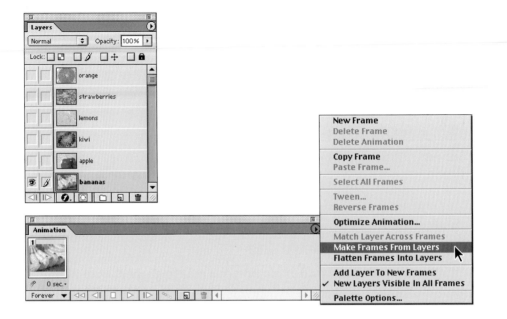

The layers in the image appear as six individual frames in the Animation palette and six layers in the Layers palette.

3 In the Animation palette, Shift-click to select all frames, or choose Select All Frames from the Animation palette menu. In the palette, position the pointer on the time beneath frame 1, and press the mouse button to display the Frame Delay pop-up menu. Choose Other. In the Set Frame Delay dialog box, enter **0.25** in the Set Delay for All Frames text box, and click OK.

Note: *To select discontiguous multiple frames, Ctrl-click (Windows) or Command-click (Mac OS) additional frames to add those frames to the selection.*

4 In the Animation palette, choose Once from the Looping pop-up menu. Then click the Play button (▷) to view the sequence of images. (To repeat the loop, click Play again.)

Now you'll reorder the animation frames so that the lemons appear first in the sequence.

5 In the Animation palette, click to select the frame containing the lemons. Then drag the selected frame to the left until a heavy line appears before frame 1, and release the mouse.

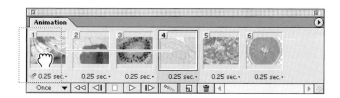

The lemons frame is now the first frame in the sequence.

6 Click the Play button (▷) to view the revised montage.

7 Choose File > Save Optimized As. Name the image **Fruit1.gif**, and click Save.

Smoothing the transition between frames

Now you'll enhance your newly assembled montage by adding intermediate frames that smooth the transition between the strawberries and the orange.

1 In the Animation palette, select the frame containing the strawberries. The image window and the Layers palette update to reflect the contents of the frame.

2 Click the New Frame button (⊡) in the Animation palette to create a new frame after the strawberries frame.

3 In the Layers palette, select the Strawberries layer, and enter **1%** in the Opacity text box.

4 Choose Tween from the Animation palette menu. In the Tween dialog box, choose Selected Layer; deselect Position and Effects, and select Opacity; enter **4** in the Frames to Add text box; and for Tween With, choose Previous Frame. Click OK.

5 In the Animation palette, choose Forever from the Looping pop-up menu. Then click the Play button (▷) to view the sequence of images. Click the Stop button (□) to stop the animation.

If desired, you can add transitional opacities between the other fruit images in the sequence.

6 Choose File > Save. If you don't save, the strawberry opacity animation will be gone as you continue this lesson.

Making an object grow in size

For the grand conclusion to the fruit montage, you'll animate the orange swelling from a small to a large size.

First you'll copy and resize the Orange layer several times.

1 In the Animation palette, select the frame containing the orange.

2 In the Layers palette, drag the Orange layer to the New Layer button (🖺) to create a duplicate layer.

Note: *Make sure New Layers Visible in All Frames is deselected in the Animation palette options menu before you duplicate the Orange layer.*

When you create a new layer in a frame, the layer is added to all frames in the animation but is visible only in the current frame.

3 Repeat step 2 to create three more duplicates of the Orange layer.

4 Double-click the Orange Copy layer to display the Layer Options dialog box. For name, enter **Orange 20%**. Then click OK.

5 Repeat step 4 for the other duplicate layers, renaming the layers **Orange 40%**, **Orange 60%**, and **Orange 80%**.

6 In the Layers palette, select and make visible the Orange 20% layer. Hide the other orange layers.

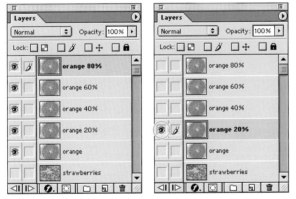

Renaming layers   *Making Orange 20% layer visible*

Now you'll create gradually larger copies of the orange.

7 Choose Edit > Transform > Numeric. Enter **20%** in the Scale Percent text box. Make sure that Constrain Proportions is selected, and click OK.

Numeric Transform	
☑ **Position**	OK
X: [0] pixels	Cancel
Y: [0] pixels	
☑ Relative	
☑ **Scale**	
Width: [40] pixels	
Height: [30] pixels	
Percent: [20%]	
☑ Constrain Proportions	

Scaling the Orange 20% layer   *Result*

When you work with layers in a frame, you can create or copy selections in the layer; adjust color and tone; change the layer's opacity, blending mode, or position; add layer effects; and perform editing tasks as you would with layers in any image.

8 Do the following for the next frame:

• In the Animation palette with the orange frame selected, click the New Frame button (▣) to create a new frame.

• In the Layers palette, hide the Orange 20% frame. Select and make visible the Orange 40% layer.

• Choose Edit > Transform > Numeric, and enter **40%** in the Scale Percent text box to resize the layer to 40%.

9 Repeat step 7 to create frames containing the Orange 60% and Orange 80% layers resized to their respective percentages, hiding the previous layer with each step. Remember to create a frame from the original (100%) orange.

10 Click the Play button (▷) to play your animation. Click the Stop button (□) to stop the animation.

11 Choose File > Save Optimized. ImageReady saves the animation as a GIF using the current settings in the Optimize palette.

12 Choose File > Close to close the original image without saving changes.

Using advanced layer features to create animations

In this part of the lesson, you'll learn some animation tricks that can be created through the use of advanced layer features, such as layer masks, clipping paths, and clipping groups.

You'll work with versions of the logo image that you saw at the beginning of the lesson.

Using layer masks to create animations

First you'll use a clipping path to create the illusion of juice filling slowly to the top of the "U" in the logo text.

1 Choose File > Open, and open the file Logo3.psd from the Lessons/Lesson17 folder.

2 In the Layers palette, hide the Photo layer, and leave the Text layer and the Juice layer visible.

The Juice layer contains a vector clipping path, as indicated by the grayscale thumbnail that appears to the right of the layer thumbnail in the palette. The clipping path is U-shaped, restricting the orange juice to appear only through the "U" in the logo text.

The orange juice currently fills to the brim of the "U." You'll move the Juice layer to define another frame that shows the "U" empty of juice.

3 In the Animation palette, click the New Frame button (🖼) to create a second frame. In the Layers palette, click to turn off the link icon (⊗) between the layer and clipping path thumbnails.

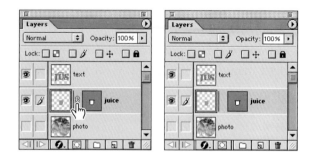

Turning off the link icon lets you move the layer independent of its layer mask.

4 Select the move tool (►⊹).

5 In the Layers palette, click the layer thumbnail for the juice layer to select the layer.

6 In the image, position the move tool over the orange color, and drag to reposition the orange color beneath the curve of the "U."

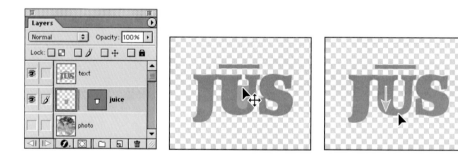

7 In the Animation palette, drag to reverse the order of frames 1 and 2.

Because you have defined the two frames by repositioning a single layer, you can generate intermediate frames automatically using the Tween command.

8 Choose Tween from the Animation palette menu. Select All Layers and Position; deselect Opacity and Effects; for Tween With, choose Next Frame; and enter **5** in the Frames to Add text box. Click OK.

9 In the Animation palette, select frame 1; in the Layers palette, select the Photo layer and show it. From the Animation palette menu, choose Match Layer Across Frames to reveal the photo in all frames.

10 In the Animation palette, select frame 1. Then click the Play button (▷) to play the animation. Click the Stop button (□) to stop the animation.

11 Choose File > Preview In, and choose a browser application from the submenu to play the animation with accurate timing. You can also select Preview in Default Browser in the toolbox.

12 Choose File > Save Optimized As, name the file **Logo3.gif**, and click Save. Then choose File > Close to close the original file without saving changes.

Using clipping groups to create animations

Now you'll create the effect of strawberries shaking inside the logo text.

1 Choose File > Open, and open the file Logo4.psd from the Lessons/Lesson17 folder.

2 In the Layers palette, make sure that both the Strawberries and Text layers are visible.

To make the strawberries appear only through the shape of the logo text, you'll create a clipping group.

3 In the Layers palette, select the Strawberries layer. Hold down Alt (Windows) or Option (Mac OS), position the pointer over the solid line dividing two layers in the Layers palette (the pointer changes to two overlapping circles), and click the dividing line between the layers. You can also choose Layer > Group with Previous.

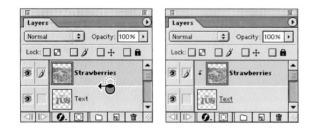

Notice that the strawberries now appear masked by the logo text. The thumbnail for the Strawberries layer is indented with a downward-pointing arrow (↲), indicating that the layer is grouped with the layer that precedes it.

4 In the Animation palette, click the New Frame button.

For the second animation frame, you'll reposition the Strawberries layer slightly.

5 In the Layers palette, select the Strawberries layer. Then select the move tool ( ).

6 In the image, drag the Strawberries layer slightly to the right, or use the arrow keys to move the layer.

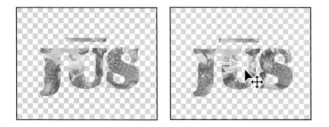